Issei, Nisei, War Bride

ISSEI, NISEI, WAR BRIDE

Three Generations of Japanese American Women in Domestic Service

Evelyn Nakano Glenn

Temple University Press
Philadelphia

Temple University Press, Philadelphia 19122

© 1986 by Temple University. All rights reserved

Published 1986

Printed in the United States of America

Library of Congress Cataloging-in-Publication Data

Glenn, Evelyn Nakano.
  Issei, nisei, war bride.

  Bibliography:
  Includes index.
    1. Women domestics—California—History.   2. Japanese
Americans—California—Social conditions.   I. Title.
HD6072.2.U52C24   1986   331.4'8164046'0899560794   85-25107
ISBN 0-87722-412-9

For my mother, Haru Ito Nakano

CONTENTS

PREFACE

When I started gathering materials for what turned out to be this book, my goals were modest. My intention was to collect and assemble a set of oral interviews of Japanese American women employed as domestics. In teaching and writing about women and work, I had become acutely aware of the dearth of materials documenting the day-to-day struggles of Asian American, latina, and black women working in low-status occupations, such as domestic service, the most prototypical job for racial-ethnic women. Little was known about the conditions they confronted, what they felt about their situation, or how they responded to menial employment. Accounts in which women spoke in their own words about themselves and their work seemed the best vehicle for illustrating how gender, race, and class intersect to shape the lives of racial-ethnic women.

Once started, the project took momentum and drew me along. Questions raised by the initial interviews led to a broadening of the study both empirically and theoretically. My new aim was to uncover the relationship between Japanese American women's experience as domestic workers during the first seventy years of the twentieth century and larger historical forces: the transformation of the economy and labor market in Northern California and the process of labor migration and settlement in that locale. How did these forces affect women's work, both paid and unpaid, and what were their strategies for dealing with the conditions engendered by these forces?

A brief account of my personal and intellectual odyssey in pursuing this project may explain how these questions came to the fore. As a sansei, a third-generation Japanese American, I felt I had two initial advantages for carrying out the study: first, I had connections that would provide access that might be denied to others, and second, I had a first-hand acquaintance with Japanese American women's situations that would help direct my inquiry toward the most relevant issues.

Access turned out to be relatively easy. Though living and working in Massachusetts, I had longstanding family ties in the San Francisco Bay Area. My paternal grandparents arrived in Alameda in 1905; many of their descendants and those of collateral relatives continue to reside in San Francisco and the East Bay. These family connections proved to be decisive in my ability to carry out the study. Relatives and their friends provided introductions to issei (first-generation), nisei (second-generation), and war brides (post–World War II immigrants) employed as domestics. Without these introductions, which amounted to being personally vouched for, I suspect that many of the women would have refused to be interviewed. Some might have refused out of modesty: many of the women I interviewed protested that their stories could be of little interest to anyone, but they were willing to talk if it would be helpful. Others might have declined in order to preserve their privacy. Some women were working sub rosa, not reporting their income or concealing their employment from relatives. Yet almost everyone I approached agreed to be interviewed, reassured that my interest was legitimate and that I would respect their confidences.

My knowledge of Japanese American (*nikkei*) women was also useful, but it proved to be more limited than I had imagined. A great deal of what the women told me was surprising, even astonishing. I came to realize that my view of nikkei women had been colored by my childhood and adolescent reactions to the strictures imposed on females in Japanese American society. As a young girl I resented the whole notion of female subordination and the socialization it entailed. I respected my mother, grandmothers, and aunts for their selflessness and hard work. I appreciated their critical contribution to the family and to the economy through their toil as farm hands, cooks, boardinghouse keepers, operatives, and assistants to their husbands. But, I vowed, I would not be like them. They were uncomplaining martyrs, catering to their husbands' demands and sacrificing endlessly for their children. Their own needs and wishes did not count. I viewed them as victims, and therefore as weak.

The eight women I interviewed in the pilot study overturned my preconceptions. These women could not be easily pigeon-holed. They were as varied in personality and character as any group of women could be. Some were, as I expected, uncomplaining and mild of speech; they denied any pain and glossed over hard times with conventional expressions of fatalism. Others, however, were outspoken and noisy. They complained vociferously about discrimination, selfish husbands, or arrogant employers. Some, as I anticipated, resisted talking about their feelings and avoided introspection. Others, unexpectedly, expounded remarkably sophisticated analyses of their work and the ties that bound them to their employers.

Most important, though, was that underneath their diversity lay a common core—a core of strength that was often hidden, but nonetheless palpable. When they talked about their hardships, they did so with pride and a sense of humor. Reviewing the interviews, I realized that these women were relating "war stories." They had suffered mistreatment and injustice and deprivation, but through determination and grit they had endured and finally overcome adversity. Like old warriors, they felt a sense of camaraderie with others who had gone through the same struggle. Most impressive was the vitality of women in their seventies and eighties, many still employed. They were enjoying life as never before. They were busy enough not be to bored, yet were spared the cares and responsibilities that burdened their earlier years.

Here was a curious contradiction. At one level these women were victims of triple oppression, trapped in work that is widely regarded as the most menial employment in our society, subjected to institutional racism of the most virulent sort, and subordinated at home by a patriarchal family system. As a result of these external forces, their aspirations and hopes had been dashed repeatedly. At another level, though, they were not passive sufferers. Ironically, the very difficulty of their circumstances forced them into a struggle for survival, a struggle that developed in them a corresponding strength and tenacity. They could look back with satisfaction at what they had accomplished. They had helped support their children, gained some measure of independence from their husbands, and won the respect of their children and community.

It became evident that static models of class, race, and sex that would treat Japanese women simply as objects of history were inadequate and misleading. To capture the contradictions and dynamism of Japanese American women's situations, I would have to take a dialectical approach to class, race, and gender, an approach that captures the struggle inherent in all relations of dominance and hierarchy and thereby takes into account not only the efforts of dominant groups to maintain their privileged position, but also the active resistance of subordinate groups striving to carve out areas of autonomy and power.

I came to view labor exploitation and control as central to all three axes of oppression. The labor systems in capitalist economies are structured to maximize profits for capital while also maintaining race and gender advantages for privileged workers—that is, native white men. The particular mechanism by which some groups are subordinated is labor market segmentation. The market is divided into separate sets of jobs, with separate wage scales, for different segments: migrants and natives, racial-ethnics and whites, women and men. Formal and informal barriers serve to keep groups "in their place."

The structure of the labor system in turn profoundly affects the family and cultural systems of workers. The harsh conditions under which migrants and people of color work, as well as low wages and insecurity, make it difficult for them to maintain family life. At best, they are valued primarily as individual units of labor, so there is little institutional support for family integrity. At worst, to the extent that kin ties may interfere with their malleability as labor, their family and community systems may be subjected to systematic attack. This has been the case for racial-ethnic migrants. Historically state policies and practices have been designed to recruit young adult migrants to fill labor needs, while also preventing them from forming or reconstituting families. The labor system also has an impact on the structure of individual households. The segregation of women into low-wage, low-status women's jobs perpetuates gender hierarchy within the home. Their secondary position in the labor market means that women remain economically dependent and must accept an unequal share of domestic responsibility.

Systems of domination set up a dialectic, however, because subordinate groups do not passively acquiesce. They frequently resist exploitation and assaults on their autonomy. Struggle takes place at many levels and in many arenas. People of color are not content to remain in menial occupations, but strive to overcome color barriers to improve their positions. Migrants find ways to form families—if not through legal means, then through extralegal stratagems. Women resent the unequal division of labor and resources, and fight with their husbands to reallocate them more equitably.

I came to focus, therefore, on labor market segmentation by race, gender, and migrant status and examined where different cohorts of Japanese American women fit into the market at different times and how they maneuvered within the constraints imposed by that structure. I also began to explore the connection between their labor market situation and their situation in the family, looking in particular at the interaction between their oppression in the labor market and their oppression in the family and between their struggles in the workplace and their struggles at home.

As I compared the experiences of issei, nisei, and war brides, I became more convinced than ever that historical process was crucial to an understanding of their situations: first, the evolution of the local economy, with its shifting needs for different kinds of labor, and, second, stages in the group's migration and settlement in relation to that changing labor market.

If I wanted to understand individual experiences, I had to relate them to these historical processes. As patterns of similarity among those in a generation emerged, it became evident that these women's experiences were not comprehensible as idiosyncratic phenomena. Rather, their experiences grew out of specific sociohistorical circumstances shared with others in a cohort. The commonalities among women of a generation or cohort came about because they encountered certain key events in the history of Japanese migration, settlement, and adaptation at similar points in their lives. Moreover, the experiences of one cohort were systematically related to those of other cohorts. What happened to earlier cohorts established patterns that shaped the circumstances and choices of subsequent ones.

I decided, therefore, to organize my analysis in terms of the history of the cohorts. I set out to study systematically the three cohorts most heavily involved in domestic service—issei, nisei, and war brides. I conducted in-depth interviews and follow-ups with forty-eight women. This group comprised fifteen issei, aged 65 to 91; nineteen nisei, aged 48 to 84, of whom twelve had been raised exclusively in the United States and seven (referred to by the special term *kibei*) had spent part of their childhood in Japan; and twelve war brides, aged 41 to 55. Fourteen issei, two kibei, and one war bride were interviewed in Japanese, and the remainder in English. In order to better understand these women's relation to the community, I interviewed over thirty long-time members about social relations in the community and key events in its history. I attempted to get some insights into the women's social worlds by attending church functions, senior centers, group meetings, and informal social events.

I gleaned additional historical information from the census and a few early surveys and from community directories, church histories, and newspaper files. Community documents from the pre-war period were, unfortunately, scarce because organizational records and personal documents were lost or destroyed during World War II. Secondary materials from the perspective of the dominant group were more abundant. State records of various commissions and hearings gave insights into the thinking of anti-Japanese elements, though the purported facts contained in these sources were often unsubstantiated and distorted. The controversy they stirred up nonetheless stimulated a number of more "objective" scholarly studies that provided useful data on Japanese immigration and economic activities before the war.

My attempts to explicate the development of the labor market and the role of female migrant labor led me to the literature on labor migration, labor histories of other racial-ethnic groups, women's work in industrializing America, and domestic service. This comparative research led me to conclude that although many of the details of the Japanese American experience were unique, the underlying similarities to the experiences of other immigrant women and women of color were more significant. I realized that the case of Japanese American women could be used to address broad issues related to the labor systems of capitalist economies, the role of immi-

grant and racial-ethnic women in those systems, and the consequences of race- and gender-stratified labor systems for the family
and cultural systems of minority groups.

I said earlier that this was a personal as well as an intellectual
odyssey. The process of writing this book has not only allowed me to
work through many ideas about the social organization of work and
its relation to labor migration and to gender and race stratification; it
has also brought me closer to my family and cultural roots.

I learned while talking to an aunt about the project that my
paternal grandmother worked as a domestic for almost twenty-five
years up until World War II. When I questioned my father about this,
he told me that his mother had been employed full-time most of her
married life, despite having eight children. Once her eldest daughter
was ten or so, she took a full-time job at one of the big houses on
Alameda's "gold coast." She rode a bicycle to work every morning,
came home in the mid-afternoon to prepare a family supper, then
returned to her employers' house after dinner to clean up their kitch-
en. Before that, when her children were small, she took in laundry,
which she did in a large tub, boiling the whites and later ironing by
hand. My father and one of his older brothers were delegated to pick
up the dirty laundry from customers and return it clean. In addition,
she supervised a massive amount of household work, aided by her
eldest daughter, who left school after the eighth grade to help at
home. My grandfather, a gardener, was a leader in the church, and a
bit of a dandy. He carried himself with dignity and, when not dressed
for work, wore a three-piece suit. He would not, as a true Japanese
male, involve himself in "women's work."

The portrait drawn by the daughter-in-law and son of a dynamic, energetic woman was at odds with my own recollection of her,
when she was in her seventies and I was six or seven. I remember her
as a quiet, often melancholy figure, dressed invariably in black, sitting in her rocker. After forty years in the United States, she spoke no
English; she rarely left the house, and never went out by herself. The
new information, as well as the realization that much of what the issei
women told me about themselves was also true of her life, made me
feel that I knew her for the first time.

The most felicitous personal aspect of the project was the involvement of my mother, Haru Nakano, as interpreter and facilitator.

Her involvement allowed her to participate in an aspect of my life that she had never known first-hand and led me to see her in a different light, as an ally and colleague. Mom was an enthusiastic and tireless associate. She made numerous phone calls on my behalf, arranged introductions to many people in the community, accompanied me on interviews, and acted as interpreter when my childhood Japanese proved inadequate to the task. Her reassuring presence and tact put the women we were interviewing at ease. This undoubtedly contributed to the frankness of many of the interviews. I grew to respect my mother's skills and to appreciate her generosity and genuine goodness.

I owe much to many people, and not least to the issei, nisei, and post-war immigrant women who shared their memories, both bitter and sweet. Over thirty other men and women also gave generously of their time and thoughts about past and present life in the community.

In order to maintain confidentiality I have used pseudonyms for all these subjects and community informants. In some cases, I have altered personal details that might reveal a person's identity.

The late Masako Minami, who for many years ran the Eden Township Senior Center in San Lorenzo, personally introduced me to a number of issei women in her area. June Sakaguchi of the Berkeley Senior Center and Kay Okamoto, who started and still runs a program for issei in San Francisco, put me in contact with women from their areas.

The theoretical perspective developed in this study was stimulated and refined through discussions with friends and colleagues. I received much food for thought, as well as specific suggestions on an earlier paper growing out of this research, from members of the Women and Work Study Group. I thank all of them—Chris Bose, Carol Brown, Peggy Crull, Roz Feldberg, Nadine Felton, Myra Marx Ferree, Amy Kesselman, Susan Lehrer, Amy Srebnick, Natalie Sokoloff, and Carole Turbin—for many years of intellectual stimulation and support.

I learned a tremendous amount about issues of race and gender through intensive sharing and collaboration with Bonnie Dill, Cheryl Gilkes, Elizabeth Higginbotham, and Ruth Zambrana. We are the only group that I know of that has done a comparative historical analysis of the effects of race-stratified labor systems on black, latina, and Asian American women. I am fortunate to be part of this group of politically committed scholars; they always remind me that racial oppression is as pervasive in our society as gender oppression.

Peter Langer and I met regularly during the period when I was writing the first draft of this book to discuss and comment on each of our works in progress. His careful reading and positive suggestions for each chapter as it emerged kept my momentum going. Scott Miyakawa, who passed away in 1981, encouraged me in the early phase of my research. His knowledge of Japanese American history was exhaustive and authoritative. I still miss him, but am grateful for having had him as a friend and colleague for many years. Terry Kovick and Rosalyn Geffen did a heroic job of deciphering my scribbled-over copy to type a clean first draft. Insook Jeong was enormously helpful in checking tables and assisting in constructing the index.

Material in Chapters 3 and 4 was incorporated from Glenn, "Occupational Ghettoization: Japanese American Women and Domestic Service, 1905–1970," *Ethnicity* 8, no. 4 (1981): 352–86; it appears with permission of Academic Press.

Mike Ames, editor-in-chief at Temple University Press, was consistently encouraging from the book's inception as an outline and abstract to its final production. His unflagging interest and patience through the long gestation period are deeply appreciated. Two anonymous reviewers for the Press provided detailed and useful suggestions for revision.

Two others must be singled out, because without them this book certainly would never have gotten off the ground. At one point I had over eighty interviews on tape and the prospect of analyzing them was daunting. They might have remained there, gathering dust, had not my friend Jean Twomey been inspired. She voluntarily undertook hours of transcribing and coding purely out of personal interest. Her enthusiasm and hard work gave me the impetus to finish transcribing, systematizing, and analyzing the data. Once this was done Jean and I spent hours discussing themes and ideas.

Even with this stimulation, it would have been easy to let the project slide. I was busy with other research, which was also important and absorbing and, because it was collaborative and funded by grants, usually took priority. The Japanese American project was a side line, relegated to weekends. This is where my husband, Gary Glenn, played a crucial role. He urged me to keep working on the project; he believed in its value and was confident that I could write something significant about the lives of these women. His overoptimism about how easy it would be to write the book turned out to be a necessary counterbalance to my tendency to agonize over my task. His enthusiasm kept me going through some difficult times. He also contributed to the work at every phase, from helping to clarify my ideas to critiquing drafts to participating in the final proof-reading. Finally, and not least, he carried much of the burden for keeping our household going, nurturing our children, and getting meals on the table, so that my time and energy could be devoted to writing. He did all these things with his usual good cheer.

PART I
ROOTS

CHAPTER 1
Women and
Labor Migration

Starting in the middle of the nineteenth century, millions of women left their homelands in Europe, Latin America, and Asia to work in the United States. Later in the century black women began migrating from the rural South to seek livelihoods in the cities of the North and South. These women were an integral, yet often unnoticed, part of a migrant stream responding to the call for cheap and willing labor in various parts of the country. They migrated initially to find work but over time became settlers, establishing families and building communities in their new surroundings.

Women came alone or, more often, as part of families, as wives and daughters. Whether single or married, they found their lot difficult. Recruited as "cheap hands," migrant fathers and husbands rarely earned a family wage. Moreover, many migrant families had destitute kin at home to support. In this context, women's labor was essential for survival. Most of these women were accustomed to toiling in the household, and they continued to do so in the new setting, manufacturing many essential goods consumed by the family, nurturing children, and carrying out a myriad of domestic chores. As keepers of the home and socializers of children, they struggled to maintain their cultural traditions, often under harsh conditions. Additionally, many migrant women were forced into a new form of labor—wage work outside the home. In a period when the ideal for middle-class married women was to remain at home cultivating domestic virtues, migrant wives had to leave their homes to seek wage employment. Long before employment became a major issue for native white women, migrant women faced the double day.

What kinds of jobs did they find? Their options were limited. Handicapped by language, lacking industrial skills, and burdened by heavy household responsibilities, they also faced a race- and gender-stratified labor market that confined them to the lowest-paid and most degraded jobs. The particular forms of low-wage employment open to them varied according to time and place, ranging from agricultural field labor to operative jobs in manufacturing. Yet one field of employment epitomized the migrant woman's experience—domestic service. From the mid-nineteenth century until the advent of World War II, domestic service was the most common employment for migrant women and their daughters. Live-in servants, laundresses, and day workers accounted for half of all non-agriculturally employed foreign-born females[1] and over 80 percent of black women during this period.[2] The long hours, heavy work, lack of freedom, and, worst of all, low status made such employment distasteful to native women, while the incessant demand for household help and the absence of specific job qualifications made it easily accessible to newcomers.[3] Even today, domestic service remains one of the largest fields of initial employment for recent migrants.[4]

Servitude in domestic employment was an experience common to the immigrant generation of many ethnic groups, European and non-European alike. The legacy for subsequent cohorts differed, however, for voluntary immigrant groups (primarily European in origin) and labor migrant groups (primarily non-European people of color).

For European ethnics, who were not strictly set apart from natives or barred from movement on purely racial grounds, the pioneer generation's sweat was an investment that benefited subsequent generations. Daughters of European immigrants moved up and were absorbed into the more advanced sectors of the labor force. High school education, often financed in part by the mother's employment, enabled many an American-born daughter of European stock to take advantage of expanding opportunities for white-collar employment.[5] As men in these groups moved into the crafts or other secure jobs in primary industries, wives began to emulate the middle-class ideal of womanhood by leaving the labor force after marriage or

motherhood. In short, domestic service was a temporary way station
for European immigrant groups, a job that bridged the transition
from the old country to the new.

The experience of racially distinct migrant groups differed. Recruited to fill temporary labor needs, they were denied basic political
and legal rights and were hemmed in by almost impermeable "color"
barriers to mobility. People of color were routinely barred from the
skilled crafts, sales, clerical work, and even the "light" manufacturing jobs that were the steps up for sons and daughters of European
immigrants. Domestic service and its close relative, laundry work,
were often the only options outside of agriculture for black wom-
en in the North, Chicanas in the Southwest, and Japanese American
women in Northern California, regardless of education or generation.[6] Settlement in the United States for these groups meant not
assimilation, but transition to the status of a racial-ethnic minority.
Women in these groups had to work outside the home even after
marriage and motherhood, and they continued to be restricted to the
same menial occupations as the immigrant generation.

For racial-ethnic women, then, employment in domestic service
became a long-term proposition, not a temporary expedient. Their
concentration in domestic service in turn reinforced their degraded
status in society. They came to be seen as particularly suited for, and
only suited for, degraded work. Racial-ethnic status and occupational position became more or less synonymous badges of inferiority. The black cleaning woman, the Mexican maid, the Japanese
housecleaner, became stereotyped images that helped to rationalize
and justify their subordination.

The universality of domestic service among migrant women and
its divergent consequences for later cohorts make it a pivotal occupation for understanding the role of women's work in ethnic migration,
settlement, and adaptation. The study of individual and group involvement in domestic work can shed light on the way migrant and
ethnic women are incorporated into the urban economy, the effects of
employment in particular sectors on women, their families, and communities, and the factors that determine mobility.

In this book the experiences of one particular group of racial-
ethnic women—Japanese Americans—and their involvement in domestic service in a specific locale—the San Francisco Bay Area—are
examined in detail. Like other migrant women of color, Japanese

women were heavily concentrated in domestic service over a substantial period of time. In the years before World War II, over half of all employed Japanese females in the Bay Area, both foreign- and native-born, were found in domestic work.[7] Though the percentage dropped after the war, as overall employment in private household work fell, Japanese American women remained disproportionately concentrated in the occupation. Three groups in particular specialized in domestic service: older immigrants (issei), older second-generation women (nisei), and post-war immigrants (war brides).

The present study examines the involvement of these three cohorts[8] in domestic service from the early years of the century to the present. It looks at the historical circumstances of their entry into this field and at the interrelations among their experiences as workers, family members, and community participants. The women's lives are viewed in relation to the process of Japanese American settlement in the Bay Area. The process of settlement is conceptualized as a series of stages that unfold dialectically. That is, the process encompasses fundamental contradictions. It involves forces that tend to break down the immigrants' original ways of life and orientation and counterforces that tend to strengthen their solidarity, identity, and cultural distinctiveness. It is also an active, rather than a passive, process: it occurs through struggle between the dominant society and immigrants and ethnic groups. The dominant society seeks to keep these groups subordinate and therefore exploitable, while the groups strive to gain a material and social foothold in the new society, using whatever opportunities are available to achieve their goals. Women play a critical role in the process. As maintainers of the family they are active in the creation and perpetuation of group culture, and their labor is an important resource in the effort to secure a viable position within the dominant society.

Although a relatively small group, Japanese American women provide an ideal case study of the role of women's labor in the settlement process. In the first place, their experience in the United States encompasses the extremes of treatment accorded migrant groups, ranging from virulent hostility and exclusion to acceptance and even esteem. This range throws into relief dialectical aspects of the process: institutional structures that constrain a group's opportunities versus the strategies devised by the group to overcome these

Women and Labor Migration

constraints; demands on groups to "fit in," assimilate, and disperse versus pressures to remain separate, distinct, and cohesive.

Prior to World War II, West Coast Japanese were subject to measures as harsh as those meted out to any group except blacks and native Americans. They were deprived of civil rights, naturalization, jobs, and land ownership, and they were eventually excluded from entry altogether on the basis of national origin. The press and demagogic politicians assailed the Japanese as an immoral and unassimilable race, whose low standard of living and high fertility threatened the survival of white Americans. The wartime evacuation and incarceration of all people of Japanese ancestry culminated a half-century of organized and unorganized anti-Japanese sentiment.[9]

The post-war period, in an almost complete reversal, saw the Japanese making rapid educational and occupational gains. Though delayed, their achievements caught up to and then surpassed those of all except the most upwardly mobile European groups.[10] The image of the Japanese also underwent a dramatic revision. They were portrayed as a model minority, quiet, law-abiding, and hardworking. Ironically, their apparent fortitude in the face of discrimination was used to refute the claim of other minority groups that institutional racism was holding them down.[11] Yet the depiction of the Japanese as a successful minority has been at best a partial truth. An accurate portrait reveals repeated failure as well as success, shattered dreams as well as achievement, and continued barriers as well as new opportunities. Even today the Japanese have not been fully assimilated into the economic mainstream, as historical patterns of employment influence current placement in the labor market.[12] A dialectical perspective is needed to capture these contradictions. Indeed, there is an underlying contradiction in the whole process of immigrant settlement, as groups seek to better themselves through what is ordinarily considered menial employment—employment that is initially seen as, and indeed may represent, opportunity for some, yet turns out to be a dead end for many.

A second reason Japanese Americans make an ideal case study is the periodicity of their history, which has rendered the stages of settlement relatively unambiguous and given rise to distinct generational cohorts. Stages in settlement were demarcated by political and social events that shaped immigration, the formation of families, and the development of community institutions. Institutional constraints confined immigration to two narrow time periods, leading to two distinct immigrant cohorts and a distinct second-generation American-born cohort. The first period of female migration was a fifteen-year span from 1909 to 1924, beginning with the establishment of the Gentlemen's Agreement of 1907–1908 and ending with the restrictive 1924 Immigration Act, which cut off entry from Asian countries.[13] The vast majority of these pioneer issei women came as wives, called over by men who had resided for some years in the United States. These women bore most of their children in the years between 1918 and 1940. This second-generation cohort, the nisei, shared the historical experience of growing up in a stable ethnic community that provided both a refuge and an anchor for identity in a hostile society. The second wave of female immigration arrived after World War II, when sizable numbers of Japanese women married Americans stationed in Japan with the military or occupation administration. Most of these women entered between 1950, when restrictions were lifted, and the mid-1960s, when such marriages became less common.[14] This cohort shared the circumstance of growing up or reaching young adulthood during the war, suffering the hardships and dislocations occasioned by the war and its aftermath, and having to adjust to life in the United States as wives of ex-servicemen and fit into an already established pattern of Japanese American community life.

The periodicity of Japanese American settlement and the existence of such clear generational cohorts makes it possible to examine the interaction of individual history and larger social history. Women's lives can be viewed as they unfold within and are shaped by the changing political economy of a given locale. Changes and continuities across the three cohorts as well as over the life cycles of members of each cohort can be traced.

Processes of Labor Migration and Settlement

The experiences of Japanese American women are a microcosm of a worldwide phenomenon—the movement of people from less developed regions to fill labor demands in more advanced economic centers. This phenomenon has been widely discussed recently as a result of the large-scale influx of foreign workers into the advanced industrial countries of the west.[15] By the mid-1970s foreign workers from Africa, the Middle East, and Southern Europe constituted about 10 percent of the work force in Western Europe.[16] The exact size of the foreign labor force in the United States is unknown because of the large number of undocumented workers from Latin America and the Caribbean region.[17] Estimates in the mid-1970s ranged from 2 to 12 million. The size and scope of modern labor migration has led some economists to conclude that migrant labor is essential to development of advanced capitalist economies.[18]

Though seen as primarily a post–World War II phenomenon linked to the drive for capital accumulation in post-industrial societies, labor migration from less advanced regions has been a critical element in the development of American capitalism since at least the mid-nineteenth century. The source of immigrants, the regions to which they are drawn, and the sectors of the economy into which they have been recruited have changed to meet the shifting demands of capitalist development. In the mid-nineteenth century, when the infrastructure of the American Far West was being built, hundreds of thousands of Latin American and Asian men were recruited to that region for "dirty" manual work. During World War I black men and women from the rural South were drawn to the industrial North to fill the need for manual and service labor, and Mexican nationals were recruited to perform seasonal agricultural work in the Southwest. In the 1970s and 1980s, female migrants are being recruited from the Caribbean region and Latin America to fill low-wage service and manufacturing jobs in the urban Northeast.[19]

Despite differences in time and place, observers have noted striking continuities in the process of labor migration and settlement.[20] First, labor migrants are drawn from "backward" areas whose economies have been disrupted and subsequent development distorted by western colonial incursions. The distortion of the economy leaves large segments of the population with their usual means of livelihood interrupted. Many are thus free to be torn from their roots and recruited to fill labor needs in the advanced regions, often the source of the original incursion. Second, migrants are recruited by receiving countries strictly to fill labor needs, not to become permanent members of the society. Thus, policies are designed to prevent long-term settlement. This intention is matched by the orientation of the migrants, who see themselves as sojourners, working abroad temporarily for economic reasons. Third, migrants serve as a reserve army of flexible and cheap labor. The jobs they fill are those shunned by native workers because they are insecure, seasonal, arduous, low-paying, or degraded. Typically, legal and administrative barriers are devised to ensure that migrants remain in these jobs and do not compete with native workers. Thus, at least in the initial stages of migration and entry into the labor market, the needs and intentions of the dominant society and the orientations and expectations of the migrants are complementary: both see the migrant primarily as a laborer, temporarily residing abroad and willing to take whatever job is available in order to earn enough to return "home" as quickly as possible.

An underlying contradiction soon becomes apparent, however. Because they are relegated to insecure, low-wage employment, migrants often find it difficult to amass sufficient capital to go back with a stake. Many thus stay longer than they intended. Willy-nilly they begin to develop a sense of community. Separated from kin, they congregate with compatriots for living accommodations, job referrals, and sociability. Those with a little capital open stores and restaurants catering to ethnic tastes. In an effort at self-help and comfort, they build institutions such as credit associations and churches. Finally, as their stay stretches into an undefined future, they may begin marrying or sending for spouses. The rise of a second generation whose formative years are spent in the host society solidifies the transition from sojourner to settler.[21]

During the transition the migrant's orientation toward employment undergoes change. As jobs begin to be seen as long-term occupations, degrading work becomes more distasteful and insecurity less tolerable. Thus occurs the often-observed rise in aspirations—the desire for a better job, a piece of land, a business of one's own. These changed aspirations clash with the ostensible reasons for the migrant's recruitment in the first place. It is at this point that hostility to migrants often erupts. In confronting attempts of migrant labor to move up, the interests of capital, independent producers (small farmers, entrepreneurs, and craftspeople), and native labor coincide. Capitalists in the competitive sector want migrants only as long as they remain highly exploitable; independent producers and native workers want to forestall competition for jobs, land, and markets. Anti-migrant movements and exclusion drives thus find wide support. Measures to keep migrants and their children in their "proper place" range from mob violence to closed apprenticeship programs to legislation aimed at prohibiting entry.[22]

All immigrant groups in the United States have encountered some degree of hostility and discrimination, but people of color have confronted more absolute and systematic restrictions. Non-European immigrants were concentrated in industrially backward regions of the United States—the South, Southwest, and West—where they were slotted into pre-industrial niches, such as agriculture, mining, and domestic service.[23] It was difficult to move from these niches into the industrialized sector. Moreover, wherever Asian, latino, and black migrant labor was used, a two-tiered, or colonial, labor system operated. The system was based on the superiority of white labor, which monopolized the more skilled, secure, clean, and supervisory jobs and who were paid on a separate and higher wage scale.[24]

The development of a two-tiered labor system requires that groups be initially distinguishable, ethnically or in other ways. Such a system can be more easily maintained beyond the immigrant generation when groups are racially, as well as ethnically, identifiable. Because of racial distinctiveness, later cohorts of non-white immigrant groups had different labor market experiences from later cohorts of white immigrant groups. Whereas the children and grandchildren of European immigrants became dispersed throughout the occupational hierarchy, latinos, blacks, and Asian Americans tended to remain at the bottom of the ladder even after several generations in the United States.

Given the barriers to mobility, how are migrants of color to escape dead-end jobs? Self-employment is the main possibility. ✓ Rather than remain wage workers, some migrants turn to entrepreneurial activity in farming, retail trade, services, or small-scale manufacturing. The Chinese and Koreans have been notable for their concentration in small businesses, as have Cubans in Miami.[25] To the extent that it relies primarily on family labor, ethnic enterprise is a throwback to pre-capitalist modes of production in which the household was the unit of production. The smallest of these enterprises employ only immediate family members and are profitable only because all members, women and children included, work long hours without pay. Self-exploitation is substituted for exploitation through wage labor.[26] Larger ethnic enterprises are part of the competitive sector in that they may employ considerable outside labor—typically recent immigrants willing to work for low wages just to get a start. In this case the ethnic entrepreneur is a middleman who provides low-cost goods and services by exploiting his or her compatriots. The exploitation is mitigated by the opportunities for mobility that exist in ethnic enterprise in contrast to the rest of the competitive sector.[27] The experience gained, as well as sponsorship by the employer, often enables the workers to start their own businesses.

Models of Labor Migration and Settlement

How are we to account for both the similarities in the initial settlement process and the divergence in the later labor experience of white and racial-ethnic immigrant groups? The traditional model, which grows out of the human capital model in economics[28] and the assimilationist school in sociology,[29] explains migration in terms of push and pull factors. Equal weight is given to conditions in the country of origin that force people to leave and opportunities in the country of destination that attract them. The human capital characteristics of migrants are invoked to explain the positions they occupy in the host economy. Thus, migrants are said to be in menial jobs because they lack industrial skills or facility in English. Upward mobility is explained by the process of assimilation. As migrants and their children absorb the values of the host society, their standards for wages and job conditions come to match those of native workers, and they are no longer willing to work in the most degraded jobs. How quickly groups assimilate and move up also depends on human capital characteristics, such as education and class-related aspirations, that migrants come with or acquire after arrival. New migrant groups come in to fill the bottom positions as older migrant groups move up.

This traditional model plausibly explains the migration and mobility patterns of European immigrants, but does not adequately account for certain features of the migration and settlement of non-

European immigrants: the role of active recruitment by the host society, the high degree of hostility toward migrants, the timing of that hostility, and the conflict in the host society between the desire to attract migrant labor and resentment of their presence. Nor does the model explain why individual migrants who may be educated and skilled are relegated to unskilled jobs, irrespective of their human capital, by virtue of their racial-ethnic status, or why certain groups remain subordinate after several generations.

The critical model, formulated to address some of these short-comings, grows out of a convergence of the dual economy[30] and dual labor market[31] models in economics and the internal colonialism perspective on race relations in sociology.[32] Although this model also focuses on the discrepancy in the economies of sending and receiving countries, the emphasis is on the exploitative nature of that rela-tionship. The advanced countries (core economies) are in a position to exploit the economies of less advanced countries (peripheral econ-omies). One aspect of this exploitation is the use of the sending society as a source of "cheap" labor. Pull outweighs push. The main dynamic for migration comes from the nature of advanced capitalist economies, the defining feature of which is the tendency toward monopoly. Monopoly firms operate in a fundamentally different way from those under conditions of competition. Their size and operating procedures enable them to reduce uncertainty through control of raw materials, financing, marketing, and labor.[33] For example, through mechanization or automation, they reduce their dependence on the vagaries of human labor, and through organizational means, such as internal labor markets, they control the remaining work force.[34] Even under conditions of monopoly capital, however, certain seg-ments of the economy remain competitive. Some processes are not easily mechanized or automated and therefore remain craftlike. Pro-duction of other goods is subject to short-term fluctuation in demand or changes in taste, so investments in technology are not worthwhile. Since their production processes remain labor-intensive, competitive industries rely on low-wage labor for profits. Corresponding to this dualism in the economy is a dualism in the labor market. The prima-ry market consists of jobs in the monopolistic sector, which are characterized by high wages, job security, promotional ladders, and bureaucratic supervision; the secondary market comprises jobs in the competitive sector, which have the opposite characteristics: low wages, insecurity, few opportunities for promotion, and arbitrary supervision.[35] Allocation to these markets follows existing divisions of race, gender, nationality, and age. The secondary market uses the most exploitable categories: minorities, women, migrants, and youth.[36]

Of these categories, migrants are the most flexible. They can be drawn to the particular geographic areas where labor needs are greatest; they are available to work long hours because they are eager to earn money quickly and are free of personal and family ties. According to this model, migrant labor serves as a reserve army, easily called up when production expands, and just as easily pushed out when demand contracts. In this way migrant workers play a critical role in advanced industrial economies, absorbing the uncertainties that remain even under monopoly capital. Their position in the economy is largely unrelated to their human capital. Their allocation to certain occupations and industries is based more on ascribed characteristics of ethnicity and nationality than on education or skills. Similarly, the mobility they achieve is determined by the degree to which capitalists and native workers permit access to the primary labor market, not by the extent of training and education that migrants and their children acquire.

Missing Pieces

These models of the settlement process have been based explicitly or implicitly on the experience of male migrants. The female side of the settlement experience has not been incorporated. Most of the existing literature on labor migration ignores women by treating migrants as undifferentiated with respect to gender or by looking only at men's experiences.[37] This emphasis on male labor is evident even in public policy, as in the enforcement strategy of the Immigration and Naturalization Service, which is aimed at apprehending illegal male workers.[38] When women *are* looked at in relation to labor migration, they are usually treated as a marginal category: as dependents of male migrants or as part of the debris left behind in the home country when the males depart. This tendency is especially evident in the sparse literature on Asian American migration and settlement.[39]

Yet, it is important to note, women constitute a large component of migrant flows. This is particularly true of post–World War II

migration to the United States, in which women have far outnum-
bered men. Among Latin and Caribbean peoples, women make up
two-thirds of all entrants,[40] and even among Asians they account for
over half.[41]

In ignoring women's labor, researchers overlook important issues. One of the most critical issues is the effect of labor systems on
the family and cultural systems of immigrant groups. Women's entry
into the labor market is often the first major change that occurs in the
family economy as immigrant groups adapt to the urban economy.
The family economy of most immigrants from rural areas was based
on household production, with women contributing unpaid labor or
engaging in informal market work (e.g., selling food) to bring in
income. As women become wage workers outside the household,
their economic role changes; their work is no longer under the control of husbands, and their contribution gains individual visibility.
These changes have profound implications for the overall family
system.

At the same time, concepts derived from the study of migrant
and racial-ethnic men's labor cannot be translated and applied un-
critically to analyzing women's labor. It is my contention that the
work of women requires separate and detailed analysis because
women's relationship to work is distinct. Their position in the labor
market is shaped not only by racial-ethnic stratification, but also by
gender stratification. These two forms of stratification interact to
create distinct labor markets for migrant and racial-ethnic women.
Second, their work is distinct from that of men in that it encompasses
a wide range of reproductive activities. These activities maintain the
current labor force (i.e., feeding, clothing, and cleaning for the male
worker) or create the next generation of workers (i.e., bearing, nurturing, and socializing children.) Sustaining family life and transmitting cultural values is an essential part of all women's reproductive
work. However, these tasks are more arduous and extensive for migrant and racial-ethnic women. In the face of a stratified labor market, poverty, and cultural oppression, family ties and psychological
and material support are both more essential and more difficult to
maintain.

Also missing from existing studies of labor migration is an adequate historical analysis of how the market for migrant labor has
varied over time and by locale. Although segmentation of the labor
market along race and gender lines remains a constant, the nature of

the segmentation has changed over time. The dual economy model focuses on the present monopoly stage of capitalism, in which segmentation occurs primarily between monopoly and competitive sectors, with the allocation of native and migrant labor following this division. During the nineteenth century, however, the primary division was between competitive capitalism and pre-capitalist independent producers made up of small farmers, artisans, and tradespeople. In California migrant and native labor was allocated according to this division.[42] Because opportunities still abounded for independent mining and farming, native workers would not accept extended tenure in labor in the competitive sector, made up of the railroads, mining, and large-scale agriculture. Migrant Asian and hispanic workers were recruited to fill labor needs in what was then the more advanced—that is, competitive—sector. Native whites predominated among independent producers.[43] Even in the late twentieth century, some remnants of independent production remain in the form of family business. This sector, though small, coexists with, and in many ways complements, the monopoly and competitive sectors by filling the interstices where even moderate economies of scale cannot be achieved.[44] Today immigrants, not natives, are disproportionately concentrated in independent production. In the period covered by this study, the division between independent production and competitive capitalism gave way to the one between competitive and monopoly capitalism. We will examine the implications of this shift for one group of workers.

In addition to variation over time, labor market segmentation also varies by locale. The way in which the local economy develops, the mix of industries, the composition of the labor force, and the relationship of the local economy to the national and international economies determine the structure of the local labor market and the allocation of different groups within it.[45] California's economy began as a colonial dependency controlled by eastern and European capitalists.[46] As is typical of dependent economies, raw materials were extracted for use in the more developed East, while manufactured products were brought in. Local manufacturing was at a special disadvantage once the transcontinental railroad allowed goods to be transported from the East on a massive scale. In San Francisco, industries that competed with eastern enterprises, such as shoemaking and cigar manufacturing, relied on Chinese labor, while industries that did not, such as street building and construction, could afford to use higher-paid white (usually Irish) workers.[47] The composition of the labor force also affected segmentation. One peculiarity of the California population was the overwhelming ratio of men to women, resulting in a shortage of women's labor for traditional female occupations such as domestic service, laundry work, and food preparation. Immigrant labor, first Chinese and later Japanese, was substituted for female labor in these fields.[48] The specialization of Asian males in domestic service was one of the unique local conditions shaping the labor force position of Japanese American women in the Bay Area.

A third missing piece is the perspective of migrant groups on their own situation. The settlement process has typically been looked at from the viewpoint of the dominant society. From this perspective migrants appear as objects rather than subjects of history. Thus, the dominant explanation of migration uses the simile of push and pull forces acting upon migrants and determining their behavior. This objectification has led researchers to depict racial-ethnic immigrant groups in one of two ways: as social problems or as victims.[49]

Undoubtedly migrant groups do create problems for the "host" society, and they are victimized. Nonetheless, they are also actors in the situation. They have to be resourceful to survive. Faced with institutional barriers to entry and mobility, they evolve strategies to take advantage of the available options and resources. For example, immigrants whose entry was prohibited made use of legal and extra-legal loopholes. Following passage of the Chinese Exclusion Act, many Chinese managed to enter as "paper sons," claiming to be children of Chinese born in the United States.[50] The Japanese used provisions in the 1907–1908 Gentlemen's Agreement to bring in "picture brides."[51]

Migrant groups have also devised a variety of strategies for coping with stratified labor markets. Some groups favor family enterprises to make use of family labor. In other groups children are sent out to work while wives stay at home to maintain the domestic sphere; in still other groups wives seek wage work in order to keep the children in school as long as possible.[52] The choice of strategies in turn has profound implications for family and cultural life and social mobility. Choosing to keep children in school sacrifices immediate economic benefits, but may further intergenerational mobility; the alternative, in which mothers stay at home and sons and daughters go out to work, may retard social mobility but help perpetuate ethnic identity by keeping children in the same occupations as their parents.

The choice of strategy stems not only from the opportunity structure, but also from cultural orientations, including notions of proper roles for men and women. In order to understand the strategic responses of migrant groups and the resulting patterns of intergenerational mobility and cultural adaptation, we need to understand how individuals interpret the conditions they confront. Not only must the larger political economy and the local labor market be taken into account, but also the subjective meaning of these structural conditions for those involved needs to be examined. We need to ask how women perceive and interpret their situations and how their interpretations shape responses to various problems and vicissitudes.

Casting a spotlight on women's labor from the perspectives of political economy, cohort history, and individual biography as this study does, can lead to a more detailed and dynamic picture of labor migration and settlement. Such a picture is a necessary first step toward developing an adequate conceptual framework for understanding the way in which racial-ethnic groups are incorporated into and move within the labor system at different stages of capitalist development.

Overview

In looking at this intersection of individual lives, cohort experience, and social structure, we begin with the broader picture and move progressively toward the finer details, starting with the political economy, moving to cohort and individual life histories, and then to the subjective meanings that individuals construct to make sense of their experiences.

Part I, *Roots,* looks at the historical and political context of Japanese settlement and women's labor force activity. The political economy of Northern California is an important part of this context. The process of immigration and settlement is the subject of Chapter 2. Japanese immigration is seen as an instance of labor migration that is specifically linked to earlier and later Asian immigration. Stages in the development of the ethnic community in the Bay Area and the position and role of women in the community are described.

Chapter 3 introduces the three cohorts of women, describing their personal and social circumstances and examining the formative historical events of their lives up until their entry into the labor market. Chapter 4 focuses specifically on Japanese American women's relationship to the labor market in the Bay Area, tracing changes and continuities from 1900 to 1970. Domestic service is seen as one of a set of occupations that make up a distinct labor market for racial-ethnic and immigrant women. This examination reveals the occupational specialization growing out of specific characteristics of a local labor market.

Part II, *Work*, deals with Japanese American women's experiences in domestic service, looking at both the structural conditions of work and women's strategies for dealing with them. Chapter 5 in this section provides a comparative framework by examining the historical relationship between female immigration, racial-ethnic subordination, and domestic service. The case of Japanese American women is shown to fit a larger pattern of immigrant entry into the urban labor market through domestic service. The continuing concentration in pre-industrial forms of labor, such as domestic service, by subsequent generations and later cohorts of immigrants is, however, a pattern specific to people of color and distinguishes the experience of racial-ethnics from that of European immigrant groups. The chapter then traces the careers of the three cohorts—issei, nisei, and war brides—covering the personal circumstances governing women's introduction to domestic work, strategies for job finding, socialization into the occupation, and factors affecting movement in and out of it over the course of a career. Typical career patterns for each cohort are identified. These careers had a dual aspect: on the one hand, involvement was dictated by specific constraints faced by each cohort at particular points in their life cycles; on the other hand, the work provided the flexibility women needed to manage their numerous responsibilities in the home.

Chapter 6 deals with experiences on the job. It begins with an analysis of the conditions workers confronted: the degraded nature of the work, the pre-modern, personalistic employer-employee relationship and the asymmetry involved in relations of subordination. Women of all three cohorts had to devise strategies to get along and achieve some measure of control over their work. Chapter 7 moves to the subjective side of the job. The degraded status of domestic work makes it difficult for workers to achieve satisfaction and maintain self-respect. We look at how these Japanese American women viewed the work and how they managed to construct meaning out of work that might be considered "meaningless." The frame of reference used to judge the work and the factors that mitigated its degrading effects differed for the three cohorts. Thus, issei, nisei, and war brides experienced varying mixtures of shame and pride, satisfaction and frustration, from the job, because they attached somewhat different meanings to it.

Part III, *Family*, deals with the second major arena of women's work. The theme of this section is the dual nature of the family as both an instrument in the survival of racial-ethnics and an arena for internal gender struggle over power and resources. Policies aimed at maximizing the exploitation of migrants as individual units of labor, and participation in a stratified labor system, had implications for the family system of Japanese and other racial-ethnic immigrant groups. Chapter 8 focuses on the struggle of racial-ethnic immigrant groups to build and maintain family life in the face of external forces inimical to the integrity of minority families.

The next two chapters focus on the internal dynamics—what might be called the gender politics—of the family. Chapter 9 is about issei families, and examines how changes in the family economy associated with migration and women's entry into the labor market affected the division of labor and conjugal relations in the issei household. Chapter 10 treats gender relations and women's position in the family in nisei and war bride families.

CHAPTER 2
Japanese American Immigration and Settlement

It is an unusually warm weekend afternoon on Post and Buchanan Streets in San Francisco. The sky is clear and sunny, but the air is slightly smoky with the fragrance of charcoal and shoyu. The pounding of taiko drums emerges over the murmur of the crowd. In the background a white pagoda-like tower juts above the block-square bulk of the Japan Center, which houses a hotel, shops, restaurants, and offices. Most of the activity today is taking place on the street in front of the center and on the pedestrian mall perpendicular to it. These are lined with tables and booths. More than half of the stalls are devoted to selling food: teriyaki, noodles, sushi, and hamburgers. Others display books, handicrafts, political tracts, and leaflets. Signs on the tables indicate the diversity of the groups participating; they range from the Japanese Progressive Alliance to the Nisei Ski Club, from the Kimochi senior services organization to the Berkeley High School Asian Student Union. Right now most of the crowd is gathered around the stage area of the plaza, watching six men and women dressed in white jackets and knee-length pants beat out complex rhythms in a strenuous melding of dance and drumming. The performance ends to enthusiastic applause and a few cheers, and people drift back toward the stalls to inspect the displays. Young adults predominate in the largely Asian crowd, but there is a goodly sprinkling of elderly folk, middle-aged men and women, and young children.

This occasion is the annual *Nihon-machi* (Japantown) street fair, begun in 1974 in an attempt to revive the community spirit that bound Japanese Americans together in the years prior to World War II. Time and events have altered the face of Nihon-machi. It no longer has a large resident Japanese population, so most of those who shop here, including those at the festival, come from outside the neighborhood and even the city. The physical environment is almost unrecognizable to those who knew it in the 1930s. Crowded rows of rundown Victorian frame houses were leveled to make way for the concrete structure that is the focal point of the "new" Nihon-machi. The small, shabby groceries and lunch counters have given way to antique oriental art shops and Tokyo-style sushi bars. The capital to build the new Nihon-machi came from Japanese, not Japanese American, sources. Still, the energy and organization invested in running the two-day festival, the range of groups participating, and the large crowds all testify to the continued strength of community ties. This spot was once the center of one of the oldest and largest Japanese American communities in North America. Its story begins in the late 1880s with the first substantial influx of Japanese immigrants.

Japanese Immigration

Although the first Japanese arrived in the United States in the late 1860s, their numbers never amounted to more than a few hundred for the next two decades. The 1890 census lists only 2,039 resident Japanese (Appendix 1). The flow of immigrants grew in the decade between 1891 and 1900, when 27,440 entered, and reached a peak between 1901 and 1908, a period that saw 51,694 admitted. Up until 1908 the immigrants were overwhelmingly male. After that, women became a substantial portion of the inflow: between 1909 and 1923, females accounted for nearly two-fifths of the Japanese admitted into the U.S.[1] The resident population did not grow as rapidly as immigration figures might suggest, because many Japanese departed after a short stay.[2] All immigration ceased in 1924 with the passage of an Immigration Act that barred entry to Asians. Japanese American immigration was thus concentrated in a narrow period of roughly thirty years.

This brief stream of migrants from Japan was part of a larger international movement of labor from Asia to the United States that took place between 1850 and the mid-1930s. During this period hundreds of thousands of Asian workers from China, Japan, Korea, and the Philippines migrated to Hawaii and California. They came in response to the call for labor—or, more to the point, for "labor willing to work for close to subsistence wages."[3] On the demand side, capitalists who controlled the dependent economies of the West needed a massive labor force to build the region's infrastructure and exploit its resources. Many hands were required for the arduous and often dangerous work of reclaiming and cultivating agricultural land, building and maintaining the railroad lines, and extracting mineral wealth from mines. Hands were also needed to clean house, cook, and launder, since there was a scarcity of women for such work. If western capitalists were to compete successfully on national and world markets, they required labor that was not only plentiful, but also cheap. They could not rely on native workers, who were in short supply and therefore expensive. Opportunities still abounded in independent mining and farming, so native workers could not be tied to low-wage employment for long. Moreover, whites who migrated to the West were drawn from the elements most committed to the independent producer ethic. They had, after all, left the East to escape proletarianization.[4] Capitalists would have to seek more malleable sources of labor elsewhere.

The U.S. presence as a power in Asia made that region a logical and attractive source. On the supply side, dislocations in the political economies of China and Japan in the nineteenth and early twentieth centuries had disrupted the means of livelihood of a substantial portion of the peasantry and other elements and therefore left them detachable from their roots. In the case of China and the Philippines, weakened or defeated central regimes had little power or inclination to keep people at home. As an imperial power the United States could exact treaties and agreements that permitted recruitment of labor under advantageous terms. Special liabilities, such as denial of naturalization rights, could be imposed on Asian immigrants, making them more controllable than native whites or Europeans.[5]

Another reason for the cheapness of Asian labor was the low cost of reproduction. The immigrants were predominantly prime-age males at the peak of their physical abilities. The burden of reproduction was borne by wives and other relatives left at home, who engaged in subsistence farming, maintained the household, raised children, and took care of the sick, elderly, and disabled. Their labor stretched the meager remittances sent by men working abroad. Administrative and legal practices prevented the entry of laborers' wives and children, thus discouraging long-term settlement and reinforcing the sojourner orientation of Asian immigrants, most of whom planned to work for a few years and return with a nest egg. The majority of Asian men did precisely that. Fewer than half—often the less successful ones—settled permanently.[6] Many of these settlers stayed on alone, single or separated from wives, for the rest of their lives. Only among the Japanese did substantial numbers of women immigrate, and then only for a few years and in smaller numbers than men.

The Chinese were the first to be recruited, starting in the 1850s, and their experiences set the pattern for the groups that followed. Legal restrictions imposed on the Chinese became the model for the treatment of other Asians. The Chinese were routinely denied civil rights and were subjected to harassing legislation, including the levying of special head taxes and local ordinances that prevented them from carrying on their businesses. At the federal level the courts ruled that the constitution prohibited naturalization of non-white immigrants who were not of African origin, a category that consisted solely of Chinese and other Asians.[7]

It was also during the peak years of Chinese immigration that a race-stratified labor system became firmly entrenched. The principle was established that Asian workers could only be hired for jobs that were too dirty, dangerous, or degrading for white men and were to be paid on a separate and lower wage scale. Generally, they were hired in industries that had to compete with eastern capital, but were barred from non-competitive fields, such as construction, that could afford to pay high wages. Even with these restrictions, the Chinese found niches in a wide range of industries and occupations throughout the state, and they constituted nearly a quarter of the California labor force in 1860.[8] Thousands of Chinese lives were lost in building the transcontinental railroad, for which they did much of the dynamiting and high-altitude work. They reclaimed thousands of acres of land for agriculture and were also employed in the burgeoning manufacturing industries, particularly cigar and shoe making.

In 1870, however, with the railroad completed and a general economic recession, widespread unemployment occurred. The Chi-

Japanese American Immigration and Settlement

nese became scapegoats. In what they themselves called the "Great Driving Out," the Chinese were expelled, often violently, from small-er towns and rural areas and were forced out of mining and other occupations.[9] Seeking refuge in urban Chinatowns, they were pro-gressively ghettoized and deskilled. Finally, in response to pressures from white labor, a federal law of 1882 excluded Chinese of the laboring class from entry. Extensions, with restrictions even on re-entry by resident Chinese, were passed in 1892 and 1902.[10]

This legislation satisfied the workingmen's groups that had led the anti-Chinese movement by cutting off one major source of low-wage labor. Still, the demand for workers was insatiable, especially in agriculture, which in California had very early taken on a pattern of concentrated large holdings cultivated by seasonal labor.[11] As many Chinese returned home and few newcomers arrived, Chinese labor became scarce, and employers looked for new sources of "cheap hands." Events in Japan in the 1880s made that country the next area for recruitment.

Prior to 1868 the Japanese government, as part of its isolationist policy, forbade citizens to leave. Following the forced opening of Japan by American forces in 1854 and the restoration of the Emperor Meiji in 1868, the new leaders of Japan embarked on a policy of modernization, which included the adoption of western technology and institutional forms. Selected students, primarily members of the gentry, were encouraged to go abroad to seek education.[12] Recalling China's experience, however, the government feared that a large out-flow of laborers would lower the country's prestige internationally. It therefore did not permit emigration until 1885, when economic pres-sures forced a change in policy. The measures used to bring about rapid industrialization and to create a modern military had brought about serious economic and social dislocations.[13] The burden fell most heavily on the small farmers, who were highly taxed to pay for modernization. The depression of the 1880s was so severe that many small farmers were unable to meet their tax obligations. The govern-ment decided that it would be judicious to allow some of the im-poverished to seek employment in foreign territories. The first sizable emigration consisted of contract laborers, mostly from Hiroshima Prefecture, bound for work on sugar plantations in Hawaii.[14] Within a few years, however, most of the outflow was directed toward the mainland, where opportunities were greater. The mainland immi-grants came from slightly better circumstances than those who went to Hawaii. Expansionism had created rising expectations among ambitious and educated youth in small towns and rural villages. Many chafed at the limited opportunities at home and took advantage of the opening to search for fortunes abroad. Others left to escape military conscription, to gain an education, or simply to taste adventure.[15]

America, particularly California, offered a siren call, a promise of unlimited wealth to anyone willing to work. The Japanese were welcomed as replacements for the Chinese. Unlike the early Chinese, they were seldom contract laborers. Nonetheless, they often worked in labor gangs or groups. Japanese boardinghouse keepers played an important role as middlemen. According to an early observer, newly arrived men made their way immediately "to Japanese boarding-houses, and from there most of them secured their first employment as section hands on railways, as agricultural laborers in field and orchard, or as domestic servants and housecleaners in the city."[16] As the latest arrivals, the Japanese worked for lower wages than other ethnic groups. As they became accustomed to the American wage structure, however, they too began demanding higher wages, staging strikes and walk-outs at strategic times to enforce their demands. It was not long before the hostility previously directed against the Chinese was mobilized against the Japanese.

The Immigrants

Studies of the social origins of the immigrants indicate that most were not, as might be expected, drawn from the poorest segment of the population. With the exception of those who went to Hawaii as contract laborers, the immigrants were "free" immigrants who paid for their own passage. According to U.S. government data, the average Japanese entrant had more money upon arrival than the average European newcomer.[17] Millis describes the majority of early male immigrants as young men "drawn largely from the most intelligent and ambitious of the middle class." In addition, he noted, there was "a smaller number of older men who had failed in business or had found farming or wage labor in Japan unattractive." A third category, those who came via Hawaii, were originally from the "poorest and most ignorant classes,"[18] but had saved enough while working on the plantation to pay for passage to the mainland. Finally, a small number, similar in characteristics to the first group, entered via Canada or Mexico.

Women immigrants, most of whom arrived some years after the peak period for male entry, were drawn from the same range of social and economic backgrounds as the men. The circumstances of their entry differed, however, in that they were not independent immigrants. They came as members of family groups—as wives, brides, or daughters. The vast majority came as new brides of men who had resided for some years in the United States. Some were accompanied by husbands who had returned to have a marriage arranged; others made the trip alone as "picture brides," married by proxy in Japan.[19]

Despite their varied pathways and circumstances of entry, the issei were remarkably homogeneous. The vast majority came from small-town entrepreneurial or rural farming families. They came almost exclusively from the four southern prefectures of Hiroshima, Yamaguchi, Kumamoto, and Fukuoka. These were among the poorest areas in Japan,[20] but an additional historical circumstance helps explain why these particular prefectures, and not other equally poor ones, furnished a disproportionate share of immigrants. An early labor recruiter, Robert Irwin, the Hawaiian consul in Japan, deliberately selected workers from Hiroshima and Yamaguchi because he had been advised that natives of these areas were hard workers who were not afraid to go to strange places.[21] Once the tradition of emigrating was established in certain villages, other residents were inclined to try their luck abroad too.

In addition to common social characteristics, the immigrants shared a cultural heritage that facilitated the formation of cohesive communities. Miyamoto points out the importance of the Japanese ethical system, which sets forth the proprieties to be observed in all aspects of social life. The primary element in this system was the concept of *giri*, literally "right reason," a term that may be used interchangeably with "social obligation" or "social responsibility":

> The duties by which an individual is guided are those
> ideas stated centuries before by the Confucian, Buddhist
> and Shinto scholars. The variety of situations to which
> these principles apply are almost endless in extent. Thus,
> one may speak of duties to oneself, to one's parents and

family, to neighbors, the community, the nation and the
supreme duty of all to one's emperor. From the requirements of duty follow other ethical conceptions such as
sacrifice, honor, loyalty and courage.[22]

This ethical system was transmitted not only in the family, but also
through schooling, which was compulsory for both males and
females under Meiji rule. The educational system established a uniform curriculum that emphasized moral principles as much as basic
literacy.

Another element contributing to a collective orientation was the
family system in which the immigrants were raised. In southern
Japan the household, rather than the individual, constituted the basic
unit of society. The household operated as a corporate economic unit
with control vested in the male head. Within the household the
obligations of individual members to others (parent to child, child to
parent, husband to wife, and so forth) and to the household as a
whole were clearly spelled out.[23] The conception of the family as the
basic unit was codified in the legal system, which made the family as a
whole responsible for the offenses of any member. It was also recognized in higher-order social organizations, where the household was
typically the unit of membership. For example, village population
was reckoned in terms of households, not individuals.[24]

The importance of the household is seen in the extension of the
family analogy to all other social institutions reaching up to the
highest level. The nation itself was conceived of as one large family,
with all Japanese being of one blood.[25]

Bay Area Japanese Communities:
Stages of Settlement

Like other immigrant groups, the Japanese tended to concentrate in
certain localities. The concentration of the population in the Pacific
and Mountain states can be explained by a combination of factors,
including proximity to Asia, the existence of West Coast ports for
vessels arriving from Asia, and the demand for labor. Once initial
immigrants had concentrated in certain areas, later immigrants tended to go to the same places, where they could count on the aid of their

compatriots. Like the pioneer Chinese, however, Japanese immigrants started out somewhat dispersed and became increasingly concentrated geographically, as well as segregated residentially, over time. In 1900 only 41.73 percent of the Japanese population resided in California, with substantial populations also found in Oregon, Washington, Montana, Idaho, Wyoming, Colorado, and Utah (Appendix 2). By 1930, 70.20 percent of resident Japanese lived in California. As geographic concentration increased, so did residential segregation, with Little Tokyos and Little Osakas springing up in cities with a substantial Japanese population. This pattern of segregation continued until World War II. The similarity in the experience of Chinese and Japanese suggests that concentration may be a stage in the settlement and adjustment of labor immigrants, at least for those groups subjected to great hostility on the part of the host society. Immigrants may be forced to congregate for protection and self-help in order to survive. At the same time, as they become oriented toward a longer stay, activities and associations with compatriots may become more important for maintaining a sense of identity. Thus, proximity to other Japanese may be actively sought.

Up until 1907 the San Francisco Bay Area was one of three main U.S. centers of Japanese population, along with the Sacramento Delta and the upper San Joaquin Valley. After 1908 the population center shifted south, with the largest concentration in Los Angeles County. Despite the shift, the Bay Area remained an area of substantial settlement. Ethnic enclaves sprang up in San Francisco itself and in the East Bay cities of Berkeley, Oakland, and Alameda. The communities were marked by a high degree of solidarity, due in part to the homogeneous character of the immigrants and their cultural orientation, and in part to their experience with discrimination in the United States. The process of settlement in the Bay Area can be divided into five main periods, each demarcated by significant historical events that shaped the nature of immigration, economic activity, and community life.[26]

Frontier Period   During the frontier period (roughly 1890 to 1910), the main body of issei men arrived. Most were single, ranging in age from their early teens to their late twenties, and averaging eight years of education.[27] The men typically started out as unskilled wage laborers in agriculture, in industries such as railroads, mining, and lumber, and in domestic service.[28] There was considerable geographic and occupational mobility during this early period as the issei moved from city to country and back or changed occupations to take advantage of new opportunities.[29] Those who managed to accumulate a little capital and know-how launched small enterprises, usually laundries or shops catering to other Japanese.[30]

San Francisco, as a port city for ships from Japan, contained one of the earliest communities. The Japanese congregated first in Chinatown and near Mission Street in the downtown area, and later in a section of the Western Addition, a district of low-rent rundown housing that became known as Little Osaka.[31]

Like other frontier communities, the Japanese community was disproportionately male.[32] The 1900 U.S. census showed 25 males for every female. Moreover, "only the bare framework of the institutional organization necessary for the wants of a normal community was existent."[33] In place of their old kin and village ties, the issei men formed mutual aid associations with those from the same prefecture (*kenjinkai*) or the same district (*gunjinkai*). They also organized rotating credit associations (*tanomoshi-ko*), through which members pooled resources and borrowed capital to finance trips or start businesses.[34]

Other cities in the East Bay soon developed concentrations of Japanese. According to informants, many issei moved to the East Bay after the 1906 San Francisco earthquake. By 1910 the Japanese populations of the four main cities were as follows: San Francisco, 4,518; Oakland, 1,520; Berkeley, 710; and Alameda, 499 (Appendix 3).

The growth in population was accompanied by a rapid acceleration of hostility directed against the Japanese:

> Anti-Japanese sentiment was on the whole more articulate and had more severe consequences in San Francisco during much of this period than in other major West Coast cities. . . . San Francisco labor organizations and other groups had developed a strong anti-Oriental voice in local politics perhaps earlier than those of most other towns, owing to the presence of large numbers of Chinese in their midst since the 1850's. For the casual, as

well as the organized xenophobe, the physical similarity
of the two ethnic groups usually seemed to override the
cultural differences, and both were seen as equally disturbing representatives of the teeming masses of Asia.
Vandalism to Japanese property; boycotting of Japanese
businesses; discrimination in housing, employment,
legal protection, and public and commercial services;
and physical assaults on Japanese residents were all familiar parts of the discriminatory pattern.[35]

The growing agitation led to a series of legal and political measures designed to reduce immigration and discourage the Japanese
from settling permanently. In 1906 the San Francisco school board
tried to segregate resident Japanese children into all-Oriental
schools. This move was viewed as a grave insult by the Japanese
government, which protested to Washington. In an effort to save
trade relations, President Roosevelt ordered an inquiry. Eventually,
federal pressure caused the school board to rescind the measure.[36]
In return, however, the Department of State pressed the Japanese
government to limit emigration. The resulting 1907–1908 Gentlemen's Agreement between the governments of Japan and the
United States closed entry to laborers and thus reduced the population of issei men. Between 1910 and 1929 more men returned to
Japan than entered.[37] However, those who remained began to think
in terms of a longer stay. The Gentlemen's Agreement contained a
loophole: it permitted the entry of wives and relatives. The issei men
went to Japan to bring back wives while others sent for picture
brides.

The Settlement Period   The arrival of issei women marked the
beginning of the "settlement" period. U.S. census figures for 1900
show only 985 Japanese women over 15. By 1910 the number had
jumped to 9,087.[38] Gulick's data show that 45,706 Japanese
females were admitted to the continental United States between
1909 and 1923, of whom 33,628 were listed as wives.[39] During this
period of family building, the sex ratio became less skewed, so that
by 1920 there was one female for every two males. The population
came to include children as well as adults. Extensive community

infrastructures developed with the founding of ethnic churches (both Christian and Buddhist), newspapers, Japanese-language schools, and business and service establishments catering to Japanese clientele.[40]

In addition, a variety of voluntary mutual aid institutions enabled the Japanese to face problems in a unified fashion: Japanese associations, prefectural and district associations, and merchant and occupational associations were formed. The communities had distinct geographic boundaries. Ethnic enclaves formed in San Francisco's Nihon-machi, on the borders of Chinatown in downtown Oakland, and around City Hall in Alameda. One of the most characteristic establishments was the bathhouse (*ofuro*), featuring deep wooden tubs heated with fires from below. Each community had at least one combination bathhouse—poolhall—employment agency at which the men congregated. By 1915 Park Street in Alameda had two blocks of shops, including a hotel, a bathhouse, a bicycle shop, a shoe repair shop, several groceries, and a sweet shop.[41] Except for jobs, the issei could fulfill most of their social and material wants within the ethnic community. According to one observer, "very few Japanese ventured beyond these comfortable environs."[42] These little ghettos were havens in a hostile world.

Meanwhile, partly in response to more permanent settlement, anti-Japanese sentiment continued to grow, and increasingly restrictive measures were promulgated to limit the Japanese economically. In 1913 the California legislature passed an Alien Land Law prohibiting the issei, who were ineligible for citizenship, from owning land or leasing it for longer than three years. The law was amended in 1920 to close the loopholes that allowed issei to purchase land in the names of their minor children. After considerable agitation in the United States against the practice of picture marriages, the Japanese government voluntarily stopped issuing passports to picture brides on February 25, 1920. Finally, in 1924, a federal immigration and naturalization law cut off all immigration from Asian countries.[43]

The Stabilization Period The end of immigration marked the start of the "stabilization" period, which stretched from 1924 to 1940. Henceforth, the growth of the population depended entirely on births. There was little room for expansion of ethnic enterprises serving a largely Japanese clientele. As the issei found their opportunities shrinking, they transferred their hopes for the future onto their children, who, by virtue of American citizenship, had rights denied their parents.[44] The issei saw education as the main vehicle for mobility and pressed their children to do well in school. They often made considerable sacrifices so that their children could finish high school and attend college.

Restrictive immigration measures created distinct generational cohorts. The majority of issei were born between 1870 and 1900, and their children, the nisei, mainly between 1915 and 1940. The Japanese community was therefore characterized by a bimodal age distribution, lacking a cohort born between 1905 and 1915. In 1933, for example, the Japanese population was concentrated in the 40 to 50 and 4 to 16 age ranges.[45] The generational split was reflected in community organizations, which developed separate subgroups for issei and nisei. The division was often along language lines, with, for example, newspapers having English and Japanese sections and churches holding separate services in the two languages. The nisei formed their own social organizations, allied with Japanese churches and community groups or sponsored by mainstream institutions such as the YMCA. The activities of these groups were prototypically American (basketball, dances, cookouts), even though the participants themselves remained segregated from their peers in the dominant culture.

By the mid 1930s the advance guard of the nisei was reaching maturity and entering the labor force. They had American citizenship and education, but the door to employment in public service and white-controlled businesses remained firmly shut.[46] Thus arose the phenomenon of the college-educated gardener or domestic. Some, frustrated by discrimination, migrated to the Midwest or East, and a few even went to Japan to obtain employment appropriate to their education and training.

It is unclear what course ethnic assimilation would have taken over the next decade under normal circumstances. The community was shattered almost overnight by the explosion of World War II. All activity ceased as the Japanese were forced to close their businesses, dispose of property, and leave for internment in concentration camps.

The Resettlement Period   The story of the war years has been told elsewhere and will not be covered in this account. We will pick up the thread with the return of the internees to the West Coast in 1945. Many, of course, did not return, but stayed in the Midwest or East, where they had relocated during the war. The majority eventually made their way back to California and undertook to piece together the remnants of their lives. Having lost savings and property, they were faced with the immediate need for shelter and work. Their success in securing these necessities was due largely to their individual efforts, but community networks were also mobilized. The few fortunate enough to own homes opened them up to other returnees. One informant recalled having thirty-five people living in her house for periods ranging from a few weeks to a year. Churches constructed dormitory facilities; other organizations set up employment referral services. The various community institutions started up again: the newspaper, the churches, and some of the businesses, although the latter were much reduced in number, since former small entrepreneurs lacked capital to start them up again.

By 1950 the Japanese population of California had reached 85,000, with the greatest concentration in Los Angeles (26,000). By this time the Japanese population in the Bay Area was returning to its pre-war level (see Appendix 3). The sex ratio, long unbalanced, had become normal except among the oldest age group.

Replacing residents who did not return were former rural dwellers who had been displaced from agriculture. Large corporate interests had extended their land holdings, squeezing out small farmers. Rather than try to start again in more competitive circumstances, many chose to relocate to the cities. These resettlers were part of the general urban shift of the Japanese population.

Despite the return of the people, the old physical communities were never fully reconstituted. In San Francisco, for example, the Japanese ghetto had been "filled in by in-migrating war workers, mostly Negroes."[47] Thus, the Japanese had to settle in widely scattered parts of the city. Harry Kitano mapped the locations of Japanese residences and businesses in 1940 and 1956, using the directories published by the two Japanese language newspapers (*Hokubei Mainichi Yearbook* and *Nichi Bei Times Yearbook*). He found much greater dispersion after the war: "In San Francisco, three census tracts embracing the former 'Little Osaka' contained more than two-thirds of the Japanese population in 1940. Sixteen years later only 46 percent of the Japanese families in the city were found in them."[48] He found similar changes in Oakland. In 1940, 29 percent of the Japanese population resided in the Japanese neighborhood; by 1956 the neighborhood, now in a new location, contained only 18 percent of Oakland's Japanese Americans. In Berkeley, where 59 percent of the Japanese lived in three adjacent census tracts in 1940, only 33 percent resided in 1956.

The post-war years also saw a continuing shift in numbers and in leadership away from the issei generation to the nisei. The remaining issei were mostly elderly and had retired from active roles in the community. Since they had never been allowed to become naturalized, they were classified during the war as enemy aliens and could not be recognized spokespersons for their families. That role was passed to the young nisei, who, as citizens, could negotiate with officials on behalf of the family. In addition, perhaps ironically, the camps had opened up new vistas for the nisei. In them, inmate labor provided all essential goods and services. For the first time, the nisei had the chance to fill jobs consistent with their education, such as teaching and office work. Kitano asserts that this experience altered their expectations so that they were no longer content with limited options.[49] The economic expansion following World War II and the Civil Rights Movement enabled many nisei to realize their new aspirations. The changes occurred too late for the older nisei and the issei, who tended to remain in service occupations. The younger nisei not only shifted into professional and white-collar occupations, but also moved into previously restricted residential areas. Although they became more integrated into the institutional life of the larger society, the nisei's primary group relations—friendships, socializing, dating—remained concentrated within the ethnic group.

Thus, the ethnic community survived the war, but its members became more scattered geographically and increasingly heterogeneous in occupation and lifestyle.

The Dispersion Period The period from 1960 to the present saw a continuation of the trends established in the post-war years.

The last vestiges of legal discrimination fell. The issei became eligible for citizenship under the McCarran-Walter Act of 1952, which also established token quotas for immigrants from Asia. The 1965 Immigration Act further liberalized entry regulations by doing away with quotas and giving preference to relatives and those in essential occupations. Because of the post-war economic boom in Japan, however, there has been little new Japanese immigration, with the exception of one major group.

During the occupation, contact between Japanese women and American servicemen resulted in many marriages. Although the exact number cannot be ascertained, an estimated 45,000 war brides were admitted into the United States between 1947 and 1975.[50] These women were more heterogeneous in social class and regional origin than the issei; moreover, in contrast to the agrarian background of the issei, the war brides tended to come from industrialized urban centers. Despite these differences, many of the new immigrants joined ethnic churches and organizations and participated in community activities.

A further shift took place in the generational composition of the community. The issei were passing away, and the nisei themselves were reaching or approaching retirement age. Meanwhile, their children, the *sansei,* were reaching adulthood and becoming visible. Raised in more affluent circumstances and freer from overt discrimination than their parents and grandparents, the sansei experienced a very different relationship to white America. Typically they interacted with whites all their lives and were culturally and socially assimilated. Possibly for this reason, the rate of sansei intermarriage has been high. It is estimated that 40 to 50 percent of sansei marry outside the group.[51]

Countering the overall trend toward assimilation (and perhaps as a reaction against it) was a resurgence of interest in Japanese culture and Japanese American history. Sansei students turned to the study of Japanese language and culture in college. During the late 1960s and throughout the 1970s, they took part in Third World Movement struggles that forced local universities to establish programs in ethnic studies, including Asian American studies. Many nisei also began to cultivate an interest in Japanese culture because they now had time for leisure pursuits. Classes in flower arrangement, music, and painting flourished.

The presence of a substantial Japanese business community in San Francisco contributed to a renaissance in Japanese performing arts in the 1970s. The Japan Center served as a focus for art exhibits and events. Television programs from Japan were broadcast on a local channel on Sunday evenings. These historical serials and contemporary social comedies had such an avid following that no community activities could be scheduled during this time.

Given this diversity, dispersion, and intermarriage, one might ask whether the concept of the Japanese American community still has meaning. The community is no longer a face-to-face group whose members interact on a daily basis. The sense of being scrutinized by watchful others no longer serves to reinforce identity or to enforce conformity. The sansei live according to the new American morality; cohabiting before marriage has become so common that it causes little comment. Still, the community serves as a reference point for orienting members' behavior, and members feel a sense of mutual obligation. Festivals, bazaars, weddings, anniversaries, and funerals are occasions for drawing together. The community is inclusive, rather than exclusive. Those who marry out of the group remain active, drawing in the non-Japanese spouse and children.

The community's solidarity was demonstrated when members organized to raise money for bail and a defense fund for Wendy Yoshimura, a young activist indicted for criminal activities connected with the Patty Hearst case, even though most of them were totally out of sympathy with her radical political beliefs. She repaid the community by being a model citizen during and after her trial. The continuity of values is also revealed in the operation of senior center programs in the Bay Area. Sansei college students were instrumental in initiating two programs and mobilizing support from various nisei groups. Both generations seem to have been motivated by *giri*, a sense of obligation toward the issei. In addition to a monthly meeting or outing, these programs provide services such as transportation, hot meals, medical checkups, advice on Medicare and social security, and home visits to the housebound. Board members and staff are primarily volunteers, drawn from all parts of the community and including all generations, professionals and non-professionals, women and men. Community networks are used to locate eligible seniors; staff members claim that no one is overlooked because *every* nikkei is known by someone in the community.

The Role of Women in the Community

Having reviewed the stages of settlement, we now turn to a more detailed examination of women's relationship to the community. Two generalizations may be made at the outset. First, from the beginning of settlement, women played a critical role in building and maintaining ethnic culture. Second, though women started out in peripheral roles in the organizational life of the community, they have emerged over time as its prime movers.

Educated women were often transmitters of formal Japanese culture, including language, literature, and art. Among the most knowledgeable informants interviewed for this study were several women who had gained familiarity with the community and its members through their work as teachers of flower arranging, calligraphy, painting, and other arts. In addition, *all* women, irrespective of education, preserved and passed on everyday aspects of Japanese culture, such as food, folk medicine, peasant lore, and customs, in their own families and in the larger community. Moreover, women were not only conservators; they were also mediators of cultural change. Employed women, especially those working as domestics, helped introduce selected aspects of American culture, such as home decoration and living arrangements.

In the initial stages of settlement, women were largely excluded from activities organized above the household unit. Their lives were circumscribed within the family by tradition and economic circumstances.

Since women were not present in the frontier period, the early immigrant institutions were created by and for men. The arrival of women changed the complexion of the community, but women were still not visible as active participants in extra-familial activities. Following Japanese custom, membership in organizations was based on the household unit, with the husband/father acting as its representative. In this role, men participated directly in church, language schools, athletic clubs, and *kenjinkai,* while women's relationships to these institutions were indirect, mediated by husbands. Involvement in these institutions was an important source of social status for men. A man employed as a gardener might not garner much prestige from his job. However, he could gain stature by becoming president of the church or donating a large sum to the Japanese school, while his wife and children basked in reflected glory. Public functions, such as dinners, were men-only affairs. Mother was expected to stay home, mind the children, and wait for father to return.

The exclusion of women from formal institutional bodies was a carryover from Japanese village life, and, as in the village, women formed their own organizations. These groups were of three main types. First were the *ko* or *tanomoshi-ko,* rotating credit associations. A typical ko was made up of twenty women who were acquainted through church, English classes, or a handicraft club. Each member put in a fixed amount each month—five, ten, or twenty dollars that she had earned sewing or doing domestic work. A lottery was held each month, with the entire sum going to the winner. Once she won, a member was ineligible to draw again, but was obligated to continue paying into the pot. At the end of twenty months, everyone had won once, and the ko came to an end. A new ko could be started, with new members recruited to fill any vacancies. The ko was a serious savings device that enabled women to accumulate a large lump sum of money for special expenses, such as a winter coat, a trip to Japan, or school clothes for children. It also served as a vehicle for women to get together, share meals, and become friends.

A second type of informal group was the handicraft club, similar to the American sewing circle. Some clubs had a commercial purpose. For example, the wife of a manufacturer of embroidered clothing ran a club to teach issei women how to do fine embroidery. The women were then recruited to do piece work at home for the manufacturer. More often the club was purely social. Women got together to learn from each other how to make beautiful or useful things for themselves and their families.

The third form of organization was the churchwomen's club, or *fujinkai.* The club's activities were strictly auxiliary: arranging flowers for the altar or preparing food for church functions. The women took no part in decision making, nor were they permitted to carry out major projects. Nonetheless, participation in the fujinkai gave women a chance to gain status and develop leadership skills within their own circle.

Pre-war nisei women were active in both female and coeducational groups. The nisei formed a plethora of overlapping clubs and organizations, ranging from the Young Buddhist Association to volleyball leagues, from YMCA clubs to chapters of the Japanese American Citizens League (JACL). The nisei preferred socializing in large groups, first because they felt more comfortable in them, and second because issei parents forbade dating. Women played active roles behind the scenes in mixed sex groups, while men were pushed forward as speakers and officers.[52]

After the war, women became more visible in public positions and were included in previously all-male ceremonial occasions. Mrs. Morita remarks: "Nowadays, if we're invited to anything, it would be Mr. and Mrs. invited. In the old days, it was just the mister. Mama stayed home with the kids and that was that."

The trend toward couple involvement is seen everywhere. Even the few remaining *kenjinkai,* originally all-male organizations, have evolved into couple clubs and are made up mostly of kibei. One woman reported that her kenjinkai meets once a month in someone's home, where they have dinner and play cards.

The change in attitude is illustrated by the following incident. Recently the management of a Japanese-owned bank gave a cocktail party for its new president and invited prominent members of the nikkei community. The bank followed the usual Japanese practice of inviting men without their wives. This caused considerable comment, but even more interest was aroused when one woman was singled out for an invitation. Mrs. Morita, the woman in question, exclaimed:

> And then I got an invitation, [addressed] just "Mrs. M."
> And then I mentioned it to somebody, who says, "Oh, my goodness, how come? You're one of the few women that's invited." I guess it was through my connection with the [senior] center. But all these guys were invited, but not their wives, you know. Just like in the old days. Mama never did go anywhere. Just stay home.

Mrs. Morita is typical of the women who are emerging as community leaders and activists. With affluence has come the leisure to get involved in community work. Many women devote endless hours to chauffeuring the elderly, making home visits, and attending meetings of various organizations. A typical community worker is Mrs. Arai, a 64-year-old San Francisco nisei who organized one of the first senior citizen programs for the issei in the 1960s. She obtained space from the city parks department, arranged transportation for outings, and persuaded professionals to donate their services. She explained that she wanted to do something to make the issei's later years more enjoyable. Another community worker, Mrs. Tsuchida, worked as a domestic before her marriage in 1937, and then helped in the family nursery business while raising four children. In 1952, when the issei finally became eligible for naturalization, she organized Japanese-language citizenship classes to help them prepare for their tests. She became increasingly active in the JACL and in unpaid social work among the elderly. When a senior center was established in her town with funds from the county welfare department, she was a logical choice for director. She was pleased:

> I wanted to do something more than a housewife. I'm not much of a housekeeper as you can see. I couldn't get involved in religion . . . so, when the JACL started up, [and] it wasn't religious, it seemed to be the thing for me.

Currently a paid staff worker, she says she would continue her work even if she were not paid.

The work of women like Mrs. Arai and Mrs. Tsuchida helps to connect different segments of the community, drawing them together to achieve common goals. The maintenance of social ties has thus emerged as an important form of unpaid labor for women. Their role as keepers of culture and ethnicity has been enlarged to encompass the community.

CHAPTER 3
Issei, Nisei, War Brides

Issei, nisei, war brides—their lives form separate but intertwined strands in the tapestry of Japanese American history. Who were these women, and what kinds of lives did they lead? The time has come to introduce the women in the three cohorts, to describe their early lives and the experiences that shaped their orientations to the labor market and the family. This account is about both the particular women who were interviewed and the larger population of issei, nisei, and post-war immigrant women.

Issei

Why did you come to the United States?
Because my husband called me. . . . I was only 18 years old, so I came here without knowing why. I came here the year I graduated from high school. My husband's cousin came back from America to find a bride for him. He persuaded my father to let me come to America. I was only 18 years old, and I grew up without going through any hardships. . . . Some people had to struggle to earn the expenses for transportation to America, but for me going to America sounded fun and I thought maybe I could study there. However, I missed the chance to study

because I had a baby right after our marriage. I attended the after-school class where English was taught to foreigners several times, but I couldn't carry on. I'd attend class for a while, then quit, then start again. I never completed the whole course. That's why I don't understand English very well. I was thinking I'd go back to Japan someday after staying awhile in America. If I had intended to remain in America forever, I would have studied hard. (Mrs. Okamura)

The backgrounds of issei women, most of whom arrived between 1915 and 1924, were similar to those of male immigrants. That is, they came from farming and small entrepreneurial families in southern Japan. Among the Meiji reforms affecting these women was the establishment of universal education in 1872. Females as well as males were enrolled in elementary school for four (later six) years, followed by an optional two or three years of middle school to learn domestic arts, such as sewing and cooking.[1] A select few attended high schools, located only in the larger cities and stressing the Chinese classics. According to a later survey, the average educational level of issei women equaled that of men—about eight years.[2] The typical issei woman was born in the last two decades of the nineteenth century or the opening decade of the twentieth. She was in her late teens to mid-twenties when she arrived, having recently married a man who had lived for some years in America, and who was employed as a wage laborer, small entrepreneur, or farmer. She was thus usually about 10 years younger than her husband.[3]

With few exceptions the women in the study fit this general profile, except for education. The domestics averaged six years, with two having no schooling and two having completed twelve or more years. Prior to marriage most lived at home and helped with farm or household work. Two women lived away, one as a maid, the other as a clerk in a hospital. Two others were employed for short periods: one worked as a laboratory assistant, another as a teacher's aide.

Marriage Following Japanese custom, marriages among the issei were arranged by a *baishakunin* (go-between). Many issei men managed to save or borrow money to return to Japan to meet their prospective brides and take part in a wedding ceremony. Others, for financial or other reasons, did not return, but had matches arranged by a go-between through an exchange of photographs: hence the term "picture marriage." A ceremony was conducted without the groom, and the union was legalized by registering it in the husband's home prefecture. Although such matches were perfectly respectable by Japanese standards, women naturally preferred to have a chance to meet their prospective spouses, however briefly. Aware of American disapproval of picture marriages, the women whose husbands did come for them made a point of emphasizing that theirs were not picture marriages.

Whether or not they actually met their spouses prior to marriage, the women in the study agreed that they had no choice but to marry, since there was no other role for women in Japanese society. Moreover, they often had little say in the selection of the husband. Daughters were expected to defer to their parents' wishes. Yet the extent to which women felt forced or manipulated by their parents and circumstances varied a great deal.[4]

At one extreme was Mrs. Takagi, who recalls that her father tricked her into going to stay with her adoptive grandfather in another town on the pretext that she would receive training to become a midwife:

> Otherwise I wouldn't have gone, you see. I knew my mother needed help. . . . I stayed one week and helped my uncle [a doctor]. I was thinking I would stay to help him. Pretty soon, they took me to see this man. I'd never seen or heard of him. He was my second cousin. You don't know the Japanese system: they just pick out your husband and tell you what to do. So I just did it, that's all. . . . I never gave my parents a fight.

Mrs. Takagi's attitude toward marriage was fatalistic: her mother and her aunt, she said, both had terrible times in their marriages; she never divorced her husband because "the next marriage might have been worse."

Another issei, Mrs. Nishimura, fell somewhere in the middle of the continuum. She was only 15 when she was persuaded by her father to marry Mr. Nishimura:

> In the Japanese style we used a go-between, and the husband would come to Japan to pick up his bride. My father

was rather new in his thinking so he told me that rather than stay in Japan to attend school, I should come to the United States. My mother told me even then that I was too young. But it's something that had to be done—so. . . . I was rather big for my age, and—. . . . But I cried at the time, and I'll always remember that. My parents felt a little guilty about it, almost as if they had forced me to come, and apparently they kept asking about me, about how I was doing, until they died.

At the other extreme we have Mrs. Shinoda, who dreamed of going to the United States even as a child:

I told my father that I wouldn't get married unless I could come to the United States.

Did your parents oppose you?

Yes, they were all against me.

How did you know you wanted to come to the United States?

I don't know. When I was small, in elementary school, we had to write an essay on "What I Wish For." I wrote in that essay that I'd like to go to America. My friends read it and told what I had written. That's funny, huh?

Mrs. Shinoda held out until her father gave in. She did not marry until she was 28, but she got her way.

Despite the pain of separation and the fear of the unknown, the majority of the women said that they left Japan with positive expectations. Just as the men came to better their lot, issei women came with their own hopes—to further their education, to help their families economically, to seek a happier home life, and to experience new adventures. They expected to achieve their goals and then return to a better life in Japan.[5]

Arrival and Adjustment The boat trip to the United States, usually from Yokohama to Seattle or San Francisco, lasted up to a month. The women report homesickness and physical illness, although they also fondly recall friendships developed with other women during the voyage.

Upon arrival, the first ordeal was getting through immigration procedures:

> Most women arrived as third-class steerage passengers for whom an inspection was a grim experience. Inspectors examined them more scrupulously than first- or second-class passengers. . . . Many questions worried the women to no end. Were their papers in order? Each wife had to have a valid passport, a certified copy of her husband's family registry, and a health certificate. Would she pass the physical examination? That she had been found free of trachoma and hookworm in Japan was no guarantee that she would.[6]

A second shock awaited many a picture bride when she encountered her new spouse for the first time. The man meeting her frequently bore little resemblance to the person shown in the photograph: "Men often forwarded photographs taken in their youth or touched up ones that concealed their real age. . . . Some had improved their overall appearance. They had all traces of facial blemishes and baldness removed. . . . Suave, handsome appearing gentlemen proved to be pockmarked country bumpkins."[7]

Mrs. Yoshida, who traveled with a number of other picture brides, recalled the reactions of some of her companions to their first glimpses of their husbands:

> A lot of people that I came together with said, "I'm going back on this very boat." I told them, "You can't do that; you should go ashore once. If you really don't like him, and you feel like going back, then you have to have a meeting and then go back." . . . Many times the picture was taken twenty years earlier and they had changed. Many of the husbands had gone to the country to work as farmers, so they had aged and become quite wrinkled. And very young girls came expecting more and it was natural.

Mrs. Yoshida herself was disappointed that her husband (sixteen years her senior) looked much older than a neighbor of the same age at home. However, many people from her village in Hiroshima had traveled to Hawaii and the United States, and she wanted to go too:

"I didn't care what the man looked like." Although her own marriage worked out well, she added, many picture marriages did not.

The newly landed issei women confronted many strange new experiences. Almost immediately they had to exchange the accustomed comfort of kimonos and slippers for constricting western dresses and shoes. The women were generally taken straight from clearing immigration to be completely outfitted.[8] Mrs. Sugihara arrived in Seattle in 1919:

> At that time ships were coming into Seattle every week from Japan, carrying one or two hundred Japanese brides. So there was a store set up especially for these new arrivals. There was a hotel run by a Japanese and also Japanese food available. The Japanese couldn't go to the stores run by whites, so there were stores run by Japanese to deal with Japanese customers. We did all of our shopping there. The lady there would show us how to use a corset, since we had never used one in Japan. And how to wear stockings and shoes.

Mrs. Okamura, who came in 1917, laughed when she remembered her first dress:

> It felt very tight. I couldn't even move my arms. That was the first time I had ever worn western clothes, so I thought they were supposed to be like that. . . . Later, Mrs. S. taught me to sew my own clothes. She had a pattern that we all used to make the same dress in different materials. So I found out that that first dress was too small.

Many issei women were appalled when they encountered the conditions under which they would live. Though most were aware that the streets would not be paved with gold, they were nonetheless unprepared for a total lack of amenities. Most followed their husbands into rural areas. Some went to remote labor camps that were built for railroad workers in the Mountain states, coal miners in Wyoming, sugar beet field hands in Utah and Idaho, laborers in lumbering camps and sawmills in Washington, and fish cannery workers in Alaska. Others, particularly those who stayed in California, went into the fields where their husbands tilled the soil as tenant farmers. In addition to working alongside their husbands, women in labor camps and farms often drew their own water, gathered wood to cook and heat the house, and fought to keep dirt out of houses that were little more than shacks. Mrs. Sugihara's experience was typical:

> We went to Seattle first and then to Oregon. . . . After we got to Oregon, we had to clear off the mountainside in order to prepare a field for planting—with shovels. Unlike California, Oregon is mountainous and the trees—pines six feet in diameter—would have to be cleared away before anything could be planted. We'd use long saws like this to cut up the pine trees. . . . During the day my husband would work [in the sawmill], then at night we would light some lanterns—kerosene lanterns—and work outside in our field. It rained a lot there, so on those days, we'd wear raincoats and work outside. That's how we made the land ready for planting. . . . We dug two wells ourselves, too. My husband would dig deep into the ground, and I would help by getting rid of the dirt he shoveled out. We were in our twenties then, so we could do everything by ourselves.

Women whose husbands resided in urban areas were more fortunate. Though they too worked long hours and kept house in crowded quarters, conditions were less primitive, and the presence of an ethnic community eased their adjustment.

As Mrs. Okamura's account indicates, earlier immigrants taught new arrivals the ropes. Though women who went to isolated rural areas got very little help in adjusting, those going straight to the Bay Area were aided by other women in the ethnic community. Living quarters were usually secured within the ghetto. Many couples rented rooms in a house and shared kitchen and bathroom facilities with several other families. Help and comfort were close at hand. Mrs. Hayashi said that the best time in her life was when she was a newly arrived bride. Her husband's friends dropped in to welcome her and bring gifts. Sometimes husbands who had worked as domestics taught their wives how to shop, cook, and clean. Community agencies like the YWCA, church missions, and the public schools sponsored housekeeping and English classes for newcomers. Six women in the study mentioned that they had attended English classes, but were unable to continue their studies once children arrived. Partly for this reason, most never fully mastered English.

In any case they rapidly became too busy to venture much outside the confines of the family and the ethnic community, except perhaps to work as domestic servants. Births followed shortly upon marriage and immigration. Large families were the norm, particularly in rural areas. Even in urban areas the issei had sizable families. A study of issei in the Seattle area found an average completed family size of 4.3 children.[9] The women in the study had somewhat smaller families, with an average of 3.4 children.

Harsh conditions drove some wives to desert their husbands, usually in the company of another man. Because of the unbalanced sex ratio, there were many detached men to whom women could turn. Several issei informants mentioned such desertions, known as *kakeochi*, in connection with disillusioned picture brides, but newspaper accounts in the Japanese-language press describe incidents involving women married for several years who left children behind. One informant reported that pictures of missing wives being sought by irate husbands appeared almost daily in the Japanese newspapers. It was rumored that runaway couples fled as far as New York or Mexico to escape detection. According to Ichioka, incidents of *kakeochi* must have been fairly frequent, judging by the number of notices and stories published in the vernacular press. The typical notice included the name of the deserting wife and the absconding "scoundrel," physical descriptions, the couple's places of origin in Japan, and photographs. For example, in September 1912 the *Nichibei Shimbun*, the main San Francisco Japanese-language newspaper, ran a notice by Suematsu Oshima of Hanford, declaring that his wife, Tora, had run off with Kenichi Ono, and offering a twenty-five-dollar reward for information as to their whereabouts.[10]

Most issei women, of course, persevered even in the face of an unhappy marriage and an intolerable workload. Issei marriages were stable and long-lasting, if not harmonious. Kitano estimates the divorce rate to have been only 1.6 percent.[11]

The issei women arrived at a time of accelerating anti-Japanese agitation. Their arrival was itself a focus of attack, since it signaled an intention on the part of the issei to settle on a long-term basis. Anti-Japanese propaganda depicted the practice of picture marriage as immoral and a ruse to contravene the Gentlemen's Agreement. As a result of mounting pressure, the Japanese government stopped issuing passports to picture brides in 1921.[12]

> Mrs. Takagi was outspoken about the racism of the period:
> I think all the [Japanese] people at that age had a real hard time.
> *They had to work hard you mean?*
> Not only that, they were all thinking we were slaves, you know, sleeping in the stable upstairs. And even when we'd get on a streetcar they'd say, "Jap, get away." Even me, they always threw stuff from up above.
> *They did? What do you mean?*
> I don't know why they did that. I was so scared. . . . One man, he was going on bicycle and someone threw cement. That night he lost an eye. But they never sued, they never reported it, because they didn't speak English. . . .
> I don't know what other people think, but we didn't have very much fun. We didn't have very many jobs.

The issei downplayed the personal difficulties they encountered as a result of racism. They avoided hostile encounters by remaining within the ethnic ghetto. Nevertheless, they were affected in a variety of ways, especially economically. Furthermore, discrimination reinforced the issei's sojourner orientation. Mrs. Amano notes that discrimination strengthened her husband's resistance to putting down permanent roots. They always rented apartments rather than buying a house, even after they could afford to do so. Her husband became increasingly nationalistic, keenly following political and military developments in Japan.

If the issei were like other immigrant groups, the likelihood of return migration diminished substantially once they started having children. Nonetheless, the issei women who were interviewed reported that they still entertained hopes of returning throughout the 1930s. The exact time when that would take place faded into the distant future as their children went through school and grew up. The advent of the war pierced even that illusion. With the exception of a small minority who accepted repatriation, any issei who had not returned before the war was destined to live out her life on American soil.

Nisei

How far did you get in school?
Oh, I just went to grammar school. And then the depression time my father couldn't hire anybody on the farm. So I was just starting high school and I had to give it up. And all the rest of them (I had three brothers and two sisters) . . . they all went to high school and I didn't get to go. . . . I was helping at home for quite a while, and then, see, my father used to raise strawberries and in the wintertime there's no work in the strawberry patch. So wintertime I used to go to work in domestic and then go back summertime to pick berries. . . . I sure worked hard, you know, in my day, when I worked for those people in C——. My day off I go home and change my clothes and put on the pants and go out in the field to pick berries. . . . I never did enjoy my young life. That's why I never wanted to marry a farmer. (Mrs. Fujitani)

The coincidence of generation and age ensured that the nisei, like the issei, shared a common historical life cycle. Most were born between 1910 and 1940. Figures compiled on internees in December 1942 indicate that the modal nisei was born between 1918 and 1922 to a 25-year-old mother and a 35-year-old father.[13] Thus, the typical nisei grew up in the 1920s and reached adulthood in the late 1930s and early 1940s. In addition, the nisei shared other characteristics and experiences that contributed to the formation of a clear generational identity.

Because of the similar occupational statuses of their parents, most nisei grew up in what might be characterized as modest, but not severely disadvantaged, circumstances.[14] While growing up the nisei were immersed in a mixture of American and Japanese culture: they spoke both Japanese and English, or often a combination of both, at home; ate corned beef and cabbage with rice; studied flower arrangement and piano; toasted *mochi* at the New Year and roasted the turkey at Thanksgiving; attended American school all day and trudged off to Japanese school in the afternoon. Reminiscences of nisei writers focus on the problem of forming a consistent identity out of the often contradictory values and norms of the two cultures.

The conflict felt most acutely was that between the self-expression valued in American society and the collectivity- and consensus-orientation of Japanese society. In her autobiography, *Nisei Daughter,* Monica Sone, who grew up in Seattle in the 1920s and 1930s, describes the dual personality she formed as she adjusted to two contrasting sets of expectations:

> *Nihon gakko* [Japanese school] was so different from grammar school, I found myself switching my personality back and forth like a chameleon. At Bailey Gatzert School, I was a jumping, screaming, roustabout Yankee, but at the stroke of three when the school bell rang and doors burst open everywhere, spewing out pupils like jelly beans from a broken bag, I suddenly became a modest, faltering, earnest little Japanese girl with a small timid voice.[15]

Out of the mixture, the values that were most complementary in the cultures flourished—almost to the point of exaggeration—in the nisei character. These were the so-called Protestant ethic (and Meiji) values of education, cleanliness, politeness, hard work, honesty, sobriety, and material success.[16]

Interestingly, the contradictions do not seem to have engendered confusion or feelings of inferiority. Rather, as Lyman points out, most nisei, although not uncritical of themselves, tend to feel that they combine the best elements of both cultures, achieving a felicitous balance, being neither too Japanese nor too American.[17] Lyman's observations are echoed by the interview subjects. Shown a continuum with one pole marked "American" and the other "Japanese," most of the nisei placed themselves halfway between the two poles or somewhat toward the American end, saying that they liked equally what was Japanese and what was American about themselves.

The nisei thus appear to be remarkably homogeneous. Yet there were differences among them. One major division was between those raised entirely in the United States and those who spent some formative years in Japan; another was between those who grew up in the country and those raised in the city.

The Kibei   A special term, *kibei,* was coined to refer to those who were American-born but spent part of their childhood in Japan. The size of this group can be gauged by the finding that 9.2 percent of the population in one evacuation camp was kibei.[18] Prior to World War II many issei parents sent their children to Japan for part of their education. Often they did this for economic reasons: the children were raised by grandparents or other relatives, freeing both parents to work full-time. Parents were also motivated by a desire for their children to receive a proper Japanese upbringing so that they would not be overly Americanized. They wanted their children to be inculcated with traditional virtues, such as respect for elders, discipline, and appreciation of the arts.

The issei parents succeeded in their aim. The kibei, especially those who came back as young adults, were seen by the nisei as fundamentally Japanese in their outlook, speech, and behavior. As a result, they did not fit into the social world of the urban nisei. The kibei tended to mix with other kibei and to marry among themselves. Of the seven kibei in the interview study, four were married to kibei, one to an issei, and two to nisei. In all but one instance, the marriages had been arranged by the families. Conformity to traditional practices is consistent with the kibei's generally low levels of acculturation.[19] Mrs. Taniguchi, an issei whose older children were raised in Japan, reported that she felt closer to her Japanese-educated daughters because they were more apt to accept her advice and take on domestic chores than their acculturated younger sisters. The kibei's "Japaneseness" proved to be a handicap in the dominant culture, however. Many never became fully fluent in English, and their occupational choices were therefore limited. Among the families in the interview sample who had sent some children to Japan and kept others in California, the kibei offspring were less successful occupationally. Kibei siblings were employed in service and blue-collar jobs, while their nisei brothers and sisters worked in white-collar jobs.

Rural Nisei The distinction between urban and rural nisei was also important, though less dramatic. Rural families retained traditional peasant values to a greater extent, particularly in communities such as Alviso and Livingston, which had large Japanese settlements. Some nisei in these communities received their education in private Japanese-language schools. Mrs. Aoki, who came to Alameda as a bride, was born and grew up in Alviso, where she attended a Japanese school. She remains more fluent in Japanese than English, so the nisei in Alameda are under the impression that she is an issei. Still other nisei attended American schools, but were segregated into "Oriental schools" set up for the Japanese and Chinese. The elementary schools in the Sacramento Delta region were segregated until the war. Overall, the rural nisei had few opportunities for developing face-to-face relations with whites.

Rural childhoods were arduous. The labor of women and children was essential in the type of small-scale farming the issei practiced in Northern California. Many issei sharecropped or worked on leased land. After the 1913 Alien Land Act was passed, the issei could not own land or lease it for longer than three years. They had to take short-term leases on small, often undesirable, parcels and work them intensively. Mrs. Aoki described her routine as a young child:

> Yes, on the farm we had to work hard. I picked the strawberries and beans out in the fields. I woke up early in the morning—before I went to school, I had to put all the baskets into the drawers of the chests [for strawberry picking]. You put six baskets in a drawer and there were twenty-four drawers in each chest. I had to do four or five chests before I got to school. And then I come home— sometimes I go to Japanese school after three o'clock and sometimes I have to come home and pick strawberries.

Schooling was often irregular because the children's labor was needed at home or because the family moved frequently to find new land to lease. Older children in large families often dropped out of school, the boys to work in the fields, the girls to help with housework and childcare. The oldest daughter became the substitute mother to the younger siblings. Mrs. Sasaki, who grew up in Courtland in the Sacramento Delta, reported:

> My father was a sharecropper. My mother did farming, helping her husband. She worked just as hard as my father did in the fields. . . . I finished the second or first year of high school—I can't remember. I had five brothers and three sisters. I was the oldest, so when the babies were born, I'd have to stay home and take care of them, so I got behind. And I started late too. My father kept moving from one ranch to another, and we couldn't go to school in some places. Myself and my brother Michan had to travel here and there with the family.

In addition, hard-pressed farm families sometimes needed out-side wages to supplement farm income. Daughters, rather than sons, could be spared from the fields. The most easily available jobs were in domestic service. Sometimes the women worked as live-in servants in the winter months and returned to help on the farm in the summer. One nisei, Mrs. Ito, was able to attend high school only because she worked as a live-in domestic for a teacher in town.

In rural areas, traditional family practices held sway. Dating was unheard of, and marriages were arranged up until World War II. All six of the women in the study who were raised in rural areas had arranged marriages; four were married to issei and two to kibei husbands. As in Japan, the parents engaged a go-between to investi-gate the backgrounds of suitable candidates and to arrange introduc-tions. Mrs. Fujii was "married off" to an issei eight years her senior when she was only 17:

> My parents, brother and sister went back to Japan in 1928. I was the only one left here. . . . My father had cancer and thought he wasn't going to live. . . . I had to get married because my parents wanted me to stay here. They thought it's too hard [for me] to live in Japan.

Because of the shortage of women, many women were married at a fairly young age, providing parents could spare their labor.

Urban Nisei   Compared with their rural counterparts, the nisei who grew up in San Francisco and other Bay Area cities had more comfortable, though not affluent, childhoods. Their parents owned small businesses, such as laundries, or were independent wage work-ers, usually gardeners and domestics. Family budgets were tight, and children were expected to help in the business or around the house, especially if there were many siblings. However, city girls usually did not have to work long hours or perform heavy manual labor. Mrs. Watanabe, who grew up in San Francisco in the 1930s, recalled that when her older sister and brother were small, her parents were em-ployed in a commercial laundry. These children were sent to Japan to be raised by relatives so that both parents could work. By the time Mrs. Watanabe was born, the parents had managed to acquire a small laundry. They were sufficiently well off that although her mother worked in the shop alongside her father, she and her younger brother and sister only helped out occasionally.

Urban children were also exposed to the dominant culture. Mrs. Nishi, a 55-year-old nisei, grew up as one of seven children; the family lived in various towns in the Bay Area as her father moved from one nursery job to another. The family finally settled in Oakland. She described her childhood in this way:

> Basically it was a happy childhood. I didn't realize how poor we were until people mentioned it. We didn't go hungry, but I remember we took turns getting a new pair of shoes, but then we didn't all need a new pair of shoes at one time either [laughs]. Living in California there were a lot of open spaces; it wasn't as built up as it is today. The kids were supposed to cut off the plant heads. But I said, "I can't stand this," so they said I could do the housework and the younger ones did the plant work. But basically the older ones took care of the younger ones. We had quite a cultural household, though there were five of us— and two came later—we had parents that took us to an awful lot of cultural events, concerts, museums. But I didn't see my first movie until I was five.

In the cities the nisei attended public schools with non-Japanese. Because of residential segregation the Japanese tended to be concentrated in certain schools, but they did not constitute the majority in any of them. They were able to mix a great deal with their non-Japanese peers in school. Conscientious and obedient students, the nisei generally did well academically. The one disadvantage they felt in relation to their non-Japanese peers was the lack of time for after-school activities. Many, if not most, nisei attended Japanese school in the afternoon. Sponsored by the churches and other community organizations, the schools emphasized discipline and character building as much as literacy; children were taught proper etiquette, including bowing, polite forms of speech, respect for authority, and such personal qualities as thrift, diligence, honesty, punctuality, and neatness. Kitano notes that the schools did not teach most nisei to speak Japanese fluently; still, they provided a social outlet and kept the children of working parents busy and off the streets.[20]

By the time the nisei reached their early teens, they were beginning to help at home and contribute to their own support. Mrs.

Issei, Nisei, War Brides

Morita started working in a store at 15, although underage, because she was big for her age. Mrs. Nishi notes that in Oakland many nisei girls worked as live-in babysitters during high school; she took her first live-in job at 14 because "I thought it would be helpful to my parents. They didn't say anything, but I just felt I should do it."

Unlike the rural women, most of the urban women managed to complete high school. Many, like their white classmates, took commercial courses to prepare themselves for office jobs. A few managed to attend business college, although parents tended to put their resources into educating their sons if funds were scarce.

With the loosening of traditional family controls, the urban nisei had moved toward the ideal of "free marriage" by the mid 1930s. Dating was still forbidden by most issei parents, but the young managed to meet through organized activities sponsored by the YMCA, the church, or other community organizations. If a couple met in this way, got to know each other, and decided to marry, they still had to gain parental consent. Before parents would approve a match, they engaged the services of a go-between to investigate, even if only in a pro forma way, the family background of the prospective partner.

The wedding itself had two parts. First came an American service with the bride dressed in a white gown. Later the bride reappeared in a kimono and traditional headdress to pose for photographs. The mixture of Japanese and western elements in Mrs. Morita's courtship and marriage is typical. Mrs. Morita grew up in San Francisco and graduated from high school in 1933. Shortly afterward, she met her husband on a camping trip on the Russian River at a spot popular among the Japanese. She was with a friend's family, while he was there with a group of his friends. Then:

> They got to start calling, and then we'd get a bunch of girls together. We always had to go in a bunch, you know [to the beach and dancing]. And then [we] kind of got together on different occasions, parties, or we still continued [at] the YMCA. But then we started meeting outside the YMCA, you know couples, stuff like that. And so then eventually it was just Harry and me. . . . My family wouldn't consent to it.
> *Why is that?*
> He lived in the country and nobody knew his family. And his family likewise—I lived in the city [and they thought] I wasn't good for country work. [Harry's family ran a

nursery.] . . . So they [his parents] did the proper thing by it. I used to visit, get to know the family. And then they sent a couple over to formally ask for my hand in marriage, the regular way. So then that's when I got married in the Buddhist Church [in 1937].

The familiar world of the nisei, with its mixture of old and new cultures, its combination of restrictiveness and comfort, came to an abrupt end with the commencement of World War II. The typical nisei was in her teens or twenties on the eve of the war. She was still single, but was likely to marry within the next few years and start her family. She might anticipate continuing her education.

The internment played a role for the nisei analogous to that of immigration for the issei. It cleaved the nisei's life into two distinct periods. It tore her from her familiar environment and set her course for an unknown future. It signaled the end of youth and the beginning of added responsibilities for the welfare of the older generation and the network of kin. It also eventually brought about unforeseen changes in her economic and social circumstances.

The War Brides

My parents said, "You made your own decision. If your husband leaves you, don't come back. Just slit your throat."
Were you scared?
Yes, but I was excited and I enjoyed it. I thought that in America there was lots of money. Everything is carefree, lots to eat. So I was very happy. Plenty to eat, plenty of clothes. I thought I was going to paradise.
Think so now?
No—opposite! American soldiers used to spend money so freely we thought that everyone in America had money. We thought it was a dream world. But I was disappointed. I speak not much English. I was sick, up and down for fourteen years. (Mrs. Langer)

It is more difficult to generalize about the social and economic circumstances of the war brides than about the other two groups.

The post-war immigrants came from diverse backgrounds: they were raised in well-to-do, middle-class, and poor working-class families; they came from all parts of Japan, from provincial towns and large cities. Not surprisingly, the women brought with them divergent values, experiences, and personal resources.

Despite their diversity, the war brides shared some important experiences. Most war brides had suffered some degree of privation and social dislocation during World War II and the economic upheaval that followed the war. One result was their employment in jobs that brought them in contact with American servicemen. For all the women, marriage to a non-Japanese meant some degree of alienation and ultimately separation from parents and other kin. Once they emigrated, the women faced difficult cultural and social adjustments not unlike those faced by the issei—a new language, cultural differences, and restricted economic options.

Social and Economic Circumstances Prior to Immigration

The women who became war brides during the 1950s and early 1960s were adolescents or young women at the end of World War II. As a result of the war, Japan had suffered massive losses of human life, as well as large-scale destruction of the environment. Families were uprooted. Young men were away, disabled, or deceased. Women and children were evacuated from the cities and sent to the countryside to escape the bombing. As the war drew on, a labor shortage developed, and school-age children were brought into the work force to aid in the war effort. Women who were still in school during the war were required to sew or perform light assembly work during school hours. Despite difficulties, most of the women in the study managed to complete high school. Among the twelve women interviewed, three left school in the ninth grade, eight completed high school, and one did post-high-school teacher training. As the economy collapsed in the closing months of the war, severe shortages of food and other essential goods developed, and several women reported suffering hunger and privation during this period.

At the end of the war, with the loss of males in the family and the ruin of family enterprises, many young women were forced to go out to seek a livelihood. Miyoshi Farrow's story illustrates the straits in which many women found themselves:

I was born in the fourth year of the Showa reign [1928] in
S—— near Kyoto. Then I went to school in Osaka. I was
15 years old when it was bombed. Our house was burned
up, so we had to move to Kobe. I stayed at Kobe awhile
and finished school, and then it was burned again. So we
had to move to D——. That time I was eighteen years old.
I found my first job at R—— Garden, a dance hall. I was
the youngest one, and I can't work the dance because I
don't know how to dance either. First day, opening, they
invite government and military officials. We girls put on
kimonos and help serve the food. The top colonel saw me
and asked me some questions, and at that time I didn't
know any English. The interpreters said come next day to
such and such office. So I went the next day and through
the interpreter the colonel asked me a lot of questions:
"Why are you working there? How old are you?" So I told
that I couldn't find a job and I had to work and then the
colonel feel sorry for me because I'm a virgin. He told me I
shouldn't work there. . . . He says, "I give you a job if you
like to come over to this office." So I took a job in that MG
[Military Government] office. I worked in the office where
they used to do pay and that sort of thing. And there I met
my present husband.

As Mrs. Farrow's story indicates, the need for employment cor-
responded with expanded opportunities provided by the American
occupation. Young women found jobs on military bases as sales,
service, or clerical workers, and in establishments catering to American servicemen as bar girls and waitresses. Later, with economic
recovery, low-paying jobs opened up in Japanese industry. However,
it was primarily through jobs related to the American military presence that Japanese women came into contact with American men. All
but one of the women were employed prior to marriage and met their
husbands on the job. Six women were living away from their families.
Thus, most of the women were relatively independent and free of
family constraints at the time of marriage.

Marriage   The shortage of Japanese males of marriageable age,
the loneliness of servicemen abroad, and contact between American
men and Japanese women made it almost inevitable that some inter-

cultural marriages would take place. Aside from any romantic element, economic and emotional security were powerful impetuses. Kazuko Frankel saw marriage to an American as insurance against want. She recalled what it was like to be hungry during the war. A high school student at the end of the war, she studied typing and obtained an office job; later she decided to switch to waitressing at a non-commissioned officers' club. She liked it better, and "there was plenty to eat." She met her first husband there. Her family was opposed, but she decided to go ahead with the marriage: "You see that time for me, base work was not too easy to find because the army forces were getting smaller and smaller. So I feel not too relaxed. I felt it would be more security to find someone to support me."

For Shizuko Howell, the desire was for emotional as well as material security. She had led a hand-to-mouth existence in the nine years since she took a job at the Honda factory in Tokyo sewing motorcycle seat covers. The pay was low and she was frequently in debt, so she quit to work in a friend's bar. Her father heard about it and came to fetch her home. She worked for a few years in his store and then returned to Tokyo to work at Honda again. She hung around her friend's bar and met her husband there. After going with him for a while, she found out that she was pregnant:

> I tell my husband I'm pregnant, but I don't want to marry. I'm afraid to go to the United States. My husband said, "If you don't want to marry me, I'd like to have the baby anyway.". . . My girlfriend said, "You're 28. It's hard for you to stay single. It's time you married. You're pregnant and he wants the child." So then I said, "Okay." [In those days] I didn't think too deeply. Because he's so nice to me. When I was sick and in the hospital, he paid my hospital bills and comes every day. Then I think I can trust him. So then I started going to fix the papers and stuff like that.

A rebellious streak, such as that displayed by Mrs. Howell, may have been another impetus for some marriages. Many of the women had shown a taste for independence before marriage. Hideko Sentino grew up in a small town in northern Japan where her father was the police chief. In the mid-1930s she signed up right out of high school for service in Manchuria. She proudly recalls that as an army stenographer, she earned "more pay than a college graduate." Etsuko Rybin, now the leader and lay minister of the U.S. branch of a Buddhist sect, ran a successful business, a small restaurant given to her by an aunt.

The women seemed to have been conscious of the inequities involved in Japanese male-female relations. Reiko Simeone recalled rebelling against the idea of marriage as a young girl after observing what happened to women:

> In Japan when I was young, I never thought I'm going to marry because in Japan, if you marry, to me it was going to the graveyard. That time, men do what they want even if they're married. A couple of years later, he'd be fooling around. I won't say everybody, but most. So I don't care for that life. That's why I thought I'm never going to get married.
> *Is that why you married an American?*
> Maybe! [Laughs.]

Thus, in addition to emotional and material security, marriage to an American offered the prospect of a more egalitarian relationship than is typical in Japanese marriages. This may have been especially important to women who had tasted freedom before marriage.

War bride marriages violated the most fundamental norms of Japanese society. First, there are strong proscriptions against marrying outside the group. Second, marriage is considered a family rather than an individual matter. All but one of the women reported initial parental opposition to the marriage. Two women, living away from their parents, simply did not notify them. For some women, already estranged from their parents, marriage simply magnified the alienation. Those who married blacks encountered the strongest disapproval. Sachiko Adair reported that her mother, after twenty years, still refused to acknowledge her grandchildren. Mrs. Inaba's wish to marry a nisei was opposed by her father, who said that American Japanese are American. Even parents who reluctantly gave their consent made it clear that their daughters were forfeiting parental support. Midori Langer's tale is unique because of her long courtship and late marriage. Yet her parents' attitudes and harsh warning are quite typical:

> My eldest brother had heard rumors about Japanese women married to American men—that after they got there the husbands deserted them and the girls were all

working as waitresses and domestics. Most of the men didn't have too much education, so he wanted to find out how much education Robert had. Since we had been corresponding for eight years, my brother wanted to read the letters. My brother was an interpreter for the occupation government, so he could judge. After reading the letters he said, "This man is educated." He is the eldest, so the others listened to him; he convinced them that it was all right. Since I was sickly, my brother had bought a [house] lot and provided for me. He told me to think about it as going on a long vacation for two years. "You can come back any time for your property." But my parents said, "You made your own decision. If your husband leaves you, don't come back. Just slit your throat."

The parental disclaimer of responsibility became important later on in that it increased the women's feelings of isolation. When problems arose, the women kept them to themselves, feeling ashamed. They did not inform their families that they were divorced or that they were working as domestics. They preferred to paint a rosy picture and suffer alone, rather than admit that they had made a mistake.

Entry Into U.S. Society   It was not uncommon for couples to cohabit before marriage or to live as a married couple in Japan for an extended period before emigrating. One couple stayed in Japan for eleven years. Except for this couple, who reported discrimination in Japan, the women indicated that as long as they stayed in Japan, life was relatively smooth. Kim, a social worker specializing in war brides, found this to be the case among her clients. She suggests that this was so because very little adjustment was required by either spouse:

> The wife continues to live in her familiar environment; she speaks her own language, interacts with her family and friends who may also be intermarried, and eats her native food. The husband likewise continues to work in the same setting, more likely on the military base, although he may spend more time with his wife. Military

benefits for dependents make them feel affluent as such benefits stretch much further in the wife's country where living is less costly.[21]

Once the couple or family moved to the United States, however, the equilibrium shifted. Now the wife faced a monumental task of adjustment. She had to learn to communicate, shop, prepare meals, and carry out other tasks in a completely unfamiliar environment, without a supportive kin network. Since the husbands generally did not speak Japanese, the women had to communicate entirely in English, a language they found difficult to master. Aside from limited services provided by social agencies, churches, and war bride organizations, they were almost completely dependent on their husbands for guidance and support. Unfortunately, some husbands were not sufficiently responsive to their wives' needs. The husbands' parents and relatives did not play a major role, since most of the couples did not settle near his kin.

Some women learned that the security and ease they had sought were not forthcoming, and they quickly became disillusioned. Many servicemen were not well educated or skilled; the military provided more security and opportunity than they could find in civilian life. Nationally, about half of the husbands of war brides were in the military, a proportion that applied to the present sample of twelve. Unfortunately, military life meant frequent uprooting and separation. Life on army posts in the American South and Southwest or in Asia was boring and lonely. Five of the six divorces in the group occurred among military families. The women cited frequent separation and the husbands' drinking, adultery, and non-support as interrelated causes of the breakup of their marriages. The breakups were doubly traumatic for the women because they were so isolated. Without job skills and, frequently, alimony or child support, these post-war immigrants were hard-pressed to find the means to support children. Both during and after their divorces, the women experienced anxiety, immobility, and recurrent thoughts of suicide. Shizuko Howell confessed: "For four years I had a hard time, but I didn't tell people. People just wouldn't understand. Sometimes I said I wished I killed myself and kill my kids. I thought about it a few times." Sachiko Adair has been on welfare for several years. She works part-time in a restaurant as a hostess and occasionally does domestic work and maid work in a motel. However, she can only work sporadically because she gets "too nervous."

The other half of the sample, those whose marriages endured, were generally better off financially and emotionally, but they too experienced adjustment problems. Loneliness, homesickness, and inability to speak English were principal complaints. Forming social connections outside of marriage was an important step in overcoming isolation. Many war brides put a great deal of effort into establishing relationships with other Japanese American women. Kazuko Frankel reports that when she first arrived in the Bay Area, she looked up people with Japanese names in the telephone book and introduced herself over the phone. When this effort did not bear fruit, she went from house to house in a neighborhood where many Japanese lived. She even made friends with other war brides she met on the bus. Through these efforts she established an extensive network of friends, many of whom meet regularly for meals and outings.

Other women worked through institutions. Reiko Simeone joined the local Japanese American church and participated in almost all of its activities. A few years before her interview, she started a newcomers' group with the minister's help. Mrs. Rybin started her own church, the U.S. branch of a Buddhist sect; she recruited members, started counseling, and now holds regular services. Other women were less aggressive but managed in their own way to form friendships with other war brides. Four women belonged to ethnic, church, or social service organizations; four were active in religious sects made up primarily of Japanese immigrants; and two participated in community organizations for Japanese newcomers. The other two were involved in friendship groups with at least three other war brides. Altogether, ten out of the twelve appeared to have close ties in the ethnic community. Thus over a period of years, though still suffering pangs of homesickness, most war brides managed to construct their own social supports, whether by using established organizations or building their own informal networks.

Despite the differences in the personal circumstances of war brides and issei and nisei, there was nonetheless a sense of fellow-feeling among them, if only because of the way they were treated by the dominant culture. As a result of their visible racial resemblance, all Japanese American women were lumped together by outsiders.

Thus, whether they wanted to be part of the ethnic community or not, their life chances were to a great extent determined by their ethnicity. As we shall see in the following chapter, issei, nisei, and war brides shared a common fate in the labor market, where they were tracked into the same narrow range of occupations. Prospective employers sought "Japanese help" without distinguishing among cohorts.

CHAPTER 4
The Labor Market

Issei, nisei, and war brides have had distinct, yet related, experiences in the work force. Their working lives were shaped by a labor system stratified according to gender, race, and migrant status. As a result of this stratification, their employment was limited to a narrow set of occupations and industries that constitute a separate and distinct labor market.

In this chapter I analyze that labor market by examining the occupational distributions of the three cohorts at decade intervals over the period from 1900 to 1970. I also consider the unique features of the San Francisco Bay Area market. Labor markets, in addition to being segmented, are necessarily localized. The structure of a local labor market is determined by the historical development of the local economy and by the mix of industries and the composition of the labor force specific to that area.[1] Thus, I compare the labor market for Japanese women in the Bay Area with that in other metropolitan areas with significant Japanese populations.

What occupations and industries constituted the distinct labor market for Japanese women? Did issei, nisei, and war brides all operate within the same market? How did the structure of the market change as the economy changed? The underlying question throughout is, why have successive cohorts of Japanese women specialized in domestic service from the time of initial immigration in the 1900s to the present?

The Pre-War Labor Market

The marriages that brought issei women to the United States were instigated by male sojourners at a point when they realized that they were not going to make their fortunes and return home as quickly as they had originally planned. They hoped that a wife would assist them in reaching their goals. Thus, quite apart from any sentimental desire for family life, men had pragmatic reasons to send for wives. A wife would provide much-needed labor in the form of services in the home and income-producing activities outside it. Any issei woman arriving in the United States could expect to pull her weight economically.

Therefore, although they were not recruited, as their husbands were, as independent laborers, issei women were quickly absorbed into the work force and played a similar role in the market by filling jobs not wanted by native workers. As early as 1915 an observer of the "Japanese problem" in California noted that

> the great majority of wives of farmers, barbers and small shopkeepers take a more or less regular place in the fields or shops of their husbands, while a smaller number accept places in domestic service, or in laundries or other places of employment. Thus a large percentage of those admitted find a place in the "labor supply."[2]

The National Picture   According to U.S. census figures, 20.8 percent of all Japanese women 10 years of age and over were gainfully employed in 1920. This is similar to the proportion of white women gainfully employed (20.7 percent).[3] Since virtually all Japanese women in the population were married, however, the issei rate of employment was in fact remarkably high. In the population at large, only 9.0 percent of married women were in the labor force.[4] Moreover, the 20 percent rate is undoubtedly an underestimate, given the Japanese concentration in agriculture and small enterprises, fields in which wives performed unpaid labor that frequently went unrecorded by census takers.

The labor market for Japanese women was closely related to the market for Japanese men. Occupational distributions for men and women reveal concentration in parallel occupations. Both men and women "specialized" in agriculture, service, and trade (see Tables 1 and 2). There are good reasons for the similarity. In the first place, a substantial proportion of women worked alongside their husbands in agriculture or in their husbands' trades, as noted above. Second, it was not uncommon for husband and wife to work for the same employer. Japanese owners of commercial laundries and nurseries were especially likely to follow the Japanese model of family labor by hiring (and often housing) the entire family. Two of the issei women reported that they and their husbands had been employed together in a laundry or nursery, and two of the nisei reported that their parents had worked in the same enterprise at some point in their careers. Third, husbands and wives often used the same personal networks to find employment and therefore heard about jobs in the same industries and firms. Finally, and most important, their labor markets were related because issei men and women occupied a similar position in the labor system. As racial-ethnic immigrants, they were excluded from the industrialized sector and confined to the "backward" agrarian and "degraded" service sectors.

It is difficult to arrive at an exact occupational distribution for issei women in the pre-war period. They frequently divided their time among housework, unpaid labor for the family farm or business, and wage work, so their primary occupation cannot be easily pinpointed. One early study furnishes data indicating the range of their activities. Strong surveyed 1,716 issei women in the early 1930s. He classified 998 (58 percent) as housewives, 438 (26 percent) as part-time assistants to their husbands, 53 (4 percent) as full-time assistants, and 227 (13 percent) as engaged in independent occupations. He notes, however, that

> undoubtedly the last two figures are too low and the first figure too high. Accuracy in this connection was very difficult to secure because many of these women speak very little English and are unaccustomed to talk to strangers, and in some cases the Japanese men prevented or interfered in the interviewing of their wives.[5]

The most comprehensive source of detailed occupational data, the U.S. census, suffers from these same problems and also overlooks important categories of women's work by systematically under-reporting unremunerated family labor.[6] The census nonetheless provides a rough estimate of the proportions of issei women engaged in various fields from 1900 to 1940. These data (Table 2) show that

TABLE 1

OCCUPATIONS OF EMPLOYED JAPANESE MEN IN THE UNITED STATES, 1900–1940[a]

	1900 No.	1900 %	1920 No.	1920 %	1930 No.	1930 %	1940 No.	1940 %
Agriculture, forestry, animal husbandry	5,345	23.9	23,860	45.4	22,454	47.3	17,733	42.9
Farmers and farm laborers	(5,102)[b]	(22.8)	(12,197)	(23.2)	(21,434)	(45.1)	—	—
Fishermen	—	—	(773)	(1.5)	(857)	(1.8)	—	—
Gardeners, nursery workers, florists, fruit growers	—	—	(10,572)	(20.1)	—	—	—	—
Lumbermen	(111)	(0.5)	(218)	(0.4)	(163)	(0.3)	—	—
Other	(132)	(0.6)	(100)	(0.2)	—	—	—	—
Extraction of minerals	168	0.8	1,119	2.1	680	1.4	—	—
Manufacturing, including lumber mills	826	3.7	6,424	12.2	3,508	7.4	3,962[c]	9.6
Transportation	6,277	28.1	4,273	8.1	2,290	4.8	—	—
Trade	198	0.9	4,510	8.6	6,732	14.2	9,125[d]	22.1
Public service	—	—	119	0.2	89	0.2	—	—
Professional services	132	0.6	1,150	2.2	1,641	3.4	1,254	3.0
Domestic and personal services	9,058	40.5	10,363	19.7	9,351	19.7	4,491	10.9
Servants	(2,960)[e]	(13.2)	(4,893)	(9.3)	(4,223)	(8.9)	(1,814)	(4.4)
Clerical work	—	—	796	1.5	744	1.6	—	—
Labor, other than farm	—	—	—	—	—	—	4,499	10.9
Other	336	1.5	—	—	—	—	258	0.6
TOTAL EMPLOYED	22,340	100.0	52,614	100.0	47,489	100.0	41,322	100.0

Sources: For 1900: U.S. Bureau of the Census, *Special Reports, Occupations of the Twelfth Census* (Washington, D.C.: U.S. Government Printing Office, 1904), table 35: "Distribution, by Specified Occupations, of Males and of Females in the Chinese, Japanese, and Indian Population Gainfully Employed, 1900." For 1920: U.S. Bureau of the Census, *Fourteenth Census of the United States Taken in the Year 1920*, vol. 4: *Population, Occupations* (Washington, D.C.: U.S. Government Printing Office, 1923), table 5: "Total Persons of 10 Years of Age and Over Engaged in Each Specified Occupation, Classified by Sex, Color, or Race, Nativity, and Parentage, for the United States: 1920." For 1930: U.S. Bureau of the Census, *Fifteenth Census of the United States: Population*, vol. 5: *General Report on Occupation* (Washington, D.C.: U.S. Government Printing Office, 1933), table 6: "Chinese and Japanese Gainful Workers 10 Years Old and Over by Occupation and Sex, for the United States and Selected States, 1930." For 1940: U.S. Bureau of the Census, *Sixteenth Census of the Population, 1940: Population Characteristics of the Non-white Population by Race* (Washington, D.C.: U.S. Government Printing Office, 1943), table 8: "Non-white Employed Persons 14 Years Old and Over, by Major Occupation Group, Race, and Sex, for the United States, by Regions, Urban and Rural, 1940."

[a]Data for 1910 are omitted because occupational figures for Japanese and Chinese were combined in the census report.

[b]Includes gardeners, nursery workers, florists, and fruit growers.

[c]Includes workers in transportation and extraction of minerals.

[d]Combines trade and clerical categories.

[e]Includes waiters.

TABLE 2

OCCUPATIONS OF EMPLOYED JAPANESE WOMEN IN THE UNITED STATES, 1900–1940[a]

	1900		1920		1930		1940[b]	
	No.	%	No.	%	No.	%	No.	%
Agriculture workers, including farm and nursery labor	13	4.9	1,797	34.0	2,041	30.3	2,525	37.7
Servants, including cooks, chambermaids, and other servants	151[c]	56.8	1,409	26.6	1,195	17.7	690	10.3
Other personal service workers, including barbers, waitresses, lodging house keepers, laundry operatives, etc.	57	21.4	951	18.0	1,463	21.7	1,579[d]	23.6
Trade workers, including saleswomen, clerks, etc.	9	3.4	369	7.0	946	14.0	683[e]	10.2
Dressmakers, including seamstresses and tailors	23	8.6	124	2.3	121	1.8	—[f]	—
Other manufacturing, mechanical workers	8	3.0	378	7.1	348	5.2	801[g]	12.0
Professionals (teachers, nurses)	5	1.9	145	2.7	329	4.9	214	3.2
Clerical workers	—	—	75	1.4	271	4.0	—[h]	—
Other	—	—	41	.8	27	0.4	201	3.0
TOTAL EMPLOYED	266	100.0	5,289	99.9[i]	6,741	100.0	6,693	100.0

Sources: For 1900: U.S. Bureau of the Census, *Special Reports, Occupations of the Twelfth Census* (Washington, D.C.: U.S. Government Printing Office, 1904), table 35: "Distribution, by Specified Occupations, of Males and of Females in the Chinese, Japanese, and Indian Population Gainfully Employed, 1900." For 1920: U.S. Bureau of the Census, *Fourteenth Census of the United States, Taken in the Year 1920*, vol. 4: *Population, Occupations* (Washington, D.C.: U.S. Government Printing Office, 1923), table 5: "Total Persons 10 Years of Age and Over Engaged in Each Specified Occupation." For 1930: U.S. Bureau of the Census, *Fifteenth Census of the United States: Population*, vol. 5: *General Report on Occupation* (Washington, D.C.: U.S. Government Printing Office, 1933), table 6: "Chinese and Japanese Gainful Workers 10 Years Old and Over by Occupation and Sex, for the United States and Selected States, 1930." For 1940: U.S. Bureau of the Census, *Sixteenth Census of the Population, 1940: Population Characteristics of the Non-white Population by Race* (Washington, D.C.: U.S. Government Printing Office, 1943), table 8: "Non-white Employed Persons 14 Years Old and Over, by Major Occupation Group, Race, and Sex, for the United States, by Regions, Urban and Rural, 1940."

[a]Data for 1910 are omitted because occupational figures for Japanese and Chinese were combined in the census report.

[b]Only foreign-born (issei) women are included in the figures for 1940. The 1940 census for the first time separated out native and foreign-born. The figures for 1930 include some native-born (nisei) women, but they probably constitute only a small proportion of the total. Because of immigration patterns, most nisei were born after 1910.

[c]Includes some waitresses.

[d]Made up of "proprietors, managers, and officials, except farm" and "service workers, except domestic."

[e]Named "clerical, sales and kindred workers" in the 1940 census.

[f]No longer separately reported; presumably these occupations are included below under "manufacturing."

[g]Named "operatives and kindred workers" in the 1940 census.

[h]Included under "trade," above.

[i]Due to rounding.

agricultural labor, including employment in plant nurseries (an early Japanese specialty), was the largest field of employment throughout the pre-war period, accounting for about one-third of all employed issei women.[7] Outside agriculture, domestic service was by far the most common form of employment. In 1900 over half of all wage-earning women were so employed; however, with only 266 counted as gainfully employed, their numbers are so small as to make the data inconclusive. Twenty years later, when 5,289 issei women workers were listed, 1,409 (or 40.3 percent of those in non-agricultural occupations) were in domestic service.[8] The number had dropped to 690 (or 16.6 percent of non-agricultural employment) by 1940, but it remained the largest single non-agricultural occupation throughout the pre-war years.[9]

The other fields in which Japanese women specialized were personal services and retail trade. The growth in their employment in services and trade from 25.0 percent in 1920 to 35.7 percent by 1930 reflects the movement of Japanese men out of wage labor and into self-employment in small business, such as Oriental gift stores and shops catering to a Japanese clientele. The women were engaged as paid and unpaid sales and clerical help in these ethnic enterprises. A small and fluctuating percentage of women found work in manufacturing, primarily in food processing and garment making. The proportion dipped from 7.1 percent in 1920 to 5.2 percent in the depression trough of 1930, but rebounded to 12.0 percent in 1940. The establishment of ethnic community institutions created a small demand for professionals: for example, teachers in Japanese-language schools and instructors in calligraphy, music, and other Japanese arts. The proportion of Japanese women listed as professionals peaked at 4.9 percent in 1930. Perhaps the most important category of female professions was midwifery. Up to the mid-1930s, issei women gave birth at home, attended by a midwife (*osamba*) trained in Japan. The *osamba* provided both pre-natal and post-natal care, starting with the preparation of layettes and the manual manipulation of fetuses to prevent breech delivery and extending to advice on breastfeeding and post-natal nursing services. Two San Francisco midwives, Mrs. Iyeki and Mrs. Kojima, were renowned for their skill and compassion.[10] Many others whose names are forgotten also practiced their skills in the pre-war period, including one of the issei in this study, Mrs. Hayashi.

Census statistics do not tell the whole story. Information garnered from community informants revealed that women engaged in a great deal of informal market work.[11] The tourist traffic in San Francisco created a demand for handmade "Oriental" goods that women could manufacture at home. Embroidery, hand sewing, and paper flower making were common home industries. The contractor, usually a storeowner or wholesaler, delivered raw materials and picked up finished products. During the 1920s a couple named Isoe sold hand-embroidered dresses to exclusive apparel shops. The husband sketched the designs and the wife taught the stitches to issei women, who then embroidered in their spare time at home. Another couple sold custom-tailored kimonos in their gift shop on Grant Avenue. The wife cut out the pieces and made up bundles, which the husband delivered to women in their homes. He paid them three dollars for each finished garment. A kimono took about two days to complete, and a financially hard-pressed woman might stay up through the night completing one.[12] Mrs. Shimada, a nisei informant, recalled that one of her chores as a child was to thread forty needles and line them up in rows before she went to sleep so that her mother could sew without stopping.

Whether in the formal or the informal market, issei women's occupations shared several characteristics. The work could be fitted around family responsibilities (e.g., it was done at home, children could be taken to work, hours were flexible); it involved tasks that were an extension of women's work in the home (e.g., food preparation, laundry, and sewing); it was in a low-technology, labor-intensive field where low wages and long hours reduced competition from white women; it took place in a family-owned or ethnic enterprise where language difficulties and racial discrimination did not constitute barriers to employment.

Because of their common characteristics, one would expect these occupations to be highly substitutable. The job histories of the women in the study support this expectation. The issei moved easily among this set of occupations but were never employed outside it. The eleven women with job experience outside domestic employment had worked in one or more of the following: farming, home laundry, commercial laundry, garment shop, plant nursery, home dressmaking, home embroidery, midwifery, and family-owned cleaning store, hotel, or nursery. In short, this set of occupations, which includes domestic service, constituted a distinct, separate labor market for immigrant Japanese women.

What about the nisei? Were they confined within the same market? The 1930s saw increasing numbers of them reaching adulthood and joining the work force. Most were still single and expected to earn their keep until they married. By 1940 the number of nisei women matched the number of issei women in the labor force. Data from the 1940 census (Table 7), which distinguishes between native and foreign-born Japanese, shows that three-quarters of all employed nisei females were distributed in equal proportions among three categories: (1) farming, where they appeared as managers, wage laborers, and unpaid family workers (24.3 percent); (2) domestic service (25.7 percent); and (3) clerical and sales work (22.9 percent). The concentration in farming illustrates the importance of daughters' labor for the rural issei family. The concentration in clerical and sales jobs reflects Japanese involvement in small urban enterprises. Nisei clerks and sales workers were employed almost exclusively in Japanese-owned firms, where their knowledge of English was useful in dealing with non-Japanese customers and vendors. Domestic employment was extensive in both city and country.

The nisei received little return on investments in education and skill training. Several of the nisei women interviewed reported taking business or typing courses, just as their white classmates did, but none was able to use her skills in the job market. Opportunities for white-collar work were limited. White business and government jobs were closed. Their only chance for white-collar work was in ethnic firms, which were generally small and marginal. There were simply not enough openings in these firms to employ all who were qualified. The resulting competition and crowding depressed wages below those offered for comparable jobs in the dominant market.

Thus, despite their American education and fluency in English, the nisei's options were almost as restricted as their immigrant mothers', and their concentration in domestic service was even greater. Over a quarter of employed nisei were listed in 1940 as private household workers, compared with slightly over 10 percent of the issei.

The Bay Area Labor Market   There is evidence that the structure of the local labor market in the Bay Area was even more restrictive for issei and nisei than the national statistics suggest. The

The Labor Market

number and proportions of issei and nisei women engaged in domestic work in the four U.S. cities with the largest Japanese concentrations in 1940 are shown in Table 3. The proportions are strikingly different in the four cities. Domestic service was the occupation of 56.7 percent of the employed nisei and 50.4 percent of the employed issei women in San Francisco. The figures for Oakland were 38.6 percent and 26.8 percent respectively. In contrast, only 19.1 percent of the nisei and 6.4 percent of the issei in Los Angeles, and 24.2 percent of the nisei and 3.3 percent of the issei in Seattle, were so employed. Private household work appears to have been a Japanese specialty primarily in the Bay Area.

A comparison of the occupational distributions of Japanese women in San Francisco and Seattle, a city with a roughly equal Japanese population, is instructive. In his study of pre-war Seattle, Miyamoto found the majority of Japanese were engaged in running small retail and service establishments, such as stores, hotels, restaurants, barbershops, and pool halls. The demand for such services

TABLE 3

NISEI AND ISSEI WOMEN IN DOMESTIC SERVICE IN FOUR CITIES, 1940

	Number in Labor Force	Number in Domestic Work	Percent in Domestic Work
San Francisco			
Nisei	494	280	56.7
Issei	367	185	50.4
Oakland			
Nisei	132	51	38.6
Issei	97	26	26.8
Los Angeles			
Nisei	1,431	274	19.1
Issei	1,363	88	6.4
Seattle			
Nisei	482	117	24.2
Issei	611	20	3.3

Source: U.S. Bureau of the Census, *Sixteenth Census of the Population, 1940: Population Characteristics of the Non-white Population by Race* (Washington, D.C.: U.S. Government Printing Office, 1943), table 38: "Japanese Employed Persons 14 Years Old and Over, by Major Occupation, Group, City and Sex for Selected States, Urban and Rural, and for Selected Cities."

Roots

grew out of Seattle's position as the stopover point for transient male labor in the lumbering and canning industries of the Pacific Northwest.[13] Not surprisingly, as Table 4 shows, in 1940 a majority of wage-earning issei (63.8 percent) and nisei (51.6 percent) women in Seattle were involved in three occupations related to small enterprises: proprietors and managers, clerical and sales personnel, and service workers outside private households.

Opportunities for small enterprises of this kind were more limited in the San Francisco area, perhaps because much of the market was already filled by the Chinese, who had arrived first and specialized in trade and services. Although the Japanese did run hotels, restaurants, and shops in the Bay Area, they catered primarily to a Japanese clientele. Thus, the number of such businesses was neces-

TABLE 4

MAIN OCCUPATIONS OF ISSEI AND NISEI WOMEN
IN SAN FRANCISCO AND SEATTLE, 1940

	Seattle				San Francisco			
	Issei		Nisei		Issei		Nisei	
	No.	%	No.	%	No.	%	No.	%
Total employed	611	100.0	482	99.9ª	367	99.9ª	494	100.0
Professional and semi-professional workers	23	3.8	26	5.4	17	4.6	33	6.7
Proprietors and managers	111	18.2	29	6.0	41	11.2	14	2.8
Clerical and sales personnel	112	18.3	151	31.3	21	5.7	96	19.4
Operatives	143	23.4	69	14.3	58	15.8	33	6.7
Domestic workers	20	3.3	117	24.2	185	50.4	280	56.7
Service workers	167	27.3	69	14.3	28	7.6	25	5.1
All other occupations	35	5.7	21	4.4	17	4.6	13	2.6

Source: U.S. Bureau of the Census, *Sixteenth Census of the Population, 1940: Population Characteristics of the Non-white Population by Race* (Washington, D.C.: U.S. Government Printing Office, 1943), table 38: "Japanese Employed Persons 14 Years Old and Over, by Major Occupation, Group, City and Sex for Selected States, Urban and Rural, and for Selected Cities."

ªRounding error.

sarily limited. The two types of establishment in which the Japanese dealt primarily with non-Japanese were Oriental gift stores in and around Chinatown and commercial laundries, in which Japanese workers, both men and women, were prominent. The best known was the People's Laundry run by the Baba brothers. Because these enterprises were so much rarer than in Seattle, only about a quarter of San Francisco's issei women were involved in the three service and trade-related occupations mentioned above.

The variation among cities underlines the importance of local labor markets. The potential size of the domestic labor force was highly elastic, since demand always exceeded supply. Where the local labor market provided other niches, fewer women "chose" domestic service. In areas where other niches were lacking, the proportion of women "forced" into domestic work rose.

The Post-War Labor Market

The breakdown of traditional barriers during and after World War II made possible unprecedented occupational mobility on the part of previously excluded groups, including the Japanese. The Japanese were particularly successful in taking advantage of the new options, but as noted in Chapter 2, mobility was by no means universal. The changes radically altered the outlook for younger and better-educated nisei. They did little to increase the options of the kibei and the older and less educated nisei, and virtually nothing to advance the chances of the issei. For issei women, particularly, the changes came too late. At the end of the war, the average issei woman was in her mid-forties to late fifties and was not in a position to take advantage of openings in white-collar employment.

The National Picture   The immediate effects of the internment for all subgroups were twofold. Women entered or continued in the labor force at a higher level than they might otherwise have done. The loss of businesses and personal property and the years without income had depleted resources. According to census data, the percentage of Japanese women in the labor force was 55 percent higher in 1950 than in 1940.[14] This increase reflects the overall movement of

Japanese women out of unpaid family labor and into the general labor force.[15]

That trend is closely linked to the second effect of the internment: namely, the shift of Japanese out of two areas of pre-war specialization, agriculture and ethnic enterprise. Several factors contributed to this shift. One was the age structure of the issei population. The modal issei man was in his mid-sixties and the modal issei woman in her mid-fifties in 1945.[16] Having invested their youthful energy and dreams in establishing their farms and businesses before the war, they no longer had the vigor to start again from scratch.

Also, the Japanese were displaced by other groups who had moved into the places vacated by their absence. Leased farm lands were often subdivided for real estate development or industrial use. Most of the small parcels owned by Japanese truck farmers were consolidated into larger holdings under the control of corporations who hired managers to farm the land.[17] Urban Japanese were pushed out of retail and service establishments. In San Francisco, Japanese-owned businesses in Chinatown were taken over by Chinese, and the Japanese were never able to regain a foothold.

Finally, and most important, changes in the economy undercut the position of small farmers and small entrepreneurs. Agriculture became even more concentrated. Land was increasingly controlled by corporate interests, who squeezed out small holders. New migrant groups had been recruited for planting and harvesting work. Japanese farm laborers and foremen who returned to their familiar occupations discovered conditions so altered that it was difficult to make a living. Thus, many rural issei and nisei migrated to urban centers and entered the wage labor force. Japanese farmers who tilled land close to urban produce markets found the suburbs and cities expanding outward and overtaking former farm lands. Both trends resulted in a long-term shift in population from rural to urban areas. Whereas in 1930 nearly half (46.2 percent) of the Japanese lived in rural areas, by 1970 only 8.9 percent did.[18]

Small entrepreneurs were also affected by post-war economic changes. Chain operations in wholesaling and retailing achieved economies of scale not possible for small, independent operators. Chain wholesalers monopolized the market formerly served by the pre-war network of Japanese wholesale produce firms. Supermarkets took over an increasing share of retail food sales, marginalizing the small groceries and produce stands run by the Japanese.[19]

The net result of these circumstances was that issei women were forced to find employment quickly and to take whatever jobs were readily available—jobs that required little experience and few qualifications. Right out of camp, the most frequently found first jobs were in domestic service and in packing sheds and factories. Mrs. Amano described the situation as "like a race." Such jobs were seen as temporary, but some issei soon found themselves resigned to long-term employment in these positions.

The implications of immediate post-war pressures, as well as the impact of longer-term economic changes, can be traced in issei employment patterns, pieced together from census data. In the post-war years, employment rates among Japanese women in the issei age group averaged 50 percent higher than the rate for non-Japanese women in the same age group.[20] In 1960, 15.3 percent of Japanese women aged 55 and over were in the labor force, compared with 10.5 percent of all women in that age group. In 1970, 13.2 percent of Japanese women 65 and over were gainfully employed, compared with 9.5 percent of all women 65 and over. The high rate is impressive in light of the issei's longevity: of the 23,750 over-65 workers, 5,226 were 80 or older in 1970.[21] The figures are consistent with the case histories of the issei subjects interviewed, many of whom were employed into their seventies and even eighties.

Issei occupations also shifted as a result of the internment and changes in the economy. Occupational distributions can be partially reconstructed from the census by using age groupings. For 1950, Japanese women 45 years of age and over; for 1960, foreign-born Japanese 45 and over; and for 1970, Japanese women 65 and over may be assumed to be mostly issei. With these groupings used as proxies, striking changes in concentration become apparent (Table 5). Issei women's involvement in two traditional areas of employment declined steeply. The proportion in farming fell by approximately a quarter between 1940, the last pre-war census, and 1950, the first post-war census. The shift out of agriculture slowed between 1950 and 1960, and then accelerated between 1960 and 1970, resulting in a 50 percent drop from 28.1 percent in 1950 to 13.4 percent by 1970. The proportion of service workers, the second major area of

TABLE 5

OCCUPATIONAL DISTRIBUTIONS OF JAPANESE WOMEN IN ISSEI AGE COHORT, 1950, 1960, AND 1970

	1950[a]		1960[b]		1970[c]	
	No.	%	No.	%	No.	%
Professional/technical workers	89	1.7	132	1.7	179	5.8
Farm, including managers, laborers	1,452[d]	28.1	1,832	23.9	410	13.4
Managers, except farm	322	6.2	529	6.9	165	5.4
Clerical and kindred workers	261[e]	5.0	138	1.8	282	9.2
Sales workers	—	—	228	3.0	193	6.3
Craft workers	55	1.1	93	1.2	35	1.1
Operatives	1,395	27.0	1,796	23.4	543	17.7
Private household workers	818	15.8	1,575	20.5	747	24.3
Service workers, except private household workers	597	11.5	924	12.0	436	14.2
Laborers, except farm	90	1.7	163	2.1	80	2.6
Not reported	95	1.8	263	3.4	—	—
TOTAL EMPLOYED	5,174	99.9[f]	7,673	99.9[f]	3,070	100.0

Sources: For 1950: U.S. Bureau of the Census, *U.S. Census of the Population, 1950*, vol. 4: *Special Reports* (Washington, D.C.: U.S. Government Printing Office, 1953), pt. 3, chap. B: Non-white Population by Race, table 11: "Social and Economic Characteristics of the Japanese Population 14 Years Old and Over, for the United States, by Regions, Urban and Rural, 1950." For 1960: U.S. Bureau of the Census, *U.S. Census of the Population, 1960: Subject Report, Non-white Population by Race, Final Report PC(2)1C* (Washington, D.C.: U.S. Government Printing Office, 1963), table 39: "Economic Characteristics of the Japanese Population 14 Years Old and Over, by Age, for the United States, by Regions, Urban and Rural, and for Selected States, 1960," and table 47: "Economic Characteristics of the Foreign-born Japanese Population 14 Years Old and Over, by Age, for the United States, Urban and Rural, 1960." For 1970: U.S. Bureau of the Census, *U.S. Census of the Population, 1970: Subject Reports: Final Report PC(2)1G: Japanese, Chinese and Filipinos in the United States* (Washington, D.C.: U.S. Government Printing Office, 1973), table 7: "Employment Characteristics of the Japanese Population 14 Years Old and Over by Age and Urban and Rural Residence, 1970."

[a]Category is made up of Japanese women 45 years of age and over.
[b]Category is made up of foreign-born Japanese women, 45 years of age and over. Data from 1960 on include Hawaii, which achieved statehood in 1958. The rise in numbers reflects the addition of the large Japanese population of that state. Removing the figures for Hawaii from the 1960 and 1970 data would make them comparable to earlier censuses; however, it is impossible to do this consistently because of the way the data are reported. Checks using available data indicate that distributions for Hawaii are not very different from those for the United States as a whole.
[c]Category is made up of Japanese women 65 years of age and over.
[d]Includes 502 unpaid family workers.
[e]Clerical and sales workers reported together.
[f]Rounding error.

specialization for women—barbers, waitresses, boardinghouse keepers, and the like—also declined. The magnitude of the decline is difficult to ascertain because of changes in the classification of occupations in the census in 1950. Some idea of its extent can be gleaned from data showing that whereas in 1940, 23.6 percent of issei women fell into the "personal services" category, in 1950 only 11.5 percent were listed as "service workers." The proportion in the latter category increased slightly (to 14.2 percent) in 1970.

Compensating for a reduction in agriculture and personal services was an expansion in two other categories—operatives and private household workers. Employment in the operatives category jumped from 12.0 percent in 1940 to 27.0 percent in 1950. The sharp increase was likely due to complex circumstances, including expanded production of consumer goods, the breakdown of discriminatory barriers, the issei movement to urban areas, and the availability of operative positions as the issei left the camps. At any rate, the proportion of issei in the operatives category declined over the next two decades (to 17.7 percent in 1970), probably due to retirement.

Domestic service also absorbed a good percentage of issei returnees, as employment in this field rose from 10.3 percent in 1940 to 15.8 percent in 1950. This rise in number and percentage right after the war reversed a gradual decline in domestic service in the decades before the war. Domestic service was especially likely to be the first job out of camp because employers frequently offered living quarters. The personal histories of the women in the study suggest that the returnees stayed in these live-in positions for a short time only. Still, data for 1960 and 1970 show lingering effects of the employment choices issei were forced to make in the aftermath of the war. Even fifteen and twenty-five years after the end of the war, the proportion of the aging issei female work force engaged in domestic work continued to increase by 5 percent each decade. Especially striking are figures indicating that a quarter of women 65 and over in 1970 were private household workers.

Nisei women also entered wage labor in order to help their families recover from the internment. They, like the issei, had higher-than-average rates of employment for women in their age group. Again, data can be reconstructed from age groupings in the census (Table 6). Japanese women aged 16 to 44 in 1950, American-born Japanese women aged 25 to 44 in 1960, and Japanese women aged

TABLE 6

LABOR FORCE PARTICIPATION RATES OF JAPANESE, WHITE, AND ALL WOMEN IN THE NISEI AGE COHORT, 1950, 1960, AND 1970

	1950[a]	1960[b]	1970[c]
Japanese women	47.3%[d]	56.3%[e]	57.5%
White women	—[f]	37.9	49.1
All women	38.7	39.8	49.3

Sources: For white women and all women, 1950, 1960, and 1970: U.S. Department of Labor, *Handbook of Labor Statistics, 1974* (Washington, D.C.: U.S. Government Printing Office, 1974), calculated from table 3: "Civilian Labor Force, by Sex, Color and Age, 1947–73," and table 4: "Civilian Labor Force Participation Rates for Persons 16 Years and Over, by Sex, Color and Age, 1947–73." For Japanese women, 1950: U.S. Bureau of the Census, *U.S. Census of the Population, 1950*, vol. 4: *Special Reports* (Washington, D.C.: U.S. Government Printing Office, 1953), pt. 3, chap. B: Non-white Population by Race, calculated from table 11: "Social and Economic Characteristics of the Japanese Population 14 Years Old and Over, for the United States, by Regions, Urban and Rural, 1950." For Japanese women, 1960: U.S. Bureau of the Census, *U.S. Census of the Population, 1960: Subject Reports: Non-white Population by Race: Final Report PC(2)1C* (Washington, D.C.: U.S. Government Printing Office, 1963), calculated from table 39: "Economic Characteristics of the Japanese Population 14 Years Old and Over, by Age, for the United States, by Regions, Urban and Rural, and for Selected States, 1960," and table 47: "Economic Characteristics of the Foreign-Born Japanese Population 14 Years Old and Over, by Age, for the United States, Urban and Rural, 1960." For Japanese women, 1970: U.S. Bureau of the Census, *Census of the Population, 1970: Subject Reports: Final Report PC(2)1G: Japanese, Chinese, and Filipinos in the United States* (Washington, D.C.: U.S. Government Printing Office, 1973), calculated from table 2: "Age of the Japanese Population by Sex and Urban and Rural Residence, 1970," and table 4: "Economic Characteristics of the Japanese Population by Urban and Rural Residence, 1970."

[a]Category made up of women aged 16 to 44.
[b]Category made up of women aged 25 to 44. Age breakdowns in the 1960 census made it impossible to include ages 45 to 54, which fell into the 45 to 64 category.
[c]Category made up of women aged 35 to 64.
[d]The data for the Japanese cover women 14 to 44. The inclusion of 14- and 15-year-olds probably depresses their rates slightly.
[e]Refers to U.S.-born Japanese women only.
[f]Separate figures for whites not available prior to 1954.

35 to 64 in 1970 can be assumed to be mostly nisei. Using these age groups as proxies for the nisei, we see that their labor force participation rate in 1950 was 47.3 percent, compared with 38.7 percent for all women in that age group; in 1960 it was 56.8 percent, compared with 39.8 percent; and in 1970, it was 57.5 percent, compared with 49.3 percent. Overall, nisei women were about 20 percent more likely to be employed than white women or all women in their age groups.

Occupational mobility was much more extensive for the nisei, to whom white-collar work was now open for the first time. Using the approximation method of age grouping, we find a 50 percent increase in clerical and sales workers within a decade (from 22.9 percent in 1940 to 34.6 percent in 1950), and a 100 percent increase in professionals (from 4.4 percent in 1940 to 9.2 percent in 1950). (See Table 7.) Employment in these two areas continued to expand in the next two decades, so that by 1970 well over half of all working nisei women were in white-collar professional, managerial, sales, or clerical positions. Not all the shift was to white-collar fields, however. The proportion in the operative category rose even more steeply in the immediate post-war era, from 7.3 percent in 1940 to 17.5 percent in 1950. Employment in this category, however, did not expand in the next two decades, but stabilized at approximately the 1950 level in 1960 and 1970. This pattern indicates that nisei took operative positions when they left the internment camps but that few young nisei became operatives as they entered the labor force, and few older nisei switched from other fields to such jobs after their initial post-war employment.

Matching the rise in white-collar and blue-collar manufacturing jobs was a dramatic fall in the proportions engaged in farming and domestic employment. Between 1940 and 1950 the proportion in these fields was halved: from 24.3 percent to 12.7 percent in farming, and from 25.7 percent to 12.4 percent in domestic work. The decline continued through 1970, when only 2.5 percent of the nisei female labor force was employed in farming, and 4.3 percent in domestic work.

These figures seem to bolster the popular image of the nisei (although it is usually men who are being described) as incredibly successful in climbing the job ladder. However, consideration of age subgroups within the larger nisei cohort reveals interesting differences in mobility. Broad occupational shifts may disguise the non-mobility of some segments. I examined occupational distributions for three age groups of American-born Japanese in the 1960 census: 25 to 34, 35 to 44, and 45 to 64. That census is the only one in the post-war period to give separate data for foreign-born and American-born Japanese. The youngest group may include some sansei, but the vast majority in the three groups are undoubtedly nisei.

TABLE 7

OCCUPATIONS OF EMPLOYED JAPANESE WOMEN IN THE NISEI AGE COHORT, 1940, 1950, 1960, 1970

	1940[a]		1950[b]		1960[c]		1970[d]	
	No.	%	No.	%	No.	%	No.	%
Professional/technical workers	300	4.4	1,469	9.2	6,159	12.5	8,693	12.1
Farm workers, including managers and laborers	1,675[e]	24.3	2,026[f]	12.7	2,567	5.2	1,789	2.5
Managers and proprietors	227	3.3	469	2.9	1,915	3.9	3,436	4.8
Clerical workers	1,574	22.9	5,507	34.6	15,234	31.0	21,606	30.0
Sales workers	—[g]	—	—[g]	—	3,504	7.1	4,969	6.9
Craft and kindred workers	39	0.6	134	0.8	676	1.4	1,686	2.3
Operative and kindred workers	504	7.3	2,787	17.5	7,793	15.9	12,874	17.9
Private household workers	1,771	25.7	1,982	12.4	3,181	6.5	3,125	4.3
Service workers, except private household workers	658	9.6	1,175	7.4	5,852	11.9	13,203	18.3
Laborers, except farm	47	0.7	124	0.8	263	0.5	701	1.0
Not reported	89	1.3	254	1.6	1,992	4.1	—	—
TOTAL EMPLOYED	6,884	100.1[h]	15,927	99.9[h]	49,136	99.9[h]	72,082	100.1[h]

Sources: For 1940: U.S. Bureau of the Census, *Sixteenth Census of the Population, 1940: Population Characteristics of the Non-white Population by Race* (Washington, D.C.: U.S. Government Printing Office, 1943), table 8: "Non-white Employed Persons 14 Years Old and Over, by Major Occupation Group, Race, and Sex, for the United States, by Regions, Urban and Rural, 1940." For 1950: U.S. Bureau of the Census, *U.S. Census of the Population, 1950,* vol. 4: *Special Reports* (Washington, D.C.: U.S. Government Printing Office, 1953), pt. 3, chap. B: Non-white Population by Race, table 11: "Social and Economic Characteristics of the Japanese Population 14 Years Old and Over, for the United States, by Regions, Urban and Rural, 1950." For 1960: U.S. Bureau of the Census, *U.S. Census of the Population, 1960: Subject Report: Non-white Population by Race: Final Report PC(2)1C* (Washington, D.C.: U.S. Government Printing Office, 1963), table 39: "Economic Characteristics of the Japanese Population 14 Years Old and Over, by Age, for the United States, by Regions, Urban and Rural, and for Selected States, 1960," and table 47: "Economic Characteristics of the Foreign-Born Japanese Population 14 Years Old and Over, by Age, for the United States, Urban and Rural, 1960." For 1970: U.S. Bureau of the Census, *U.S. Census of the Population, 1970: Subject Reports: Final Report PC(2)1G: Japanese, Chinese and Filipinos in the United States* (Washington, D.C.: U.S. Government Printing Office, 1973), table 7: "Employment Characteristics of the Japanese Population 14 Years Old and Over, by Age and Urban and Rural Residence, 1970."

[a] Category is made up of American-born Japanese women.
[b] Category is made up of Japanese women aged 14 to 44.
[c] Category is made up of American-born Japanese women 25 years of age and older.
[d] Category is made up of Japanese women aged 35 to 64.
[e] Includes 1,231 unpaid family workers.
[f] Includes 816 unpaid family workers.
[g] Clerical and sales workers reported together.
[h] Rounding error.

As Table 8 shows, the occupational distributions of the three age groups are dramatically different. Those in the youngest group, born after 1925, are about three times more likely to be professionals than those born before 1925, and four times more likely to be clerical workers than those born before 1915. In contrast, the two older groups are two and a half times as likely to be operatives, four times as likely to be private household workers, and twice as likely to be in other types of service occupations as those born after 1925. Overall, close to three-quarters of those born after 1925 are in white-collar

TABLE 8

OCCUPATIONS OF AMERICAN-BORN JAPANESE WOMEN
BY AGE GROUP, 1960—PERCENT OF NUMBER EMPLOYED

	25–34 Years	35–44 Years	45–64 Years
Professional/technical workers	19.9%	7.7%	10.1%
Managers (except farm managers)	2.3	4.5	5.3
Clerical workers	45.9	28.6	11.9
Sales workers	5.2	8.8	7.0
Crafts workers, foremen	1.0	1.5	1.8
Operatives	8.0	19.4	21.9
Private household workers	2.3	6.6	12.7
Service workers (except in private households)	7.9	13.6	15.0
Farm workers (including managers)	2.4	6.0	7.9
Laborers (except farm and mine workers)	0.5	0.5	0.8
Occupation not reported	4.6	2.7	5.7
TOTAL[a]	100.0	99.9	100.1
NUMBER EMPLOYED	17,330	21,067	10,556

Source: U.S. Bureau of the Census, *U.S. Census of Population, 1960: Subject Reports: Non-white Population by Race: Final Report PC(2)-1C* (Washington, D.C.: U.S. Government Printing Office, 1968), table 39: "Economic Characteristics of the Japanese Population 14 Years Old and Over, by Age, for the United States, by Region, Urban and Rural, and for Selected States, 1960," and table 47: "Economic Characteristics of the Foreign-born Japanese Population 14 Years Old and Over, by Age, for the United States, Urban and Rural, 1960."

[a]Percentages do not add up to 100 because of rounding errors.

fields—professionals, managers, and clerical and sales workers. In contrast, less than half of those born between 1916 and 1925 and only one-third of those born before 1915 were employed in white-collar fields.

There seems to be a marked discontinuity in the experience of those growing up and reaching adulthood prior to the war and those attaining their majority after it. Those who were adults and entered the labor market *before* the war remained stuck in the traditional Japanese job market after the war. Those who became adults and entered the labor force *after* the war were able to enter the white-collar job market at the beginning of their careers. Thus, many of the nisei who penetrated the dominant labor market were probably not themselves mobile: they had never been in the restricted Japanese job market. This finding confirms the dual labor market model, which asserts that once workers enter a particular market, they remain in it for the rest of their working lives.[22]

One might expect the war brides to have better job options than the issei and older nisei did when the latter groups first entered the labor market. They arrived after the war-time changes described above, and, in addition, many had previously worked in office, technical, or semi-professional jobs in Japan. However, they were also immigrants, who might be expected to fit into the typical immigrant market of service and manual jobs. Even highly skilled and educated immigrants typically experience downward mobility following migration.

In contrast to the numerous studies of pre-war issei and nisei economic activities, there are no parallel studies of war brides' employment. Research on war brides has been concerned almost exclusively with issues of cultural adjustment and marital conflict. For example, Strauss interviewed thirty wives and fifteen husbands in Japanese-American marriages in the Chicago area in the early 1950s and reported only the bare fact that "the Japanese wives sometimes work, either because they are childless and hence bored, or because extra income is desired; but they are not career-minded."[23] The latter description—"not career-minded"—is echoed by Schnepp and Yui in their study of twenty couples in St. Louis.[24] The only other discussion of war brides' employment is Kitano's two-sentence account in his book on Japanese Americans. He describes the war brides as a marginal group in the Japanese American community and notes:

"Certain behaviors commonly associated with marginal populations (e.g. less stable occupations) are sometimes seen in this group. One common pattern of employment involves serving as waitresses in Japanese restaurants."[25]

The census, despite its limitations, remains the best source of information. Although no census separates out the war brides as a group, it is possible to piece together evidence about their occupational distributions from the 1960 census, which at least provides breakdowns by foreign-born and native-born status and age group. Because of the limited period of earlier immigration, it may be assumed that foreign-born women born after the 1924 cut-off year are predominantly war brides—that is, the group aged 20 to 35 in 1960 (see Table 9).

Using this group as an approximation of the war bride population, we conclude that the distribution of the war brides group deviates markedly from those of issei and nisei. More than half of the war brides were either operatives (30.6 percent) or service workers employed outside private households (24.9 percent). The latter figure supports Kitano's observation about the prevalence of waitressing. The war brides were also disproportionately involved in private household work (7.7 percent). This proportion was lower than that of the issei (12.0 percent in 1960), but higher than that of the nisei (6.5 percent) or whites (4.1 percent).[26] As might be expected of workers who speak limited English, the war brides are underrepresented in the clerical and sales categories. However, the proportion in professional and technical occupations (9.4 percent) is higher than expected. Perhaps those with special training or post-secondary education were more successful at gaining employment in their fields than those with high school education and previous employment in lower-level white-collar positions were in locating appropriate white-collar jobs.

Further details about employment that might not be revealed in aggregate data can be gleaned from the job histories of the twelve women in the interview study and from information they and others provided about other war brides. This evidence must be interpreted cautiously; the women cannot be assumed to be typical of the war bride population, since they were deliberately chosen because of their involvement in domestic work. It is unlikely, however, that their situations are unrepresentative of the war bride experience in the Bay

TABLE 9

OCCUPATIONAL DISTRIBUTION OF FOREIGN-BORN JAPANESE WOMEN
AGED 20 TO 35, 1960[a]

	No.	%
Professional/technical workers	481	9.4
Managers, officials, except farm	90	1.8
Clerical and kindred workers	642	12.6
Sales workers	164	3.2
Craft workers, foremen	96	1.9
Operative and kindred workers	1,565	30.6
Service workers, except private household workers	1,270	24.9
Private household workers	394	7.7
Farmers, farm managers, farm laborers, and foremen	166	3.2
Laborers, except farm and mine	11	0.2
Not reported	231	4.5
TOTAL EMPLOYED	5,110	100.0

Source: U.S. Bureau of the Census, *U.S. Census of Population, 1960: Subject Reports: Non-white Population by Race: Final Report PC(2)-1C* (Washington, D.C.: U.S. Government Printing Office, 1963), table 47: "Economic Characteristics of the Foreign-Born Japanese Population 14 Years Old and Over, by Age, for the United States, Urban and Rural, 1960."

[a]This group is assumed to consist primarily of war brides.

Area. First, they discussed their alternatives in terms of what other war brides they knew were doing. Therefore, their frame of reference was broader than their own job histories. Second, the women were quite varied in educational attainment, past occupation, and current economic circumstances. That such disparate individuals were involved in domestic work indicates that war brides' choices were similar across social and economic levels.

According to both the women themselves and informants, waitressing in Japanese restaurants is indeed a common form of employment. Opportunities are plentiful because of the plethora of Japanese restaurants in the San Francisco area. Two women worked in restaurants: one was currently a hostess, and one had been a cook. Several women mentioned that they chose some particular line of work because they did not want to wait on tables, thus indicating an awareness of waitressing as a common source of employment for war brides. Light assembly work and sewing were also mentioned as major alternatives. Two women had worked as operatives, and three in needle trades.

The war brides had fewer opportunities for informal market work than the issei had had in the pre-war period. In the post-war economy, hand manufacturing has been exported to low-wage regions of Asia and Latin America, so there is little call for home industry. On the other hand, the post-war growth in women's employment has created a demand for childcare services, which other women can provide at home. Two women had at one time or another sat for a working neighbor's children for pay. Some divorced single parents obtained income from several sources: formal employment, informal work, and even welfare. Mrs. Adair, a single parent with three daughters, received funds from Aid to Families with Dependent Children, worked a few hours a week as a hostess in a Japanese restaurant, and periodically took other part-time jobs, such as cleaning rooms in a motel and caring for elderly folk in their homes. Mrs. Osborne was employed half-time as a nutrition coordinator for a Japanese American senior center, managed the apartment house in which she lived in exchange for reduced rent, and cleaned houses on weekends.

Though seven of the twelve war brides had worked in semi-professional and white-collar capacities in Japan, they found it difficult to use their job experience to obtain similar employment in the United States. Only two managed to continue their previous occupation. Mrs. Simeone, trained as a dental assistant, worked in this field in the United States until arthritis forced her to stop. Mrs. Rybin combined her experience running her own business in Japan with knowledge gained working in a drapery shop in America and put it to use in running her own drapery shop. The other five went into waitressing, factory work, and domestic service.

In spite of the changes in the economy since issei immigration, the labor market for war brides in many ways paralleled the issei labor market in the pre-war period. That is, much of the war brides' employment was in traditional women's work transferred to the market (sewing, serving food); it took place within ethnic businesses (e.g., waitressing in Japanese restaurants); and it did not interfere with family responsibilities, either because the hours were flexible (e.g., domestic work) or because the work could be done at home (e.g., babysitting.) This kind of work takes place outside the industrial economy. Like the issei, the post-war immigrants were confined to the least advanced sectors of the economy.

The Post-War Bay Area Market   How typical was the situation of Japanese in the Bay Area? That is, did the labor market in the Bay Area continue to be different from labor markets in other cities? Information on this issue was readily available only for 1970. Occupational data on Japanese women in the San Francisco–Oakland, Los Angeles–Long Beach, and Seattle-Everett metropolitan areas for that year are displayed in Table 10. Post-war economic changes appear not to have homogenized the local markets, which remained distinctive. The differences were not as dramatic as before the war, but they were substantial.

The Bay Area market differed in two ways from the markets in Los Angeles–Long Beach and Seattle-Everett. The first was the much lower proportion of Japanese women in operative jobs. Japanese women in the Bay Area were half as likely to be in such positions (7.7 percent versus 16.6 percent and 16.4 percent). Second, domestic service, at 11.5 percent, remained a major source of employment; proportions for the other cities (around 3 percent), though greater than those found among whites, indicate that domestic service was a relatively minor category. These two patterns are likely related, in that the dearth of light manufacturing and food processing—industries that typically rely on a work force of minority women—restricted a principal alternative to domestic work in San Francisco–Oakland. The Seattle-Everett market also had some peculiarities, partly reflecting the continued specialization in ethnic enterprise. As before the war, Seattle-area Japanese had higher concentrations in occupations related to service and retail trade establishments. The proportion in clerical and kindred occupations was about 25 percent lower in Seattle than in the Bay Area and Los Angeles–Long Beach. Although all of the reasons for the differences cannot be pinpointed, it is safe to say that both the composition of the local economy and historically established traditions shaped local labor markets for Japanese immigrant and second-generation women.

TABLE 10

OCCUPATIONS OF EMPLOYED JAPANESE FEMALES, 16 AND OVER,
FOR SELECTED STANDARD METROPOLITAN STATISTICAL AREAS, 1970

	San Francisco–Oakland		Los Angeles–Long Beach		Seattle–Everett	
	No.	%	No.	%	No.	%
Professional/technical workers	1,228	16.4	3,156	14.9	426	14.9
Managerial workers/administrative employees	253	3.4	795	3.8	162	5.6
Sales workers	350	4.7	1,166	5.5	175	6.1
Clerical workers	2,970	39.8	8,679	41.0	881	30.7
Crafts workers	138	1.8	325	1.5	69	2.4
Operatives	577	7.7	3,507	16.6	472	16.5
Laborers	44	0.6	255	1.2	49	1.7
Farm managers and farm labor	131	1.8	165	0.8	82	2.9
Service workers	915	12.3	2,443	11.5	463	16.2
Private household workers	858	11.5	681	3.2	86	3.0
TOTAL EMPLOYED	7,464	100.0	21,172	100.0	2,865	100.0

Source: U.S. Bureau of the Census, *Census of the Population, 1970: Subject Reports:* Final Report PC(2)-1G: *Japanese, Chinese and Filipinos in the United States* (Washington, D.C.: U.S. Government Printing Office, 1973), table 14: "Family Income, Poverty Status, Weeks Worked and Occupations of the Japanese Population for Selected Standard Metropolitan Statistical Areas and Cities, 1970."

The Continuing Stratification of the Labor Market

The employment patterns of issei, nisei, and war brides from 1900 to 1970, which reveal extreme concentration in a narrow range of occupations, confirm the continued existence of labor market segmentation. In the pre-war period, immigrant and second-generation Japanese were almost completely excluded from the more advanced sectors of the economy and confined to the pre-industrial sector of agriculture and personal services, or to interstices in the economy where it was difficult for monopoly capital to achieve economies of scale. Japanese workers, women as well as men, were employed in fields where low technology, low capitalization, and labor-intensive methods made "cheap labor" necessary and desirable.

Economic and social changes in the post-war period led to a breakdown of traditional barriers. The Japanese were able to penetrate many areas of the economy from which they had previously been excluded, such as state and local government and white-owned businesses. This resulted in dramatic changes in occupational patterns. Especially noteworthy was the movement of nisei women into professional and clerical employment.

These shifts, however, disguise the more subtle forms of stratification that have continued to the present. First, issei, older nisei, and kibei have remained captive in the pre-industrial sector and have been unable to penetrate the dominant labor market to any significant degree. Second, although a considerable proportion of Japanese women are integrated into the dominant female labor market at the level of broad occupations, they remain differentiated from other women within these categories. It is beyond the scope of this chapter to detail the differences, but the following is an example of segregation at the sector level. In the 1980s nisei women are employed in white-collar jobs in the same proportion as white women; however, nisei white-collar workers are disproportionately found in government, especially at the local level, while being underrepresented in private industry.[27] This pattern suggests continuing discrimination in the private sector. Third, Japanese American women are still tracked into certain stereotyped occupations. Traditional patterns of tracking are particularly relevant to the question of why Japanese American women continue to be recruited into domestic service in the Bay Area. Finally, as the experience of the war brides illustrates, segmentation by migrant status is still pervasive. Though better educated and more skilled than pre-war immigrants, war brides ended up in similar kinds of service, domestic, and operative jobs. Ironically, they experienced downward mobility as a result of moving to the more advanced industrial center.

Overall, it appears that issei, older and less educated nisei, and war brides function within the same labor market in the Bay Area: one made up of service occupations, including domestic service, and manual positions in light industry. The three cohorts diverge primarily in terms of different distributions within that market.

PART II
WORK

CHAPTER 5
Careers in Domestic Service

Japanese women are not, of course, the only group for whom domestic service has been important. In fact, from the mid-nineteenth century up to 1930, domestic service was the largest single field of paid employment for all women in the United States.[1] To understand what is unique or typical about Japanese women's experiences, one needs to look at the development of domestic service as a female occupation and the situation of other groups who specialized in it.

Domestic Work

Fortunately, ample information is available. As part of the resurgence of interest in women's work, some sociologists and historians have turned their attention to this pivotal occupation.[2] Domestic service provides a strategic entry point for analyzing the impact of industrialization and urbanization on women's labor, since it functions as a transitional occupation in the shift from unpaid work in the household to wage employment outside it.

The character of the work itself is transitional in that it incorporates features of both unpaid family labor and paid employment. The work takes the woman outside her own household, where she sells her labor for wages. Yet it retains key features of unpaid household work: it involves no capital investment, little division of labor, and a low level of technology;[3] it produces simple use value rather than marketable commodities;[4] and it takes place within a separate women's sphere, where relations between employer and employee are personalistic and work arrangements are casual and unregulated.[5]

Even more to the point, international historical comparison reveals domestic service as a major setting for women's employment primarily in the transitional stage of industrialization. In Chaplin's words, "it occupies this unique status in part by default, for this is the period when the lowest proportion of women engage in paid employment according to most census definitions."[6] At an earlier stage women (and men as well) are occupied in unpaid production, mainly in agriculture and handicrafts; at a later stage, domestic service declines in importance because a large proportion of its potential work force is drawn into employment in manufacturing, clerical, and sales occupations and commercial services.

During the transitional phase, a growing urban middle class seeks household help to maintain its affluent lifestyle at a time when there are neither adequate commercial services nor sufficiently advanced household technology to substitute for labor in the home. On the supply side, the process of industrialization displaces labor from traditional agrarian pursuits without providing industrial employment for the entire population. Some of this displaced labor becomes available for household employment. Thus, in nineteenth-century Europe as well as mid-twentieth-century Latin America, migrants from rural areas made up the majority of urban servants.[7]

Domestic Service in the United States In the United States, the high water mark for household service came in the second half of the nineteenth century. Whereas nearly two-thirds of all non-agricultural female wage earners were in service in 1870, the proportion had dropped to slightly over one-third by 1900, to one-fifth by 1930, and to one-twentieth by 1970.[8] It should be noted, of course, that the actual numbers employed in service *doubled* between 1870 and 1910 (from slightly less than a million to about two million), and then held steady until World War II. The drop in percentages reflects the fact that the number of women employed in other fields increased dramatically during these years.

Careers in Domestic Service

Even in the mid-nineteenth century, the availability of land and other opportunities created a perpetual shortage of labor for domestic service. Few men were found in service, so that by 1870 domestic service was already 85 percent female. Native white women also turned to other endeavors, including factory work and teaching. Investigations of the conditions of work life for servants revealed that despite the somewhat higher compensation (if room and board were added to wages) and the safer, healthier environment offered by a private home, young women still preferred the relative freedom of the factory or shop.[9] Thus, servants were increasingly drawn from the most tradition-oriented groups and those lowest in the status hierarchy and most marginal in the urban economy—that is, recent immigrants and migrants from rural societies and members of subordinate racial-ethnic castes.

Irish, German, and Scandinavian immigrants were heavily concentrated in domestic service in eastern and midwestern cities.[10] Historical studies of specific cities suggest that the majority of women from these three nationality groups worked as servants prior to marriage.[11] Glasco, for example, concluded that domestic service "was almost a universal experience of foreign born girls" in Buffalo, New York, during the mid-nineteenth century: "virtually every Irish girl during adolescence spent several years as a live-in domestic."[12] Interestingly, women from other European immigrant groups apparently avoided service; only a small percentage of Italian, Russian, and Polish women were so employed.[13]

In the Southwest, where Anglos had taken over territories inhabited and farmed by Mexican peasants and become the ruling caste, the ranks of domestic service were filled by Mexican American women, both native-born and migrants from below the border. From the 1880s up to World War II, domestic service was, next to agriculture, the largest field of employment for Chicanas.[14] In El Paso, Texas, for example, Spanish-surnamed females accounted for 65.4 percent of all servants and 64.8 percent of all laundresses in 1910.[15] In cities with large Mexican populations, such as El Paso, "almost every Anglo family had at least one, sometimes two servants: a maid and laundress, and perhaps a nursemaid or yardman."[16]

In the post–Civil War South, blacks were the traditional servant caste.[17] At the turn of the century, recent black migrants from the

South were also heavily concentrated in service in the North.[18] Indeed, domestic service and related employment such as laundry work were virtually the only occupations open to black women prior to World War I.[19] The number of blacks employed as servants and laundresses in the North increased rapidly during and after World War I, when foreign immigration slowed to a trickle. Efforts to recruit southern blacks to work in the North were stepped up, apparently with some success.[20] Since that time, blacks have constituted the majority of domestic workers. In the 1970s black women were five times as likely to be found in this field as white women. Even among blacks, however, the proportion of employed women in domestic service fell in the 1970s, from 16.4 percent in 1972 to 7.4 percent in 1980.[21] Thus, the search for household help continues. Even with severely curtailed immigration, domestic service remains a major entry occupation for recent immigrants, especially those from Latin America and the Caribbean. Between 7.0 percent and 10.9 percent of female immigrants were employed as "private household workers" according to records kept between 1961 and 1971.[22]

Domestic Service in the Processing of Immigrants The concentration of immigrants and rural migrants in domestic service raises an interesting issue about the role of the occupation in the "processing" of agrarian or traditional peoples into an urban society. Domestic work places the newly arrived worker in a distinct position in relation to the urban economy. What kind of position is it, and how does it affect the occupant?

One view, based on European and Latin American examples, depicts domestic work as a "bridging" occupation, one that fosters the acculturation and social mobility of immigrants and migrants from traditional societies.[23] For example, looking at nineteenth-century English servants, Broom and Smith argue that live-in employment cut off ties with kin that might have hindered social mobility, while providing servants with a chance to acquire middle-class demeanor and skills. The more ambitious sometimes used these advantages to leave service and found their own service establishments, including hotels, stables, and haberdasheries. The patronage and endorsement of the employer helped ensure the success of these enterprises.

The other view, based on American examples, particularly the case of blacks, depicts domestic work as a "ghettoizing" occupation, one that traps and further disadvantages those who engage in it. According to Salmon, the isolation, long hours, and physically exhausting nature of the work effectively removed workers from normal social relations and prevented them from maintaining or developing alternative job skills.[24] Katzman argues that a further barrier was the low status of the occupation in the United States, compared with the situation in Europe. Because of the stigma attached to service, Katzman notes, those who chose domestic service tended to be the most traditional women and those least prepared for social mobility.[25]

Though individual mobility was rarer in the United States than it was in Europe, intergenerational mobility did occur. Its extent varied according to race and ethnicity. For European women, domestic work functioned as a starting point for both the individual and the group. Most European immigrant domestics were young, single, live-in workers. The typical servant entered service upon leaving school in early adolescence and worked until her early or mid-twenties. After marriage she left service and usually did not return. In addition, although an immigrant woman might not move up the occupational ladder, her daughter usually did. American-born daughters of immigrants for the most part shunned domestic service[26] and entered the expanding white-collar fields of clerical and sales employment. Thus, the group's involvement in domestic service continued only as long as new immigration from the mother-country continued.

Blacks, on the other hand, experienced neither individual nor intergenerational mobility. Black domestics were predominantly married women working to support their children. They preferred to live out.[27] Because they were primary breadwinners, they could not leave the labor force. Domestic work was thus a lifetime, not a short-term, proposition. Moreover, institutional barriers prevented their daughters from moving out of service. Blacks were barred from many industries until the 1930s and from offices and stores until the 1950s so that several generations of black women were confined to domestic service or related employment. For blacks, domestic service operated as an occupational ghetto.

Mexican American women, similarly ghettoized in the ethnically segmented labor markets of the Southwest, experienced virtually no mobility out of domestic and other service occupations. Camarillo found little change in the occupational patterns of Chicanas in Southern California between 1900 and 1930. "Regardless of nativity and regardless of whether one was a second-generation descendant of Mexican-born parents or a first-generation descendant of one of the earliest Mexican settlers in California, the likelihood of upward mobility was almost nil."[28]

Japanese American women represent an important intermediate case that suggests that each of the views is partially correct. In the pre-war period domestic work played a dual role for issei and nisei. On the one hand, it provided a port of entry into the urban labor market; the non-industrial nature of the job, the low level of technology, and the absence of complex organization made it accessible. Its menial status reduced competition from native born white women, who had better options. It was also a vehicle for acculturation. Through domestic service the issei acquired knowledge of American housekeeping techniques, Western family relations, and some rudimentary English. For most domestics the job provided their only face to face contact with members of the dominant culture. On the other hand, once the Japanese began in it, domestic work operated as an occupational ghetto. The same characteristics that made it accessible separated it from the more advantageous occupations and more advanced industries. Labor market segmentation set up barriers that prevented Japanese women from moving into other labor markets. Formal and informal tracking systems directed successive cohorts—issei, nisei, and then war brides—into the occupation. Social segregation contributed to occupational concentration by isolating Japanese women and making them dependent on ethnic networks for information about jobs and connections to ease entry. These ethnic networks provided access to the few occupations in which other Japanese already had experience, but provided little or no access to other occupations. Until recently, Japanese women were denied resources and connections needed to move into other fields.

As for intergenerational mobility, the Japanese took a path intermediate to that of European immigrant groups and that of blacks and Chicanas. Theirs was a three-generation (or perhaps a two-and-a-half generation) mobility process. The immigrant generation worked as live-out domestics, usually as a permanent career after marriage, just as blacks and some Chicanas did. Their daughters, the nisei, were also confined to domestic employment in the pre-war labor market. However, their career patterns differed from their mothers'. Like Irish and German immigrant women, the nisei worked as domestics while single, often as live-in school girls, and left service upon marriage. The next generation, the sansei, as well as members of the nisei generation who reached adulthood after 1940, resembled second-generation European American women. As noted in Chapter 4, they prepared for white-collar careers and moved into them in great numbers.

The San Francisco Bay Area Up to now the discussion has focused on the national picture, with an emphasis on eastern and midwestern cities. The labor patterns in the Far West were anomalous in many ways. California, in particular, underwent rapid economic development in the second half of the nineteenth century and suffered a chronic shortage of labor in all fields. This meant that native workers, women as well as men, had ample opportunities for employment outside domestic service. In contrast to the national distributions, in California up until 1880 more women worked outside domestic service than in it.[29] Moreover, female labor was scarce since the population was still imbalanced in favor of men, who migrated west in larger numbers than women. Asian men not only supplied low-wage manual labor for railroad construction, manufacturing, and agriculture, but also substituted to some extent for white female labor. Starting in the 1850s, Chinese laundrymen and cooks provided commercial services that replaced women's unpaid labor in the home, and Chinese houseboys and cooks took the place of female servants. Katzman notes the peculiarities of the domestic labor situation in the West in this period: "The demand for servants was greatest in the West because of its distance from the ports of entry of European immigrants and from the source of black servants in the South. This resulted in a unique situation: in 1880, California and Washington were the only states in which a majority of domestic servants were men."[30]

The demand for servants was reflected in the wages of the West Coast, which were the highest in the nation by a large margin. After Chinese immigration was cut off by the Exclusion Act of 1882, white women entered domestic service to take up some of the slack. More women were now available, in part because their share of the population had grown and in part because the pace of industrialization from 1880 to 1900 was slower in the Far West than in the Midwest, reducing women's employment options. After 1880 more women worked in domestic service than out of it. Moreover, in contrast to a national trend that saw a reduction in the ratio of servants to households, the number of servants per thousand families in California increased from 49 to 53 between 1880 and 1900.[31]

Despite, or perhaps because of, their diminishing numbers, the Chinese continued to be highly prized servants through the 1900s. The Chinese houseboy was the symbol of upper-class status in San Francisco. Women's magazines hailed "John Chinaman" as a boon to the household economy. The Chinese worked for one-third of the wages of white servants and still paid for their own food and clothing; they did not need separate quarters but were content to sleep on the kitchen floor or in a shed. Moreover, they worked hard and did not venture to bring company into the house.[32] However, as Katzman notes, employers also reported some faults:

> But they were also wily; they used the Christian Sunday School merely to learn English. Conversion led them to assume "sanctified airs" and shirk their work and neglect their duties "so as to hurry away to evening school." . . . As the Chinese adjusted to the American environment, they began to demand higher wages and better conditions. Mistresses reacted as they had to the independence of blacks and immigrants, interpreting their requests for adequate housing in the home as a license for theft. Moreover, they were considered disloyal and irresponsible for leaving positions. A mistress complained that no matter how badly their services might be needed, they left without any advance notice. Despite these faults, "as has so often been said, in many respects they are the best servants that we have ever had."[33]

By the mid-1920s the immigrant Chinese were retiring or dying out. One author declared that "the old-time Chinaman, however famous in California's history, is now passing fast. Whereas a few years ago hundreds of mansions on Nob Hill were managed entirely by these servants, now not many of these domestic employees remain."[34] As the Chinese servant became extinct, paeans of praise were sung in his memory. Nostalgia cast a rosy glow over the master-servant relationship.

Japanese Men and Domestic Service Japanese men preceded the women into domestic service. Just as Japanese men succeeded the Chinese in railroading and agriculture, they also followed them into domestic service. They were only a partial replacement in that the Japanese never constituted as large a proportion of the California labor force as the Chinese did in the mid-nineteenth century, when they made up perhaps a quarter of it.[35] The white population had grown so rapidly by the time the Japanese started immigrating in substantial numbers in the 1890s that the Japanese, both immigrant and native-born, never made up more than 2 percent of the California population.[36] Moreover, for the Japanese, domestic service was intended to be merely a stopgap until something better came along.

Many young men gained a foothold in the United States as "Japanese school boys." This designation was reportedly coined in the 1880s by a Mrs. Reid, who enrolled a few Japanese students in her boarding school in Belmont, California. These students paid for their tuition and board by doing chores and kitchen work.[37] The term came to refer to any live-in Japanese apprentice servant, whether or not he was involved in formal education. (Many so-called school boys were mature men in their late twenties or early thirties.) The job itself was the education; it provided the new immigrant with an opportunity to learn English and become familiar with American customs. In return for his services, the school boy received token wages of about $1.50 a week in 1900 ($2.00 a week by 1909) in addition to room and board, compared with the $15.00 to $40.00 a month earned by trained servants. It has been estimated that at the height of male immigration (1904–1907), over 4,000 Japanese were employed as school boys in San Francisco. By 1909 their number had diminished to around 2,000.[38]

Still other immigrants earned their first wages in the United States as "day workers." They hired out to do yard chores and house-cleaning on a daily or hourly basis. Groups of men from the same prefecture sometimes took lodgings together and advertised their services. Newcomers were invited to join the household and were quickly initiated into the work. Millis found 163 Japanese day work firms listed in the 1913 San Francisco city directory.[39] In addition, issei who had their own businesses sometimes acted as agents for day workers. Advertisements for a Japanese nursery started by three brothers in the 1880s began including notices such as the following, which appeared in the Alameda *Argus* in 1900: "Japanese Help. Also first class Japanese help for cooking, general housework, or gardening, by day, week or month, furnished on short notice."[40] By 1905 the numbers of Japanese seeking day work were substantial enough to support ethnic employment agencies in San Francisco, Oakland, and Alameda.

Some of the school boys graduated to become "professional" servants, butlers, or cooks.[41] For the most part, however, domestic work was temporary. One contemporary author noted that "the Japanese, unlike the Chinese, are too ambitious to remain at one post if there is a better chance for them elsewhere."[42] Studies of issei occupational histories indicate that a domestic job was frequently a first occupation for the new arrival. After learning the ropes, most issei moved on to agricultural or city trades.[43] Thus, the high point of male employment in domestic service occurred in the peak years of male immigration.

In the Bay Area, many day workers graduated into a specialized branch of domestic service—gardening. The Japanese gardener was an independent contractor who traveled from house to house to service a regular clientele on a daily or weekly basis. He became a status symbol throughout California, but the indoor male domestic had largely disappeared by 1930. The early association of Japanese men with domestic service, however, paved the way for women's subsequent entry.

The men's involvement had established in the public mind the stereotype of Japanese as domestics. This mantle was inherited by issei women when they arrived. The Japanese had a reputation for being willing and dedicated workers and were much in demand. The men also facilitated the women's entry by serving as role models. By the time the women entered the work force, there were well-established networks for finding jobs. Earlier immigrants helped later arrivals to place advertisements and passed on the tricks of the trade.

Prospective employers asked the advice of the neighbor's Japanese gardener when seeking household help. Some men acted as formal middlemen and established employment agencies for household workers. Thus, it was not long after the arrival of the women that the "Situations Wanted" columns of Bay Area newspapers, which prior to 1908 had been dominated by advertisements from "Japanese school boys," began to include such messages as "Japanese girl wants situation to assist in general housework and taking care of baby. Address, Japanese Girl, 1703 Park Street."[44]

The path was clearly marked. Several questions remain: What were the circumstances that launched the women on the journey? What factors influenced them to continue in domestic work on a long term basis? What led subsequent generations of Japanese women to also enter domestic work?

Issei Careers

Issei women were the pioneers. Ninety-one years old at the time of the interview, Mrs. Yoshida arrived in 1909 as a picture bride. Her husband, sixteen years her senior, had lived in the United States for almost twenty years and had managed to acquire a laundry in Alameda, which the couple ran together. Since they had one of the few telephones in the Japanese community, they began acting as agents for day workers. Employers called to request help for cleaning, painting, and other jobs. The Yoshidas referred the requests to the issei men who dropped by, collecting a token ten-cent commission for each referral. By 1912 Mrs. Yoshida had two small children and felt that they needed extra income:

> I started to work because everyone went on vacation and the summer was very hard for us. The cleaning business declined during the summer. . . . I bought a second-hand bicycle from a friend who had used it for five years. I paid $3 for it. My husband disapproved of my doing day work. He said, "Stupid." So at night I went to the beach and practiced on that bicycle. At night nobody was at the beach, so even if I fell down, I didn't feel embarrassed. And then I went to work. I worked half a day and was paid $1. . . . We didn't know the first thing about house-

work, but the ladies of the house didn't mind. They taught us how at the beginning: "This is a broom; this is a dustpan; when you finish that work bring it back here." So that's how we learned. Those Caucasians taught us everything and then very properly paid us money. . . . And we worked hard for them. We always thought America was a wonderful country. At the time we were thinking of working three years in America and then going back to Japan to help our parents lead a comfortable life. . . . But we had babies almost every year and so we had to give up that idea. [She had ten children between 1910 and 1923.]

Mrs. Yoshida's account reveals several elements common to the lives of issei women who entered domestic work in the pre-war period. First, the Yoshidas' intention of accumulating a nest egg and returning to Japan was shared by other immigrants. In this context, wage work could be viewed as a temporary expedient, and even the most menial employment would not reflect on a family's social standing.

A second common element was the economic squeeze experienced by many issei families, especially after children arrived. Not only did children have to be fed and clothed, but money for remittances to parents and other relatives had to be set aside. Most of the women in the study were married to gardeners, whose modest earnings fluctuated with the seasons and economic conditions. As Mrs. Yoshida's case illustrates, even those who owned their own businesses found that their small enterprises did not generate a steady enough income to support a growing family.

Women who lost their husbands or whose husbands were unable to work were in even worse straits. Mrs. Shinoda was part of this group. Her husband, a college graduate, was killed in an accident in 1928. She was 39 and had two young sons:

I started work after my husband died. I went to Japan to take my children to my mother. Then I came back alone and started to work. My sons were ten and eight. . . . And I worked in a family. At that time I stayed in the home of a professor at the University of California as a

live-in maid. . . . I got the job through another Japanese
person. She was going back to Japan, so I took her place.
What kinds of things did you do?
Cleaned house, and cooking and serving food.
Did you know how to cook and things like that?
No, I didn't at first. The lady told me.

Factors like these pushed issei women to seek wage work, but
what factors drew them particularly into domestic work? The basic
limiting condition was the structure of the labor market. In addition,
family responsibilities, inability to speak English, and lack of marketable job skills limited their aspirations. Among their restricted
choices, domestic work offered some advantages. The main attraction was its flexibility. Those with heavy family responsibilities, such
as Mrs. Yoshida, could work part-time or seasonally; then, during
times of extra financial pressure, they could take on additional jobs
or work more days or longer hours. Another pull was the sheer
demand for day labor, especially among the growing number of
middle-class urban families who could not afford live-in servants.
The demand was so great that, as Mrs. Yoshida and Mrs. Shinoda
noted, employers were willing to hire someone inexperienced and
unable to speak English and train her on the job.

Finding a Job Because they were unfamiliar with American institutions, the immigrants relied on informal social networks within
the community for job placements of all sorts. It could be argued that
this reliance on ethnic ties contributed to the concentration in domestic work, since ethnic sources provided a great deal of information about fields in which earlier immigrants had gained a foothold
and none about other possible lines of work.[45]
At any rate, the know-how for obtaining domestic jobs was
widespread as a result of the early experience of issei men as school
boys and day workers. Issei women sometimes turned to educated
acquaintances to help them place advertisements in the newspaper,
but more frequently they relied on informal job referrals. They heard
about openings through relatives, friends, or acquaintances working
as gardeners or domestics themselves. Sometimes, like Mrs. Shinoda,

they inherited a position from another issei who was taking another job or returning to Japan. The departing worker personally introduced and helped train the new employee. Somewhat more formal mediating was performed by domestic employment agents in the community. Some issei did this kind of placement as a sideline; two examples described earlier were the Japanese nursery and the Yoshidas' laundry.

Job placements were also initiated by employers. As the Japanese gained a reputation for domestic work, employers began making requests through Japanese churches, businesses, and social organizations. Moreover, once a worker secured one job, she could easily obtain additional jobs through employer referrals. Thus, the employer's social network was another important mechanism for locating jobs. Mrs. Amano noted that once she started working, she had no problem finding new, often better, jobs:

> When they're playing cards, they talked about the help—
> if someone knew who is a good worker. They would give
> the other ladies my name and they would call me. Then
> I'd go and see. If I liked it better than the other place, I'd
> quit the other and move to the new one.

The reliance on personal referrals is one aspect of the match between Japanese cultural preferences and the characteristics of the occupation. Japanese culture, with its emphasis on social proprieties, requires the use of intermediaries in a variety of "delicate" social arrangements, from requesting a personal favor to negotiating the terms of a financial transaction. The issei could thus be expected to feel more comfortable when introduced to a potential employer by a friend or acquaintance acting as a go-between. At the same time, the personal nature of the employer-employee relationship in domestic work required a sense of mutual trust and compatibility. A third party who knew and could vouch for the other person established the trust needed to smooth entry. It is no wonder that both employer and employee preferred personal referrals to impersonal mechanisms.

Entry: School Girls and Day Workers   The women who started in domestic work prior to World War II entered in one of two ways. One group began as apprentices, like the school boys who preceded them. In fact, the term "school girl" was used to refer to these apprenticeship positions. A woman typically found a school girl job soon after her arrival and before she had children. She was thrust into the position without intending a long-term career in domestic service. The job was arranged by the husband, another relative, or a friend. Wages were nominal, and the employer provided training in housekeeping techniques and American cooking. Many of the issei women simultaneously attended English language classes. The job was thus seen as part of the socialization of the newcomer. In many cases, however, it portended the beginning of a career in domestic work. Unlike the men, for whom a school boy job was a temporary way station, the issei women tended to get locked into domestic work once they started as school girls.

The experience of Mrs. Takagi, who arrived as a 19-year-old in 1920, illustrates this mode of entry. Mrs. Takagi's husband's parents had immigrated with him, and the couple lived with them in Oakland:

> I was here twenty-eight days, and my mother-in-law took me to the first job on the twenty-ninth day. So I didn't even know "yes" or "no." I was so scared to go out then. . . . The first time I went, she taught me all the things I said. . . . They had a coal stove, a big one. Burned coal just like a Japanese hibachi. It has a pipe inside and heats the water from down below. I had to bring the coal up; all the time I went up and down. Then I had to wash diapers. Me, I grew up on a big farm, so I never had to do that. When I came to America I didn't know anything. So I just had to cry. She said, "What happened to your eyes?" . . . Then she gave me $5.00 and gave me a note and said to take it home. . . . My mother [in-law] and father [in-law] said, "Oh, that's big money." They thought it was supposed to be $5.00 a month.

Mrs. Takagi was fortunate in having an employer who treated her as an apprentice and encouraged her to attend English classes: "She put a hat on me, put a book in my hand, and gave me carfare. She said, 'Go to school.'" After six months, Mrs. Takagi became a housekeeper for a banker and later worked for a wealthy widow before finally settling into day work.

The second group entered as part-time day workers after the arrival of children, when family expenses began to outrun income. Mrs. Yoshida, whose experience was discussed earlier, was part of this group. In these cases the women entered domestic work more deliberately and initiated the job search themselves after deciding that they needed to work to make ends meet. Other issei women working as domestics provided both the inspiration and the means to secure employment. Mrs. Yoshida's account indicates that her husband attempted to discourage her employment. Conflict between husband and wife is even more apparent in the case of Mrs. Amano. She began day work in her mid-thirties after several years of taking in laundry:

> When the kids got to be in junior high school, Mrs. S——
> said, "Why don't you go out to work?" Other people
> with small children did go out to work, but Mr. Amano
> was sickly when he was young, so he didn't want the
> children left alone. He said, "What if the children get
> hurt. You couldn't get their lives back. The children are
> worth more than a few dollars. Just as long as we have
> enough to eat that's enough." So I went out secretly to
> work in one place. And that one became two and that
> two became three. By three I stopped [adding more jobs]
> because by that time my husband found out and of
> course there was still work at home because I was still
> taking in home laundry.

Mrs. Amano's decision to secretly defy her husband illustrates the dialectical nature of issei women's involvement in domestic wage labor. On the one hand, circumstances beyond their control forced them to seek employment: their husband's inability to provide adequate support and the needs of parents and other relatives in Japan. They had to travel in unfamiliar neighborhoods and enter strange households without any experience of the work or knowledge of English. Some confessed that they felt fearful and helpless in the beginning. Yet, on the other hand, some women actively sought out employment, even in the face of opposition from husbands. And some women who got into school girl jobs more or less passively continued in domestic work even without great financial pressure.

These instances suggest that employment, even in a menial capacity, provided resources that women could not get anywhere else.

Staying In The benefits provided by employment partly explain not only why some women wanted to go into domestic work in the first place, but also why they were committed to remaining in it. The most obvious benefit was an independent source of income. Because pay arrangements in domestic work are informal, women could keep the exact amount of their earnings secret from husbands. Some women reported keeping their own bank accounts and using their earnings to make purchases for themselves or their children without asking their husbands. A second benefit in some cases was the material and emotional support provided by employers. Several domestics mentioned learning a great deal and having their horizons expanded by contact with employers. Mrs. Takagi's employer visited her in the hospital when she was sick and gave her money to go to Japan to retrieve her son. She credits this employer with helping her weather many personal crises. For women cut off from kin ties, the connection with employers could be a valued resource.

These kinds of personal motives were only a minor factor in the continuity or discontinuity of women's careers, however. The multiple responsibilities carried by issei women brought a number of situational contingencies into play. Career patterns varied a great deal from one woman to another, depending on the husband's line of work and the family's financial needs. Issei women engaged in domestic work continuously or intermittently as their sole occupation or as a supplement to other work, for a few hours or for fifty or sixty hours a week. Moreover, an individual woman might display different work patterns at different stages of life. Even the most continuously employed women took occasional leaves because of illness, the birth of a child, a trip to Japan, or other contingencies.

Beneath the variability, however, certain regularities can be discerned. In general, the careers of women trained in school girl positions shortly after arrival tended to be less casual than those of women who started as day workers after the birth of children. Former "school girls" tended to work exclusively in domestic service, put in full-time hours, and be continuously employed. The later-entering women were more likely to work seasonally, vary their hours in domestic service according to the volume of work in the family business, or combine domestic service with home industry, such as sewing, embroidery, or taking in laundry.

Most issei worked the longest hours during the years when their children were young, in the 1920s. Although a time of heavy domestic responsibilities, it was also the period of greatest financial need. Moreover, they were still young and energetic enough to carry the double burden of work in and out of the home. By the late 1920s, by dint of dual wage earning and frugality, many issei families had managed to attain a standard of living somewhat lower than that of native-born white Americans, but not inferior to those of many immigrant groups in the East.[46] The depression that followed shortly afterward was a set-back. Several women mentioned that their husbands were unemployed or underemployed during the 1930s. Women tried to increase their work hours, but it was hard to increase their earnings. Wages for day workers fell as low as fifteen cents an hour. As the 1930s progressed, some of the older issei women's children were old enough to begin working. The added income permitted some women to reduce their work hours.

Returning to Work After World War II   Issei domestic workers were perhaps the group least affected occupationally by the war. Of the domestics who did not return to California after release from internment camps, some found manual jobs in factories or packing sheds, while others were forced to take live-in domestic positions in order to secure sponsorship and a place to stay. Many in both groups eventually returned to the Bay Area and re-entered their former occupation. Many issei had reached the age when parents normally retire in Japan. Instead of retiring or slowing down, they stepped up their efforts and increased their work hours.

Housing was an immediate problem because of the wartime boom in California. Many returnees had to take temporary quarters in churches, rooming houses, or hostels. Some, like Mrs. Takagi and Mrs. Ikeda,[47] secured live-in housekeeping positions and thus obtained living quarters. The lucky ones found apartments. Once housing was secured, jobs had to be located quickly. The urgency felt by the returnees is evident in Mrs. Amano's description of how she found jobs after returning:

> Everyone put ads in the paper. I advertised in the *Berkeley Gazette*. At the time I took two or three houses. I worked four days, some half, some whole days. Everyone said if you didn't hurry up and find a job, all the good ones would be taken. So I thought I'd better hurry up and find a job.

Post-War Entrants   Women who resumed domestic work were joined by other issei who had not done this type of work before the war. The new entrants were drawn from three sources. First were women who had farmed before the war. The switch to domestic work sometimes occurred in conjunction with the migration from rural to urban areas described earlier. Mrs. Sugihara and her husband farmed in Oregon and California before the war, but afterward settled in Berkeley, where he became a gardener and she a day worker:

> Gardening was the easiest thing to do, since when we came out of the camps we had very little that we owned. . . . I didn't do any housework before then. . . .
> *How did you find your first housecleaning job?*
> Well, they seemed to come one right after another. At first, right after we left camp requests for housecleaners would come to the church, so that was one method. Also through friends. The Caucasian employers were looking for Japanese to hire, and so they'd pass on the information among themselves. As a result we'd find out about many available jobs.

Families who resumed farming in rural areas close to cities found that suburbanization was creating opportunities for day work near home. After five years in Berkeley, the Sugiharas bought a small farm in Concord. They did a little walnut growing, and Mrs. Sugihara supplemented their income through part-time housework in the rapidly expanding suburbs of Walnut Creek and Lafayette.

A second group of entrants were urban women who had been employed in occupations that they were unable to resume. Three issei in the study group fell into this category, including Mrs. Hayashi, who had been a midwife in San Francisco, and Mrs. Taniguchi, who had run a laundry with her husband in Berkeley. Instead of going back to Berkeley, the Taniguchis settled in San Francisco, where community groups had set up an agency to place the returnees in day work jobs. Both she and her husband signed up. They wrote down the addresses and showed them to bus drivers to get directions:

> We hadn't gone out of our house very much when we lived in San Francisco [before moving to Berkeley], so it took us quite a while to learn how to get around. Now I can go just about anywhere I want to in San Francisco. In fact, I was just discussing this with a friend today, and we concluded that it's because we're so poor that we had to use the bus for getting around, and as a result we can go just about anywhere by ourselves even without a car.

Moreover, she found that she preferred day work to laundry:

> Even if I were offered a laundry job again, I wouldn't take it. It's too hard. But housecleaning I'd gladly do. . . . Well, I did laundry work for a long time, but I had to do the same thing over and over again. Housecleaning, though, involves doing all sorts of things in different rooms, so four hours pass by rather quickly.

The third group comprised women who had not done any form of paid work prior to the war. An example is Mrs. Kawai,[48] who had engaged in various forms of unpaid labor, including helping in her uncle's store, taking care of her husband's nursery business, and assisting her husband in his duties as a caretaker at a nursery school. She started working for wages after returning from camp because, she said, "It would have been hard for us if I hadn't worked." She inherited her first job from her daughter, who was leaving it: "I would call her up the night before and learn whatever I didn't know. My daughter went to work with me at first and taught me whatever I didn't know—I didn't know how to use the vacuum cleaner—and that's how I learned."

Post-Retirement Entrants   Still another major entering group consisted of those who found their first jobs in domestic service long after the post-war adjustment period. These women began domestic work as a post-retirement career after age 65, following retirement from other jobs. Three issei fall into this group. Each had at least two prior positions as farmer, nursery worker, weaver, charwoman, cook, or dishwasher. Domestic service was undertaken not only for financial security, but for personal well-being. One member of the post-retirement group was an issei widow, Mrs. Togasaki, who farmed with her husband until the war and then worked as a flower sorter in a nursery until her retirement at 65. Seventy-five at the time of our interview, she had done day work three days a week for ten years:

> My friend was working in a beauty shop and someone was looking for a person. I had told everybody when I retired I wanted to do domestic work part-time. . . .
> *What's the main reason you're working now?*
> I'm getting social security and another dividend coming in. I have those two, but after I pay what I have to pay, rent, I don't have any extra left. So, for spending money.
> *If you had enough money to live comfortably, would you still work?*
> I don't have to work even now, but if I stay home all day, I start to recollect the bad old days. So even half a day I go to work. . . . I think of my troubles when I'm alone. I work and can forget about everything.

Working in Later Life   A group of elderly issei domestic workers sitting around a senior center probably appear indistinguishable from one another; yet they turn out on further inquiry to be quite varied in terms of how they got where they are. Some would have been working continuously in domestic work since starting as "school girls" shortly after arriving some fifty years previously. Others would have started as day workers when they were already mothers and worked sporadically or continuously since then. Still others would have been working as domestics since the end of World War II as a result of the economic dislocation caused by the internment. Finally, there would be elderly women who have been domestics only for the last few years, following retirement from other jobs.

Still, regardless of their career paths, what is striking is their propensity to keep working long after most workers have retired. A remarkable number of issei domestics remain employed into their seventies and eighties. For some, financial considerations are still important. They are self-supporting or have to supplement other sources such as savings or social security to make ends meet. In the past some kept working because social security benefits were not extended to private household workers until 1950.[49] Unpaid family workers and domestics accumulated no credits before then, so some kept working for a few extra years to qualify for benefits. Now, however, most of the issei interviewed deny any overwhelming financial need. Other factors make it difficult to retire, even when they think it is time to do so.

Those who have worked for one employer for a long time feel a sense of obligation to remain. Long-term domestics report that their employers plead with them to continue working. Many find these personal appeals hard to refuse. Mrs. Hayashi's case is typical. At 84, she lived with her son in the East Bay and commuted once a week to San Francisco:

> I retired four years ago when I was hit by a car. My son asked me to come and live with him here. But if I stay home, there's nothing to do. It's not good for me. The one lady I work for now I started to work for over thirty years ago. I had retired, but she begged me to come back. So now I just work four hours on Thursday. I go in the morning, work for four hours, and stay with a friend on Thursday night and come back Friday. . . .
>
> *What do you do in the four hours?*
>
> Oh, it's just play. I work for only three hours. Then she fixes an elaborate lunch. She sets the table with china and silverware, and makes it very pretty. Then we have lunch. Even though I don't understand English, she just jabbers away. Then the lady cleans up and washes the dishes. So it's just play. . . .
>
> *Then you think you'll keep working?*
>
> Well, I don't know how long. I don't know which one of us will die first. Maybe because she's younger than I am, I will die first.

Although other women worked longer hours (the range among the issei was from nine to thirty-two hours a week), their relationships with employers and reasons for working were similar to Mrs. Hayashi's. Most had worked for the same employers for a long time. They continued working, they said, because work gave them a financial cushion and kept them busy and healthy, and their employers needed them. The impression gained from their stories is that their employers depended on them as much for social companionship as for actual cleaning help. They had relieved elderly workers of most heavy physical labor and gave them only light chores. Some issei women, like Mrs. Hayashi, described their jobs as "just play" (*asobi*).

Perhaps the most fundamental reason for continuing to work, according to the issei themselves, was that they liked to work. This attitude stemmed in part from the Meiji-era ethic instilled during their youth. Equally important, hardships in the United States established habits of industry and thrift that they could not easily relinquish. Mrs. Taniguchi was perhaps the most articulate in expressing the complex of personal ties, habits, and values that kept her working:

> Lately because I'm getting old and it's hard for me to go up the hill, the missus comes to pick me up, saying I shouldn't strain myself. That too is an indication of their appreciation for my work. So I can't really quit so easily. Also, since I have an income from working, I can give contributions to the church and help out friends who get sick without being miserly about it. In that sense I value the opportunity to work. I'd like to continue working as much as I can. If I were married to a rich man, of course, I wouldn't need to work. But in our case, we had so little to start with and we gradually saved up to where we are today. So the habit of working is ingrained in us.

By the 1970s most issei women were widows. Employment enabled them to be independent. Just as some women once took jobs in opposition to their husbands' wishes, some later persisted in the face of their children's objections. According to Mrs. Nishimura:

> My children didn't like me working as a domestic. My oldest son, the one who went to Japan after the war, told me that I shouldn't be a domestic and I should do sew-

ing instead to earn some extra money. But when I was head of the women's club, sewing would take up so much of my time and I was told that domestic work was easier. . . . My children tell me too that since I've had such a hard time, they don't like my working now, either. They keep asking me when I'll quit. But my work now isn't that hard, and I'll get old quickly if I just stay at home.

Thus, even in old age issei women found that domestic work provided certain satisfactions, despite its definition as menial employment. Working meant independence and keeping active and feeling needed.

Nisei Careers

The nisei's entry into domestic work was also conditioned by their limited options in the labor market. In rural areas the main alternatives were farm work, picking produce, or packing it, and in urban areas they were sales, service, or clerical positions in ethnic enterprises. Mrs. Morita, who grew up in San Francisco and graduated from high school in the 1930s, bluntly summarized her options:

In those days there was no two ways about it. If you were Japanese, you either worked in an art store [Japanese gift store] where they sell those little junks, or you worked as a domestic. . . . There was no Japanese girl working in an American firm. Maybe one or two in all of San Francisco. How they got it I don't know, but no jobs were open to Orientals until after the war.

Three of the nisei in the study had clerical jobs before World War II, and all worked in Japanese firms. White-collar employment in ethnic enterprises offered higher status than domestic service, but the pay was low and the hours were long. These jobs also entailed extra expenses. Firms were concentrated in San Francisco, so those living outside the city might spend considerable time and money on commuting. The worker also had to buy and maintain an appropriate wardrobe. After graduation, Mrs. Morita obtained a job as clerk in a Japanese firm through her father's connections. When her father died, two years later, she stayed home and took care of things for a while. When she decided to go back to work, she assessed the advantages and disadvantages of the careers open to her:

> I had graduated high school, but the only kind of job open, like I said, was salesgirl in Chinatown, which would mean eating out and silk stockings. You wore silk stockings those days. And a fresh dress every day. As opposed to domestic work, where you go and change clothes into a smock or uniform. Then you get fed too. So that would be more economical, you know, in our family situation, too. . . .
>
> I realized I could save more by doing domestic, so that's what I did. I got a part-time job in the cafeteria at Galileo High. They paid ten cents an hour. At that time that was big pay! So I worked that job for two hours, 11:30 to 1:30, and then I went to my domestic job in the afternoon, for which I got $7.00 a week and carfare, $7.50 total. I worked from 1:30 to 7:00.

In short, despite its low status, domestic work offered some advantages. Part-time jobs were available, and less desirable jobs could always be dropped and traded for better ones. Thus, even when white-collar work was available, some women chose domestic jobs.

Finding a Job Given the history of Japanese women in domestic work, finding a job was no problem. Such jobs were often offered to the nisei without any specific effort or intention on their part. Some women described the entry process as "falling into" the work. When asked how she got her first job, Mrs. Nishi said of herself and her older sister: "We never intended to go into that kind of work, but someone who knew my parents said there's someone who's looking for some help, and would one of your daughters like to, and that's how it always happened. . . . [Later] it was always through someone." If entry was more calculated, the worker usually asked a friend or acquaintance for a referral. Rural women needed a relative or other connection in the city to find positions there. Such arrangements were typically made by the parents through an intermediary. There were also ethnic employment agencies, as mentioned previously, but informal networks were the most prevalent source of jobs.

Entry and Socialization: Nisei School Girls   Even taking into account their limited options and the ease of finding domestic jobs, the degree of specialization in domestic service among the young nisei remains striking. In San Francisco itself the proportion approached 60 percent, and in Oakland it reached nearly 40 percent. What additional factors explain this concentration? Sociocultural factors seem to have come into play and interacted with economic factors. The nisei job histories and interviews with informants indicate that, with a few exceptions, nisei women were tracked into domestic work through the evolution of the Japanese school girl role.[50] For both economic and social reasons, domestic service was viewed as an appropriate occupation for young single women. Traditional Japanese education for girls ended with several years of training in domestic arts. It was also customary for daughters of prosperous rural families to spend a few years serving in cultured urban households to acquire social graces.[51] Apprenticeships in domestic service can be viewed as an adaptation of these practices, as well as a variation of the Japanese school boy role. Through domestic service, daughters received training in homemaking skills, while also supporting themselves and saving for marriage. Seven of the twelve nisei and one of the four kibei who returned to the United States before World War II gained their first employment experience as school girls.

School girl jobs included both live-in and day work positions. In both urban and rural areas in Northern California, some nisei girls began work as live-in domestics while attending high school, much as the issei school boys had done. One gets the impression that parents were concerned that their daughters work in respectable and cultured families. Thus, they tended to choose situations with teachers or other professionals and business executives. A typical case is that of Mrs. Nishi, who was the second of seven children. Her father was employed in a Japanese nursery, and the birth of two more children when she and her sisters were teenagers created financial hardships at home. During her senior year she decided to take a live-in job in Piedmont and attend high school in Oakland:

> I thought it would be helpful to my parents to go out and do that. They didn't have to feed me; they didn't have to buy any clothes for me. I took care of my own clothes.
> *How did they feel about it?*
> I really don't know. The only thing they worried about was whether I'd be running around. . . .
> *Was that a common thing for the nisei?*
> It's kind of interesting that Japanese parents would let their girls go and work as school girls and live in, but the Chinese people didn't. I had [Chinese] friends who did work as school girls, but they went home every day.

Mrs. Nishi disliked being a live-in school girl because her employers treated her like a servant, but her sister had good experiences and was generally treated like a member of the family.

It was even more common to find a school girl position after leaving school. In such cases the placement was seen as a "finishing" experience. This view is particularly evident among women from farm backgrounds. Two nisei and one kibei ended their educations without finishing high school and were sent to sewing school in San Francisco. Live-in situations were secured by family friends, and they earned room, board, and expenses doing household chores.

The experience of Mrs. Aoki, whose family raised strawberries on leased land near San Jose, was typical of these women.

> Well, you know, when I was fifteen, my mother passed away. So that's why my father told me to go to sewing school. So I was a school girl when I was fifteen years old. . . . That was the first.
> *You worked a whole day or a half a day?*
> Just a half a day. I stayed there, room and board, and she paid me ten dollars a month. The wage was low. I went to sewing school in the morning and came home in the afternoon and helped with dinner. . . . I didn't know anything, because I wasn't used to using Caucasian things or to American food.

As Mrs. Aoki's last remark indicates, despite being born and raised in the United States, rural nisei were largely unfamiliar with the mores of the dominant culture. Domestic work provided one of the few avenues for them to observe the habits and lifestyles of white Americans, and employers were willing to train inexperienced girls. Mrs. Sasaki, who grew up in the Sacramento Delta, described her entry and training:

> A friend of ours asked me if I wanted to do domestic work, so I guess that's how I started working. These people that I worked for had a ranch in C——, and I came along with them to San Francisco. I started doing the school girl job, so I could go to sewing school. . . . She had a Chinese cook and a lady to manage everything. So I helped her, making beds, changing sheets, and ironing and doing dishes. . . . It's a different type of thing living with *hakujin* [Caucasians] and with my family, so I learned a lot of different things. All in all I worked about 4 or 5 hours, and lived there with them.

Attending sewing school while living with a Caucasian family in the city accomplished two objectives. First, the young woman acquired the tailoring and sewing skills considered essential for wives and mothers. Second, she learned something of city life and the ways of families from the dominant culture, thereby gaining sophistication and breadth.

City girls were more likely to finish high school and enter school girl jobs after graduation. The jobs they took, however, were not usually live-in positions. They worked part-time in order to acquire cooking and other domestic skills. Mrs. Tanabe, a nisei who grew up in Alameda, explained that her family could not afford to send her to college, so she worked as a type-sorter on a Japanese newspaper in San Francisco. A year later, she said:

> Being an only child I felt like I needed to learn how to do different homemaking [things]. So I applied for a school girl job on a part-time basis. And that was interesting. I feel like I learned my—I didn't even know how to boil water. You know when you're an only child, your mother did everything. You learn quite a bit.
> *Who taught you?*

Well, the lady of the house. I didn't even know how to set a table. Or she would say, "Make me a cup of tea." So that was interesting.

A similar account was given by Mrs. Watanabe:
I went into domestic work because my father couldn't afford college anyway. And then I didn't know how to cook. So I thought I'd learn how to cook and like that. I only did part-time work. [I got the job] through a friend that was working, and she got sick and couldn't work.

Most of these jobs started in the afternoon, leaving the mornings free, theoretically for attending school, although none of the women in the study did. A typical routine was described by Mrs. Watanabe: "[I started] work at one o'clock. I prepared dinner, did a little dusting, and I think I did the bathrooms too. I served dinner, then washed the dishes and came home. It was about seven o'clock. That's all I did—part-time work: it was easy work."

Staying In By describing their school girl jobs as an alternative to college, as only part-time work, or as a way to learn domestic skills, the nisei minimized their significance as jobs. They apparently did not view domestic work as a "real" occupation, nor did they plan long-term careers in domestic service. Like European immigrant servants of the late nineteenth and early twentieth centuries, they expected to leave service upon marriage. Because many nisei did not marry until the outbreak of the war or after it, the projected course of their careers could not be played out. However, of the seven who worked while single and married before the war, five did leave domestic service shortly before marriage. Three became involved in assisting their husbands in farming or nursery tending, and two "stayed home" for two years.

Prior to marriage the seven worked an average of six years each. Three worked for only two or three years while attending sewing school; the others worked for six to ten years, delaying marriage until their middle or late twenties, presumably because their families needed their wages.[52] Mrs. Fujitani's career is illustrative of the experience of those who graduated into full-time domestic service while still single to help support parents and siblings. The eldest of six children, she dropped out of school after the sixth grade to help on the family's strawberry farm. In her late teens she found a live-in position by walking up to the largest house in town and knocking on the door. She was taken on and trained, and subsequently remained as the housekeeper for fourteen years. Her wages enabled her younger brothers and sisters to complete high school, and all of them went into white-collar occupations. Finally, in her mid-thirties, resolved not to wed a farmer, she had an arranged marriage with an issei, divorced and eleven years her senior, who was a cook for the railroad in an East Bay city. She left domestic service until after the war.

Three married nisei worked as domestics before the war. Mrs. Aoki started out as a school girl at 15 and was a live-in domestic for several years prior to her marriage in 1927. Her husband was a gardener, and she continued in domestic service for fifteen years, first as a housekeeper and then as a day worker, until the war started. She was able to work despite having three children because her father lived with the couple and took care of the children and the house. The second employed mother, Mrs. Ito, was a school girl before her marriage in 1934. She dropped out of service for several years, until financial necessity impelled her to seek part-time domestic work, even though she did not want to leave her children. The third, Mrs. Murakami, took her first school girl job *after* marrying at age 17 and coming to the city. She attended secretarial school and worked as a secretary in a Japanese firm for three years. When she had her second child and no longer had the time to commute, she turned to full-time domestic work.

Re-Entry and Post-War Entry The post-war period was one of frustration for some older nisei, who had their horizons expanded in camp only to see them shrink once again. These were women who found in the internment camps their first opportunities to work in the fields for which they were trained, but were forced subsequently to return to domestic service. Mrs. Watanabe, for example, graduated from a San Francisco high school in the late 1930s. Although she took the business course, she was unable to find office employment and worked as a domestic for four years: "But then when I went to camp, I worked as a secretary. Can you beat that? With what I learned in high school! My shorthand and typing." The animation in her voice testified to the personal significance of this job. This experience, and her two years as a clerk in a printing shop in Chicago, were obviously the highlights of her work life. They colored her attitude toward domestic work, which she resumed upon returning to California because she was unable to find anything in her preferred field.

Choices available in camp and in the East and Midwest were not forthcoming in California. The returning nisei were faced with the monumental task of adjusting, and they had to act quickly. Jobs had to be secured immediately, and domestic jobs were often the most accessible, especially for those who had held them before. Some nisei families took live-in positions, with the wife acting as housekeeper and the husband as gardener, in order to solve their housing problems. From there, it was easy to get back into domestic service. Several of the women who had retired from school girl jobs returned to domestic work in the period immediately following the war, this time as day workers. They were joined by women who had never done domestic work before and were drawn into it as they adjusted to post-war changes. These new entrants fell into three categories. The first comprised former farm women who migrated to urban areas. Unlike the issei, most of whom never returned to farming, many nisei attempted it for a while. The Fujiis' story illustrates some of the changes nisei farm families faced. Mr. Fujii had been a ranch foreman in the Sacramento Delta. After the war the Fujiis returned with their seven children to the ranch where they had worked. They gave up farming and moved to the Bay Area in 1948:

> The reason is that there weren't enough Japanese [workers]. They were too old, and young people didn't want to do hard work, so it was hard to get people. The girls finished school and they started working in Sacramento. So instead of being separated we thought if we went to the city they could stay at home and work.
> *What did your husband do?*
> Gardening. His uncle was a gardener in Berkeley, so his uncle taught him a little bit.
> *And what about you?*
> Housecleaning.

The second group consisted of younger kibei women who had spent the war years in Japan. The poverty and hardship of the war years and post-recovery period led them to seek escape. Armed with citizenship, they were able to emigrate back to the United States. Two of the kibei interviewees fell into this category. Both did domestic work as their initial job after arriving; as in the issei generation, relatives and friends arranged apprenticeship positions for them.[53] The third group comprised older nisei women who either had not been employed before or had been employed in some other field. These women had reached middle age and were unable to take advantage of openings in white-collar work. Moreover, many nisei were still affected by racial discrimination. Even in the 1960s there were still many visible pockets of discrimination. Because she cared for her elderly parents for some years, Miss Ishida had little employment experience:

> Then in early 1964 I decided to go out to work, and I went to all the stores and applied for jobs, but they weren't hiring too many minorities at that point, and I wasn't too young either. I guess I must have been around 51. They said they weren't hiring anybody but they would let me know. So I kept phoning them and going back to see if there was. In the meantime I had to earn some kind of money, 'cause I just couldn't stay idle. But I don't really remember who I used to work for then, but it was through a recommendation from somebody and I've been working [as a domestic] ever since, off and on.

The post-war entrants were later joined by women who turned to or returned to domestic work after their children reached school age or left home. Their entry was a response to the "empty nest" stage. They were more likely to say that they were working part-time for *kozukai* ("pocket money"). A kibei, Mrs. Yamamoto, decided to go to work in 1960 when her children were all in high school:

> Everybody was going to school and everybody else was working, so I had spare time. So I go to work so I can go downtown and go shopping and buy something.
> *How did you happen to go into domestic work?*
> That's the funny part. Most Japanese ladies have to work and I don't speak English. Everyone was doing it, so I

thought I'd try it. I put an ad in the newspaper, the
Oakland Tribune. And I got two jobs right away. I got so
many telephone calls, but I took these two.

In the post-war period the nisei went straight into day work
without first serving an apprenticeship in school girl jobs. As mature
women, they presumably had sufficient experience from doing their
own housework. However, they had to learn techniques for getting
the work done in the time allotted. They learned by trial and error or
turned to more experienced friends and relatives for advice. Mrs.
Noguchi, a kibei, said:

People come to ask me how I do it, so I told them you start
from above, upstairs, and then I do the vacuuming. I told
them whatever I know. Keiko (a friend) was going to start
domestic work, so I told her how. We do housecleaning in
our own homes, but it's a bit different to work for someone else.

The Past into the Present: Contemporary Nisei Careers

Since day work offers flexibility and is easily entered and left, the
hours worked and continuity over time vary a great deal within the
study group. The maximum hours worked during the peak working
years ranged from seventeen to forty-eight a week. At one end of the
scale is Mrs. Kaneko, a 60-year-old kibei who has worked forty to
forty-eight hours during her six-day weeks almost without interruption, from her return to the United States in 1937 to the present. At
the other end are several women who never worked more than half-
time. The majority (ten women) worked between twenty-five and
forty hours a week during their peak working years. Generally these
were the years just after the war, when even older women and women
with children had to earn as much income as possible. Three nisei
worked six days a week, piecing together up to twelve half-day jobs
to get forty-eight hours of work during this period. As the nisei
reached middle age, most reduced their hours, so that only a few
worked more than twenty-five hours a week by the mid-1970s.

Like the issei, the nisei took advantage of the flexibility of domestic work to take extended leaves and to expand or contract their
working hours as circumstances changed. Although some women

worked more or less continuously in domestic service, they varied the type and extent of the work over time. Mrs. Hori, an 83-year-old Hawaiian-born nisei, started out with a job processing sugar. After coming to the mainland, she worked in a sugar processing plant, as a laundress, as a maid in a sorority house, and, finally, as a cook in a private household. For the past two years, since she reached 80, she has worked only part-time. Only two subjects from the nisei/kibei generation were fully retired, one at age 63, the other at 65. Four others moved into other lines of work. The remaining ten women aged 60 or over continue to be employed as domestics. These include the two oldest nisei, Mrs. Hori (83) and Mrs. Murakami (79), who worked sixteen and twenty hours a week respectively, as well as three other women over 65.

The seven remaining nisei were still below retirement age at the time of the interview, so only time will tell whether they show the same drive to work in old age as the issei. Still, many nisei express attitudes similar to those of their elders.

The nisei and kibei can, like the elderly issei, be divided into those who were continuing domestic work from the past and those who had entered it more recently. The former group started working either before or after the war because of financial pressures, and they continued working for the same reasons. The pressures were not as great as in the past, but most were married to self-employed men, primarily gardeners, and they worried about saving enough for retirement. Many were working full-time when interviewed, but planned to cut back when they were more secure. Mrs. Sasaki, a 63-year-old nisei, worked five days a week: "I thought, as long as I'm able to, I'd like to work. . . . If I could I'll try to keep up until I'm 65 and then I'll work about two or three days at most. . . . My family thinks it's good for my health."

Mrs. Ito, another continuously employed domestic, said she now worked just for a bit of *kozukai*, and domestic work was flexible enough to let her "run down any time I want to" to see her daughter in San Jose. She said, "If I didn't work, that's that, I mean I'm just as happy," but when asked if she would stop working if she did not need the money, she contradicted herself:

> Well, I don't think so. I think I'd still keep on just to keep
> myself active. My mind going. Gosh, no life then! I think
> I'd be pretty stupid . . . and it's boring. So I like to keep

my mind busy and do something. Something I can gain
out of it. Instead of just social run-around—that's easy to
do. But I don't go too much for it.

The more recent entrants also continued working to keep busy
and for extra income, since those were the main reasons they entered
in the first place. Thus, Mrs. Yamamoto, when asked why she kept
working, said:

It's no use to stay home. And I can have money and can
buy for the grandchildren. I can have spare money. If I had
money, I wouldn't work. . . .
What would make you stop working?
If I got sick or someone else got sick, I'd have to take care
of them and would stop working. As long as I'm all right,
I will work.

There was another reason for working besides wanting to keep
active and to earn money. The nisei, like the issei, had long-term
employers who relied on their continued services. Like the issei, the
nisei felt a sense of obligation to their employers. Women's statements
that they would quit working if they had no financial need seem to
clash with their expressions of commitment to particular employers.
Mrs. Yamamoto, for example, worked for one employer for fifteen
years and said that she would never quit that job, even though she
also said she only worked for the money:

*If you inherited a large amount of money, would you keep
working?*
I don't think so. If such money came, I would quit. Just
obachan's [old lady's] place I won't quit. If she said,
"Come," I will come. She has no one. She's rich, so if she
gets sick, cousins, everyone comes, because they think
they'll inherit. Then she gets well and no one comes
again. *Hakujin* [Caucasians] say, "I'm going to give you
something in my will," but when they die, they leave
nothing.

The Japanese value system, with its emphasis on duty, evidently
retains a strong hold on the nisei.
All in all, then, barring an unforeseen change in circumstances—the main ones cited being ill health or new family respon-

sibilities, such as babysitting for an employed daughter—the nisei see the future as a continuation of the present. They expect to remain in domestic work until retirement, eventually reducing their hours, but remaining employed two or three days a week. Only the younger women speculate about the possibility of change. Mrs. Morita, aged 58, still regrets not having tried to get a secretarial or typing job earlier and occasionally mentions her intention to look into the possibility. Mrs. Hiraoka, a 49-year-old kibei, says:

> I should do something different work, but you know, I guess time goes by, and I guess I should go to school to learn something.
> *You've thought about it?*
> Yeah. I think after Katie [daughter] finishes college, I'll think about it. I should learn something, do different work. . . .
> *What kind of thing would you like to do?*
> If I go to school? I think a grocery checker. I thought about it.
> *What would you like about it?*
> Now, because they make pretty good money.

Mrs. Hiraoka and Mrs. Morita are the only ones who spontaneously mentioned the possibility of change. Many women denied having considered other alternatives. More often the women mentioned some notion, but without much specificity or enthusiasm. Mrs. Ito was typical when she said that she used to think about trying something else—like office work—but no longer: she would not want to sit at a desk all day. Anyway, she concluded, it did no good to think about such matters at her age. She would rather spend her time and energy thinking about her children, visiting them, and making her own home more comfortable.

War Bride Careers

Unlike the husbands of issei and nisei, who were clustered in a narrow range of occupations, the husbands of war brides were deployed throughout the occupational hierarchy. The war brides were also heterogeneous in marital and family status. Therefore, the economic circumstances underlying their entry into domestic service were more varied than those of the issei and nisei.

The financial exigencies pressing upon the three war brides who were divorced single parents were unmistakable. Quite simply, they had to find a source of income or some means to augment other, inadequate sources of income, such as welfare, child support payments, or another low-paying job. The married women living with spouses can be roughly categorized according to three levels of financial need. Four women married to blue-collar, lower-white-collar, or retired men can be characterized as needing to work for extra income. Two women whose husbands earned middle-class salaries had extraordinary expenses. Mrs. Schickel, whose husband was a librarian, had incurred huge medical bills during a chronic fifteen-year illness; she had recently recovered and was determined to help pay off these debts. The other, Mrs. Rybin, was married to a unionized transit driver but needed a part-time job to pay for travel and other expenses associated with her activities as an unpaid minister. Finally, three women, the wives of professionals or managers, had little or no financial incentive to work, other than a desire for personal spending money and extra luxuries for the family. All three had reached the empty nest stage where they had little to do at home and were seeking something to occupy their time and keep them busy.

Eleven of the twelve had worked, though not in domestic service, while still single in Japan. Half found jobs immediately after arriving in the United States, mostly in semi-skilled operative or service jobs. The other half were out of the labor force for periods ranging from a few years to fifteen years while they raised children. Because they had switched occupations or had gaps in their employment, most of the war brides were middle-aged when they entered domestic work. Their average age at entry was 42.8, the youngest being 36 and the oldest 57. The women themselves considered their age a major factor in their choice of casual part-time employment. Mrs. Farrow had stayed home until her youngest child was 10. She explained her dilemma: "Now the children are grown up and I wanted to work, but I was too old to work."

For the war brides, then, even more than for the issei and nisei, domestic work was a mid- and late-life career. In this respect they mirrored the overall trend in private household work, which in the post-war economy has become increasingly "gray"—that is, the field is increasingly composed of older women, the typical private household worker being six years older than the average woman in the labor force.[54] Older minority women in particular are much more likely to be found in domestic service than younger white or minority women. In 1981, 10.2 percent of minority women over 35 were private household workers, compared with 1.6 percent of those aged 16 to 34.[55] As domestic service declines as an occupation, it attracts few young recruits. Therefore, it is increasingly made up of women who have been in it for some time and those who enter it in middle age, like the war brides, or in old age, like the issei, because options are so limited for older immigrant and minority women.

Entry   As might be expected, the degree of choice exercised in the entry process varied with women's economic circumstances. At one pole is Tomiko Inaba, whose story of how she was forced into the work is strikingly similar to that told by Mrs. Takagi about her introduction to domestic work over forty years earlier. Raised in a middle-class Tokyo family, Mrs. Inaba married a nisei employed as an administrator with the occupation forces in 1947. At the time he told her that he intended to remain permanently in Japan. Not long after the marriage, however, he announced that his parents, who lived in the Bay Area, needed his help, so the couple returned to the United States. He was unable to find a position that paid as well as his army job, and he became a postal worker, moonlighting as a barber. By the late 1950s he was having trouble supporting his elderly parents, wife, and four children, even with two jobs. Finally, her mother-in-law demanded that she go out to work to help her husband:

> First time, when I was told to do housework, that I had to go to work, I'm shook. Because in Japan I had one [maid]—and to do it myself! To come to America and do housework, I thought was so hard. But it couldn't be helped. . . . So I went to work, into housework. Oh, I'll never forget it. I came back home and I'm shaking in the body all over. Because I had never done anything like that before. Whole hour of vacuuming and that. . . . Then little by little I got used to it, my body, no shaking, no nothing. From then all along, I did housework.

At the other end of the pole is Kimiko Bentley, who chose to work although she had little financial need to do so and her husband, a certified public accountant, strongly objected. After the Bentleys' only daughter left for college, Mrs. Bentley was increasingly lonely, and therefore homesick. When a nisei friend informed her about an elderly neighbor seeking household help, she jumped at the chance, despite her husband's opposition and the potential disapproval of her family in Japan:

> Housework is the lowest job, is it not? That's a secret I'm working from my family in Japan. Because if they know, it's a shock to them. Well, I think in America too, isn't it? He [her husband] wants me to quit. He doesn't want me to. He hates that I'm working in housework, but there are no jobs. . . . He said if I want to work, first, go to school, English school, then get another job. . . . Even here some Japanese people think I'm very poor because I'm working now, housework. Some people don't understand.

Women at both extremes, those "forced" into the work and those who "chose" it in the face of external opposition, experienced some tension and were therefore conscious of the forces pressing on them. In contrast, those in the middle, who encountered little or no compulsion in either direction, drifted into the occupation almost without conscious decision because jobs were readily available. Aiko Loring, for example, was married to a sales manager in a large company and had no evident financial need to be employed, but when her three children were grown, she became restless, feeling that she had "nothing to look forward to." She fell into part-time domestic work: "Way it was, I just didn't have nothing to do. Kids were big and everything else, so when a girl came over and asked me if [I wanted a job], I said, 'Well, I never done it, so—but let's try it.'"

Whatever degree of personal choice was involved, entry into domestic work was usually effected through personal networks within the ethnic community. Eleven out of the twelve women found their initial jobs through friends and acquaintances or through ethnic community organizations. Four of these first jobs came from other war brides, two from nisei acquaintances, one from an issei in-law, and four from an ethnic church or service organization. The twelfth woman obtained her job through a German American neighbor who was ill and asked her to take over her housekeeping jobs for several elderly German Americans.

If Mrs. Loring simply "fell into" the work when a job was proferred, others entered it deliberately and requested referrals. Here the ethnic community was influential in that it provided role models. The importance of exemplars is apparent in Miyoshi Farrow's account of her decision to try domestic work. When asked how she found her first job, she replied:

> From a friend. When I first started thinking about working housework, a friend of a friend, she worked a long time and she saved money and went to Japan. I heard that story, so I thought someday I might do that. And the children were growing bigger and a friend of mine's working. So I said, "This time I'm going to start it and save money to go back to Japan." Otherwise I never could go to Japan, from my husband's pay, you know. Because I had two big ones and I thought they'd go to college.

When a community agency was the source, employer demand for *Japanese* help was crucial. Agencies were simply the conduit for requests from employers for "Japanese ladies." Two of the single parents were directed to domestic work by agencies serving war brides. Mrs. Adair had divorced her army sergeant husband seven years previously and moved with her three daughters from Detroit to San Francisco. She began working part-time as a hostess in a Japanese restaurant to supplement her welfare payments. When her boss cut her working hours, she confided her economic problems to the nisei social worker attached to her newcomer club. This social worker referred her to an elderly Caucasian woman who had requested a home care worker. Another single parent, Mrs. Osborne, was employed as an outreach worker for a Japanese American senior services program. She loved her job, but it was funded only as a twenty-hour-a-week position. The nisei head of the program told her that the hours could not be expanded, but put her in touch with clients seeking weekend housecleaning help.

Staying In   For the war brides, more than for the issei and nisei, domestic work was a marginal form of employment. Not only did most war brides work part-time, but they tended to work fewer hours per week than the other cohorts. Seven of the twelve war brides worked sixteen or fewer hours a week; of these, two worked eight hours or less. Of the remaining five, only one worked more than thirty hours a week. This woman was working thirty-two hours at the time of the initial interview, but later increased her hours to fifty-six when her daughter entered college. She was the only war bride to work full-time as a domestic at any time. For two of the women, domestic work was a second job used to augment wages from other part-time employment. Thus, the majority of war bride domestics were either housewives doing a little paid domestic work on the side or employed women moonlighting as domestics.

Their employment, even more than that of the issei and nisei, was largely underground and therefore not recognized officially. Overall, more than a quarter of the issei, nisei, and war brides spontaneously mentioned, without being specifically asked, that they did not pay income taxes or social security. Three other war brides claimed that their husbands did not know what they earned, so it is unlikely that they reported their earnings on tax forms.

These patterns fit in with what has been described as the growing "casualization" of private household work.[56] Michelotti reports that a higher than average proportion of domestic workers are moonlighters, using domestic service as a supplementary source of income.[57] Domestic workers are also outside the formal economy in that they frequently do not report their income or pay into social security. The head of a New York City committee on the exploitation of workers estimated that 90 percent of that city's domestics were not covered by social security.[58]

The marginality of employment was reinforced by cross-pressures on war brides to get out of domestic service. Husbands' objections to their wives' involvement in a degraded occupation were a common source of pressure. Another was the women's own discomfort about the status of the work, especially as they anticipated disapproval from family and friends in Japan. These feelings of status degradation will be discussed more fully in the chapters that follow. What is important to note here is that war brides may have experienced more ambivalence about continued employment than the issei or nisei.

Despite the seeming precariousness of their commitment, many war brides have stayed in this line of work for extended periods. Four of the women had been working as domestics for twelve to fifteen years when interviewed. Five had worked for four to six years, and the other three had worked for two years. Inertia and the lack of viable options can partially explain this career continuity. However, given the cross-pressures to which war brides were subjected and the fact that they felt ashamed enough to conceal their employment from relatives in Japan, it is surprising that a woman like Mrs. Bentley would continue working as a domestic for twelve years. Why did she? Again, the answer seems to be that employment, however menial, offers resources that women value: a private income, a sphere of independence, a chance to do productive work. These benefits were important for the war brides, who had few other resources. Mrs. Bentley said of her own income, "I can do with it what I want." Like three other women, she kept the amount of her earnings secret from her husband. I was asking her about her hourly rate just as her husband walked through the room. She glanced up conspiratorially and shook her head. After he left, she whispered the amount into the tape recorder. Kazuko Frankel also kept her husband in the dark about how much she earned and maintained her money in a separate account on the grounds that "It's none of his business."

For women far away from kin and lacking other social support, domestic service performs a double function. It keeps the mind occupied so that they do not get homesick, and it provides a ready-made set of relationships, so that they do not feel so isolated. Aiko Loring described the woman she worked for as "more like a friend" than a boss. Hideko Sentino says that she had little in common with other war brides, who were usually less educated than she, and had trouble communicating with issei and nisei women because their values were so different. She felt most at ease with her employers, in whom she confided and from whom she got help when she needed it.

These last few examples seem to have taken us full circle. Despite changes in economic and social conditions, many of the same factors that drew issei into domestic work drew the war brides in decades later, and some of the same elements that motivated the issei and nisei to continue working also kept the war brides involved in the face of familial opposition and societal denigration. These women probably will not continue working into their seventies and eighties as the issei have done, but for the near future at least, most plan to continue.

CHAPTER 6
On the Job:
Conditions of Work
and Strategies for Coping

From Live-In Service to Day Work

Domestic service encompasses a variety of situations: full-time and part-time live-in jobs; full-time and part-time non-residential positions with one employer; and day work. Until World War I, live-in service was the most common pattern in the United States. Room and board represented a large part of the worker's compensation, with a small additional payment in wages. The merging of residence and work place stood as a marked exception to the increasing separation of production from the household and the accompanying segregation of work and non-work life brought about by industrialization. For the live-in domestic, there was no clear line between work and non-work time. Work hours were open-ended, and the domestic was "on call" for most of her waking hours. She had little time for her own family or outside social relationships. As other forms of wage work that gave workers greater autonomy expanded, the confinement and isolation of domestic service grew more onerous. Observers noted that women preferred employment in factories and shops, even though wages and physical amenities were frequently inferior.[1]

Before World War II, Japanese domestics occasionally worked as live-in help. As might be expected, those who did so were those from "pre-industrial" backgrounds (i.e., rural women) or those who had family attachments and obligations (i.e., single women and widows).

Although some live-in domestics said that they liked being included in the household and treated as a member of the family, many were troubled by the absence of boundaries to limit work hours and duties. Mrs. Nishi recalls that she had to go straight home from high school every afternoon. She undertook one major cleaning task, such as dusting or ironing, then prepared supper and cleaned up afterwards. After this she was supposed to be free to study. However, her employers frequently expected something extra: babysitting when they went out, preparing and serving dinner to guests, or tutoring the children in their homework. Dinner parties on weeknights were a special bane:

> Dinner would be at eight o'clock, and they'd have some guests who passed out from drinking. Finally at ten she'd say, "Could you send for dinner?" So I'd have homework, but I'd have to serve the dinner. I remember I put the serving dishes in the oven to wash the next day. By the time you finished serving and washing, I'd have to do homework after midnight. . . . I was a terrible student. I'd fall asleep in class.

Most issei and nisei found the combination of constraints on their freedom and lack of restraints on employers' demands in residential service unacceptable. Live-in service also interfered with married women's family responsibilities. Thus, Japanese women preferred non-live-in positions.

Up until the 1930s full-time non-residential positions with a single employer were fairly common. Issei women worked either as all-around household help for middle-class families employing only one servant or as "second girls" in multi-servant households, performing a variety of tasks under the direction of a housekeeper. Full-time positions gave workers stable employment, set hours, and a chance for private life. However, to provide all-around services, they had to put in an extended day, which typically began with breakfast clean-up and ended with clean-up after the evening meal. The day was broken up by an afternoon break, during which the issei usually returned home to prepare a meal or do chores. Mrs. Iwataki described a typical work day during this period, which began at 6:30 in the morning when she left home to catch a trolley. She arrived at work just before 8:00; then: "Wash the breakfast dishes, clean the rooms, make lunch, and clean up. Go home. Back at five to help with cooking dinner and then do the dishes. Come, go, and back again. It was very hard. I had to take the trolley four times."

Partly because of these extended hours, and partly because of the greater availability of day jobs, all of the married women in the study eventually turned to day work. They worked in several households for a day or half-day each week and were paid on an hourly or daily basis. The work day ended before dinner, and schedules could be fitted around family responsibilities. Many women worked part-time, but some women pieced together a forty- or forty-eight-hour week by combining full-day and half-day jobs. These women preferred all-day jobs because they disliked having to rush to clean two houses in a day and travel between them. However, full-day positions were not always available, and women often had to settle for ten or twelve separate day jobs.

The trend toward day work accelerated after World War II. All of the women who entered domestic work after World War II, including the war brides, elderly issei, and middle-aged nisei, started off as day workers with more than one employer. The shift to day work is attributable in part to workers' preference for freedom from constraints and flexibility in hours and to some workers' wish to hide their employment, since part-time jobs were easier to conceal from the government. It was also due in large measure to changes in the economics and size of contemporary households. Most of the homes in which the Japanese day workers were employed were modest. In San Francisco many employers live in apartments and do not need or cannot afford more than a few hours of outside help each week.

The evolution from live-in service to non-residential jobs to day work contributed to the modernization of domestic work, which now corresponds more closely to industrialized wage work. Work and non-work life are clearly separated, and the basis for employment is more clearly contractual—that is, the worker sells a given amount of labor time for an agreed-upon wage. Yet as long as the work takes place in the household, it remains fundamentally pre-industrial. Whereas industrial workers produce surplus value, which is taken as profit by the employer, the domestic worker produces only use value.[2] In a society based on a market economy, work that produces no exchange value is devalued.[3] Whereas industrial workers are integrated into a socially organized system of production, the household worker remains atomized. Each domestic performs her tasks in isolation, and her work is unrelated to the activities of other workers. Finally, whereas the work process in socially organized production is subject to division of labor, task specialization, and standardization of output, domestic labor remains diffuse and non-specialized. The work consists essentially of whatever tasks are assigned by the employer.

The next sections examine the implications of these pre-industrial features for conditions of work, concentrating on three areas: duties and routines, wages and benefits, and relations with employers. Under each area, the responses of workers to these conditions and their strategies for dealing with them are discussed.

Duties and Routines

The content and definition of domestic service has shifted along with historical changes in the economy and the family. Before the industrial revolution, the work of servants in America was not very different from the work of other members of the household. Since most goods consumed in the home were still produced there, a major portion of servants' duties consisted of what would today be considered production, including spinning, cultivation, food preservation, and manufacturing such consumables as soap and candles as well as household implements.[4] Similarly, in pre-industrial Japan, servants were engaged as extra hands in household production. In prosperous farm families, for example, servants were used as laborers in the field or in silk worm cultivation.[5]

With industrialization, domestic service came to refer to a narrower set of activities—namely, "personal services which resist packaging or mechanization."[6] More specifically, it referred to care and maintenance activities: cleaning, laundry, preparing and serving meals, childcare, and the overseeing of these. The early censuses make no distinction between the public and private sphere. They classified as domestic service any jobs involving these particular activities, whether they took place in a private household or public establishment. For example, cleaning women in offices and waiters in restaurants were included in the same category as housekeepers and maids. Since 1950 the census designation has changed to "private household workers," restricting "service" occupations to those working in public settings. Thus, the identifying criterion is now the *setting* of employment rather than its *content*.

Today domestic employment is defined in terms of a loosely conceived set of "domestic" activities taking place in a particular setting, the household. Interestingly, even though the core consists of housecleaning and laundry, women classified as domestics perform a variety of other tasks, which include not only productive activities, but also expressive functions. The main "other" tasks mentioned by the women in the study were sewing (alterations, repairs, and dress-making), arranging flowers, gardening, rearranging furniture, running errands, chauffeuring and accompanying employers on business calls, tutoring children, babysitting, preparing and storing meals in advance, baking, companionship, and nursing care. In some cases these activities were explicitly assigned by the employer; in other cases they were voluntary "extras" undertaken by the worker to increase the variety and interest of the job. Companionship is perhaps the most common implicit duty and seems to loom larger as job tenure increases. In the case of elderly or isolated housewife employers, it emerges as the central one. Several women mentioned that they got very little done in the way of actual housework. Their employers looked forward eagerly to their "visit" and spent a great deal of the time talking to them or preparing snacks or meals, so that the time invested by the employer might be as great as that put in by the worker. Other examples will be discussed below in the section on relations with employers.

In the majority of situations, the most important duties were cleaning and, especially in the earlier period, laundry. Before World War II, laundry and housecleaning were two equally time-consuming household chores. Employers frequently hired different workers for the two sets of tasks. Laundry was viewed as less skilled and more menial work, and was often assigned to women of color, such as the Japanese.[7] Two issei and one nisei mentioned taking in laundry at home when their children were young and they were unable to go out to work. Ironing was also a specialty of some issei. Many issei, however, did both laundry and housecleaning, and both were arduous jobs because of the low level of household technology. Cowan suggests that the availability of household help slowed the adoption of labor-saving devices by middle-class housewives.[8] The issei's accounts confirm this by showing that employers stressed hand labor. Workers were expected to scrub floors on their hands and knees, wash clothes by hand, and apply elbow grease to waxing and polishing. Some sense of the work and of the typical practices in the pre-war period is conveyed by Mrs. Murakami's description of her routine. She began work in 1921.

> When we first started, people wanted you to boil the white clothes. They had a gas burner in the laundry room. I guess you don't see these things any more—an oval-shaped boiler. When you did day work, you did the washing first. And if you were there eight hours you dried and then brought them in and ironed them. In between you cleaned the house from top to bottom. But when you go to two places, one in the morning and one in the afternoon, you do the ironing and a little housework.

The physical demands of the work are apparent in this description. At least two women, one issei and the other nisei, felt that the strain of combining such hard labor with heavy responsibilities at home had wrecked their health.

Many tasks formerly dependent on strength have been made easier by technology. With automatic washing machines, driers, and permanent press fabrics, laundry is no longer the heavy manual job described by Mrs. Murakami. Many women still did laundry as part of the job, but this involved sorting clothes, putting them in the washer, transferring them to the drier, and then perhaps doing some "touch up" ironing. Formerly several issei were hired principally to iron. They found it less taxing than housecleaning because they could stand in one spot. Two issei still took occasional ironing jobs, but such jobs were scarce. Mrs. Uchikura, who had retired from her job as a hospital charwoman, placed some advertisements in the paper in the late sixties looking for ironing work, but found few takers. She then had to turn to housecleaning.

Housecleaning too is somewhat less strenuous today, in part because of changes in employers' demands and in part because the domestics are no longer willing to push themselves too much. The pre-war issei were known for their willingness to do almost anything—a view held not only by community members, but also by social historians and pro- and anti-Japanese commentators.[9] Many nisei interviewed believed that, even today, the elderly issei worked harder than the nisei. Mrs. Sasaki said: "Issei ladies, they don't complain too much, and they do more work. The customers demand they do so much, and I guess they do it willingly, more than the nisei." The issei themselves, however, claimed that although they once worked as hard as they could, they no longer did so. Some cut back because they no longer felt capable of exertion. Others said that their employers had relieved them of the heaviest jobs by hiring someone else to do floors and windows, leaving them with lighter chores, such as dusting, vacuuming, and waxing furniture. Mrs. Takagi said that her employers would not let her do outside work any more. Mrs. Hayashi discussed her work as "just play." Some of the middle-aged nisei said that they did not push themselves either. They were so experienced that the work no longer seemed difficult. Mrs. Ito, a nisei, said that she learned about easier ways of doing things and new products from her friends who also worked as domestics. Evaluating the difficulty of the work, she concluded:

> I think it's kind of easy. Once you get used to it there's nothing hard. I don't have to push myself. You can go at your own pace. . . . Usually I vacuum and dust; some places have lots of silver, so I have to polish that up. All the flatwares; sometimes you do just a general cleaning; maybe do certain rooms especially good. I iron shirts—one place I do some washings—some curtains. They're easy, just washing them. . . . Usually at first they tell me what they want. But nowadays they don't even know what goes on [laughs]. You know, just leave it up to me.

As Mrs. Ito's remarks indicate, the women developed and followed their own routines for getting the work done. The employer might have signified at the beginning what needed to be done, but the worker organized the work to accomplish the tasks in the time alloted. Mrs. Simeone, a war bride, was typical in that she had developed a general routine but was flexible enough to handle special requests: "Usually I go to the kitchen first. I wash everything, clean the refrigerator and oven, then mop. Whatever they ask me to wax, I do. I do each room, one at a time, dust and vacuum." Another typical routine for a four-hour day, broken up by lunch, was described by Mrs. Togasaki, an issei.

> I usually dust first, but then there are places where I change the sheets. Every week change the sheets and then

dust. Then vacuum. That takes till noon. Then I eat
lunch. In the afternoon, I clean the kitchen, stove, and
clean the oven. It's not set. Today if the oven is dirty, I
clean the oven. Of course, everywhere there's laundry,
when you do day work.

The routines the women followed were similar to those they
established for doing their own housework. The big difference between doing housework at home and doing it for pay was the pressure to finish within a defined time period. The women had to work
steadily and quickly, as shown in such remarks as: "You can't let
things go." "You can't stop and take a break too long." "I don't want
to get behind." "You have to keep watch of the time." "You want to
finish that place in four hours; you can't fool around." To clean a
house or apartment completely in four hours requires a fast and
constant pace that makes the work tiring. Thus, Mrs. Uchikura, who
was accustomed to heavy work as a charwoman in a hospital, nevertheless said: "Doing hospital work is easier than doing housework.
Housework you have to work as hard as you can. You have to clean
everything. Scrub." Mrs. Frankel described domestic work as
"hard—healthwise, it's hard labor." Mrs. Inaba said that even
though she had done her own housework for fifteen years, the first
time she went out and did four straight hours of housecleaning in
someone else's home, she was exhausted. Thus, despite improve-
ments in household technology and smaller households, domestic
work remains a physically demanding occupation.

The women described the work as not very complicated in that it
involved skills that they learned while growing up or that were easily
acquired on the job. Nevertheless, they also reported that the volume
of work and the pace at which it had to be done made it more arduous
than their own housework. It took them some time and experimenta-
tion to learn techniques to get the work done quickly and to minimize strain.

Wages and Benefits

Because of its atomization, domestic work remained invisible and
was not subject to regulation until after World War II. Domestic
workers were excluded from the protections won by industrial work-

ers in the 1930s, such as social security and minimum wages.[10] Sporadic attempts to organize domestics in large cities rarely reached more than a small minority, and Japanese American women appear never to have been part of any organizing efforts. Thus, no collectivity represented their interests. It goes almost without saying that they received none of the benefits accorded organized workers, such as sick days or paid vacations. If a worker did not work, she was not paid, and when the employer went out of town, the worker was put on unpaid leave. (The issei, of course, never took vacations themselves.)

Because there were no industry standards, wages varied according to idiosyncratic factors. Informants and subjects reported that the going rate for day workers around 1915 ranged from fifteen to twenty-five cents an hour. The top rate had risen to around fifty cents an hour by the late 1930s. Full-time domestics earned between $20.00 and $45.00 a month in 1915, while school girls earned from $2.00 to $5.00 a week. I was unable to find wage data on other semi-skilled occupations in the Bay Area, but other studies have found that domestic wages during this period compared favorably with those of factory, sales, and other low-level female occupations.[11]

Some of the variation in wages can be attributed to market factors. Wealthier and larger households were expected to pay more. The rate in some communities was higher than in others, probably due to the balance of labor supply and demand. Compared with other Bay Area cities, Alameda had a higher proportion of Japanese seeking domestic work and earning the lowest wages. Still, the seeming arbitrariness of wages is striking. Some workers were willing to work for less than the going rate, and some employers were willing to pay more than they had to to get a worker.

It may be useful to examine the process by which wages were set in individual cases. Generally the employer made an offer, and the worker either accepted it or looked for another job at a higher wage. Although the shortage of workers may have established a floor for wages, the effect was not uniform. What employers offered depended a great deal on personalistic factors. Sometimes the worker benefited if the employer wanted to keep her for personal reasons. At other times, an employer used her knowledge of the worker's personal situation to push wages down. Both these elements are evident in Mrs. Takagi's story. Her employers liked her and paid her more than the going rate. During the depression, however, employers cut back on help, and Mrs. Takagi could not find enough work to fill the week. One employer knew about her plight and offered her an extra day's work if she would take a cut in pay.

> She said to me, "I tried another girl because you get the highest wages. I tried a cheaper one, but she wasn't good; she never put the clothes away and never finished the ironing. . . . What do you think—take $3.50 and I'll keep you. I'll give you two days a week." I wanted the money—I was trying to save money to get my son [from Japan]. So I said, "Fine." She said, "I'll never tell anybody." Here, a month later, she told every friend. . . . Everybody said, "You're working for so and so for $3.50 and here you're getting $4.00." See, that's the way all the jobs were. A lot of people worked for $2.50, so I was just crying.

Mrs. Takagi weathered this crisis and did not have to take cuts from the others, but she felt humiliated at being caught out, and the memory of the incident still smarts.

Domestic work today continues to lag behind industrial employment in worker protection and benefits, but at least workers are now covered by social security and federal and state minimum wage laws.[12] Some community members feared that the issei would not apply for benefits because of past bad experiences with the government and their disdain for welfare. Contrary to expectation, the issei were not reluctant to do so once they were given information and instructions. At the time they were interviewed, all of the issei were receiving social security, as were all of the eligible nisei and kibei. Three of the study sample were receiving it for previous non-domestic employment. It would appear that issei and nisei were more likely than other domestics to report at least some of their earnings, so that they would be eligible for benefits. All of the nisei and kibei who were asked said that their employers paid into social security; six nisei and three kibei said that the employer also paid the workers' share. Half of the war brides (six), however, did not report their income for social security or tax purposes. Thus, like many domestics, they will not qualify for benefits. These women are working part-time for personal spending money and savings or are moonlighting for extra income, so the amount may not seem significant enough for them to go to the bother and expense of reporting it. Some women mentioned employers who lied about making social security payments or terminated the worker's services when she reached the level for mandatory reporting, but only Mrs. Aoki had actually had this happen to her.

As for wages, women in this study were earning more than the federal minimum wage—in some cases substantially more. Average wages rose from $1.00 or $1.25 an hour in the early fifties to between $2.50 and $5.50 by the mid-seventies. With the retirement of elderly workers and the scarcity of new recruits, the demand for workers became acute. Employers were willing to offer higher wages and a lighter workload to retain help. Among the women interviewed, the top earners were getting $5.00 to $5.50 an hour in 1976. Some women were paid by the day—usually $20.00 or $25.00 for a four- to six-hour day. The median was $3.00 an hour, with younger workers (those under 55) earning more, an average of $4.00 an hour.

As in the past, the range of wages was wide and the rate of pay idiosyncratically determined. Despite the privatized nature of domestic work, most workers were aware of the going rate, since their friends tended to work in the same field. Thus, some workers knew that they were receiving less than the market rate, while a few indicated that they were earning more. Workers also sometimes accepted different rates from different employers. In all these cases, both interpersonal dynamics and "human capital" (i.e., the value of skills, strength, speed, and so on) figured into the calculations.

Since most of the women worked for the same employer for some time, problems arose not so much from starting pay, as from the lack of raises. Once a woman was in a job, she tended to stay on at the same wage at which she started. Generally the women reported that it was easier to start a new job at higher wages than to get a raise in the old one. Mrs. Noguchi, for example, worked for many years for a couple who paid her three dollars an hour and never gave her a raise. She quit, partly because of the pay, and a few months later they offered her five dollars an hour to come back because they were dissatisfied with her replacement. Obviously they valued Mrs. Noguchi's services, but did not think it necessary to grant her periodic raises. Mrs. Aoki said that rather than ask for a raise, she would quit and start at a new place. Only half of the women indicated that one or more of their employers gave them automatic raises. Once one employer did so, it broke the ice and made it easier for them to ask the others. Still, almost all the women indicated that they found it difficult to ask for a raise. Sometimes it was because the employer was elderly or ill and relied on the worker, but the most common reason mentioned was the personal nature of the relationship with the employer: "She's so nice that I don't like to ask." If they asked and were refused, they would feel hurt and have to leave. Even if the raise was granted, the employer might be resentful. Mrs. Hiraoka, who asked for raises every two or three years, said, "Certain people are so nice, it's hard to ask. So I'm going to wait for the right time to come." Thus, although workers were in sufficient demand that employers could not take advantage of them as they might have before the war, they could exploit the workers' feelings of obligation and the pervasive norm of "niceness" to keep wages down. This was apparent in Mrs. Loring's case when she described her employer as "more like a friend." She noted that she had not received a raise in seven years: "They never offered a raise, but they're so nice. Like at Christmas she—the doctor [her husband] gave me some money and told me to buy something."

The obverse situation occurred when the employer offered higher than market wages because she was especially attached to the worker or preferred her company. Mrs. Inaba, a war bride, started working for one woman in the early sixties at fifteen dollars for a six-hour day; by the mid-1970s she was getting twenty dollars for three or four hours: "They gave that to me because [she said]: 'You do it just so, you're very particular.' She doesn't care about the money. 'Any amount if it's you.' So the money part was good. But my body was used up." In another case, an issei, Mrs. Nishimura, said that she was already getting more than the average wage, and yet:

> They're offering to raise my salary. But I tell them that since I'm old, I'm very slow. They say I'm doing a good job, though. A very good job I'm told—although I really shouldn't say this. And I'm such an all-purpose person. I can do anything . . . sewing, everything. So they are eager to have me work.

As this example shows, aside from personal relationships, workers took into account their level of effort or efficiency in estimating what they ought to get.

It is interesting that on this basis many women deliberately asked for wages below the market level. Women near or past retirement age are likely to feel that their services are not as valuable as those of younger women. Mrs. Togasaki, a post-retirement entrant, took a job left by her friend Mrs. Noguchi. She accepted $2.50 an hour, even though Mrs. Noguchi told her that she had been getting $3.00. A number of women indicated that they asked for less because they did not want to strain themselves. If they were paid more, they would be expected to (or feel obliged to) work harder. Miss Ishida has had a lot of problems with her health over the years:

> Unless you work for someone that has a lot of money, of course they expect you to do a lot more if they pay you a lot. Whereas I don't get paid that much, but they don't expect that much out of me. That way I don't have to extend myself that much.

Perhaps the most scrupulous in this regard was Mrs. Uchikura, who would not accept more than a dollar an hour, even in the early 1970s, and refused carfare because:

> My daughter says, "Mama, a slow person like you—it's a wonder they use you." I'm so slow—really slow. Everyone says, "Even though you're slow, you clean very well," so they hire me. If you do it faster you finish faster, but I'm slow. It takes me longer and that's why it's cheap. Yes, I said to myself: a dollar an hour is enough because I'm slow, and I don't need carfare. Everyone said they'd give it to me, but I said, I don't want it. I'm slow and if I got carfare I'm afraid they wouldn't use me. Rich people give it to me without saying. Ordinary houses, a dollar an hour [straight].

Although Mrs. Uchikura was rather extreme in her modesty, the general statement that one had to be worthy—that is, extra efficient or hard-working—to deserve higher pay was shared by many issei and nisei. This may be a legacy of the Meiji cultural values that the issei internalized and passed on to the nisei.

Employer-Employee Relations

As these various incidents involving wages suggest, the relationship between employee and employer is perhaps the most distinctly pre-industrial, as well as the most problematic, aspect of domestic ser-

vice. The relationship has been described as feudal[13] or pre-modern.
According to Coser, the traditional servant role was

> rooted in a premodern type of relationship in which par-
> ticularism prevails over universalism and ascription over
> achievement. . . . While post-medieval man is typically
> enmeshed in a web of group affiliations and hence subject
> to pushes and pulls of many claims to his commitment,
> the traditional servant . . . is supposed to be entirely
> committed and loyal to a particular employer. . . . More-
> over, while in other occupational roles the incumbent's
> duties are largely independent of personal relationships
> with this or that client or employer, particularistic ele-
> ments loom very large in the master-servant relation-
> ship.[14]

Although the totalism of the traditional servant-master relationship has been reduced under conditions of day work, relations
between white employers and Japanese domestics retain two essential and interrelated characteristics of the earlier period—personalism and asymmetry.

Personalism pervades the employer-employee relationship. Employers are concerned with the worker's total person—her moral
character and personality, as well as her work skills. The domestics in
the study in turn judged their employers on moral and charac-
terological grounds. For example, they spoke approvingly of employers who were good Christians, neat and clean in their habits,
intelligent, well-educated, and happy in their family life, and disap-
provingly of those who were dirty or messy, lazy, insensitive, lax in
disciplining children, disrespectful toward relatives, or who drank
too much. The importance of the personal can also be seen in the
women's preference for personal introductions in job placement.
Personal placements were seen as a more reliable way of finding a
compatible, trustworthy employer than more impersonal means,
such as advertisements. Mutual trust and compatibility were important because employer and employee were thrown together in a situation in which there was little privacy. The worker had access to the
most intimate regions of the household and might become privy to
family secrets. The worker in turn was open to constant scrutiny by
her employer.

A sense of mutual obligation, a carryover from feudal values, also colors the tie between employer and employee. The domestic is expected to demonstrate loyalty, while the employer is expected to concern herself with the worker's welfare. This mutuality was viewed as a positive feature by some workers interviewed. Mrs. Watanabe recalled that at the start of World War II, her employer urged her to come to live with her for protection. Mrs. Shinoda remembered her first employer's concern fondly: "That lady was really nice. She would turn on the light and the heat in my room and stay up waiting for me to return. Usually she would go to sleep early, but even if I returned late at night, she would wait up for me with the room heated up."

The tie is pre-modern in the sense that obligations transcend purely economic or instrumental considerations. The commitments are often lifelong and continue even when the terms of the original "contract" can no longer be fulfilled—for example, the domestic can no longer perform the same duties, or the employer can no longer afford to pay adequately.[15] Thus, many elderly domestics, issei and nisei, reported that they were treated with special consideration by long-time employers. They were picked up and brought home from work and relieved of heavier duties. Mrs. Kawai, a 72-year-old kibei, said: "Now the places I go, because I'm old, they know I'm weak. So it's just a hobby. Talk, talk, and then going home, they take me home, because it's hard." The obligation is reciprocated in that workers often maintain a lifetime commitment to employers. This commitment, as noted above, is what keeps many older domestics working past retirement age. Younger women who would like to cut back also refuse to abandon their older employers. Mrs. Suzuki, a kibei, had been employed for over twenty years by an elderly retired professor; even though she wanted to spend more time babysitting for her daughter, she tried to go a half-day every month to help the woman maintain her independence:

I don't charge too much. She's a professor, retired now— 84. I mop the floors and do things for her. She's very particular, so she doesn't want anyone else. So I can't quit. I'm stuck. She's nice, so I don't mind helping her. Her family is in Los Angeles. She has a family but they don't help her. When her son comes she says she's fine. She's blind, but doesn't tell him she's blind. She's afraid that he'll put her in a nursing home. So I help her. My husband helps, too, doing her gardening. [Mr. Suzuki is a factory worker, not a gardener, by profession.]

For many women the relationship with particular employers was analogous to family ties. They described their situations as "just like a family thing" or said that their employers "treat me like a member of the family." For some issei and war brides, the tie was charged with emotional significance: it substituted for kin ties that they never had or were lost when they left Japan. Mrs. Takagi, an issei, was especially close to her second employer, Mrs. Cox, whom she described in these terms:

She was a Christian. Any time I came down with a sickness, she said, "Call a doctor." If I go to the hospital, she came every day. She was almost a second mother. If I didn't have her help I would have been badly off. I went to Japan and she gave me help with that.

Mrs. Howell, a 43-year-old war bride, has had two unhappy marriages, but received a great deal of emotional succor from her elderly employers:

I'm working for all German peoples. I'm working for one 97-year-old lady, 92, then, 65, and I have one 70 and one 80. Old people look like my grandmother. . . . I'm so comfortable because these people can give me love: I can give love. I enjoy every four hours that I'm working. . . . My momma died when I was young. That's probably why I like old people. I can depend on them: I can trust them. That probably means I didn't have enough love when I was young.

Despite the intimacy, however, there remained a not-quite surmountable barrier of status, reinforced by cultural and racial differences. Thus, the familial attitude of the employer usually took the form of benevolent maternalism. Mrs. Fujii's employer pressed on her food or discarded clothing. Other women reported similar gifts and bonuses (usually in lieu of higher wages). Even Mrs. Takagi, who formed close and long-lasting ties with her employers, recognized the employers' need to perform acts of "noblesse oblige." She said she had learned to accept gifts, including old clothes and furniture, even when she did not want them. Otherwise, the employer was apt to feel that the worker was "too proud" and withhold further gifts and bonuses.

Thus, the second main feature of the employer-employee relationship was its *asymmetry*. Traditional mistress and servant roles exhibited in pure form the relation of superior to inferior. Servants dressed in distinctive uniforms to mark their stations in life and used deferential forms of address when speaking to the mistress and guests. In many situations, including contemporary American society, the domestic belongs to a distinct and subordinate racial-ethnic group. Thus, the domestic worker is set apart not only by contrived badges of inferiority, but by physical and cultural differences. Differences may be perceived as even greater in the case of immigrants, who do not speak the language of the dominant culture or speak it with an accent. When social distance is great, the domestic may be treated as a "non-person." Mrs. Kono complained bitterly about one employer she particularly disliked: "She didn't look at me as a human being. Her furniture, her house, were more important." Mrs. Takagi recalled employers who displayed contempt for servants and fed domestics with table scraps. She was once offered a lunch consisting of asparagus stalks whose tips had been bitten off by her employer's son.

Because of the stigma attached to domestic service, workers were sensitive to the implication that their employers considered them mere servants or housecleaners. Mrs. Suzuki complained that many employers "think they can do anything. Only a few families treat you real well. So many people, you work for them, and they treat you like a servant." The younger nisei and the war brides were more likely than the issei and older nisei to resent being treated as menials. Mrs. Nishi, perhaps because of her personality, found it grating to work as a school girl. In contrast to her sister, who always seemed to be treated like one of the family, she said, "I always worked for awful people."

> I used to rail when the son would bring his friends and ask
> me to teach them how to jitterbug, and he'd say, "This is
> our maid." I'd stand there and say, "I am *not* your

maid!". . . I had to dress up in that maid's outfit when they had dinner parties. It was all part of it about how phoney these people were that I worked for.

Similarly, Mrs. Osborne declared that an attitude of superiority was what bothered her most about some employers:

I'll never be rich. I don't care how much they are going to pay me, you know. I don't care. If there is an uncomfortable feeling or they think I'm just a housework person, I'm not going to work. Even if they pay me fifty dollars an hour—no! I [have to feel] comfortable with working with that family.

In addition to these overt expressions of inequality, however, there are also more subtle and indirect ones. For example, in an asymmetrical relationship, the lower-status person has to be attuned to the feelings and moods of the higher-status person. Mrs. Fujii knew when an employer was displeased because "I'm under her and she's tops, so I could always tell what she's thinking. I think if I'm demanding of her [i.e., in a position of authority over her], then I probably won't feel what she wants to do." Mrs. Taniguchi inadvertently provided an insight into how this sensitivity develops when she described her approach to domestic work:

At first, since I hadn't had much chance to enter Caucasian homes, I was a little frightened. But after I got used to it, it became very easy. And I concluded after working for a while that the most important thing in this type of job is to think of and be able to predict the feelings of the lady of the house. She would teach me how to do certain things in the beginning, but after a month or two, I gradually came to learn that person's likes, tastes, and ideas. So I try to fulfill her wishes—this is only my way of doing it, of course, and so, for example, I'll change the water in the vase when it's dirty or rearrange wilting flowers while I'm cleaning house. In that way I can become more intimate with the lady of the house in a natural way and the job itself becomes more interesting. . . . Sometimes I plant flowers in the garden without being asked . . . so then I'll start to feel affection even for that garden.

Although her employers certainly may have appreciated Mrs. Taniguchi's aesthetic sensibilities, it is doubtful that they were as aware of and responsive to her thoughts and feelings as she was of theirs.

The personalism and asymmetry of employer-employee relations were complementary. The supposed inferiority and differentness of the domestic made it easy for the employer to be generous and to confide in her. The domestic was not in a position to harm her or make excessive demands, and secrets were safe with someone from a completely separate social world. This complementarity between personalism and asymmetry and the role of racism in promoting asymmetry were shrewdly observed by Mrs. Okamura, a 78-year-old issei:

> I'd been working for a lady for two hours a week for a long time, but she didn't even give me a chance to work. After my arrival, she kept talking and going on and on. For me, housework was much easier because even though I didn't understand English well, I still had to say, "Is that so?" "no" and "yes." After long talks I would start to sweat. I preferred to do my work, but this old lady was always waiting for me.
>
> There are some things you can talk freely about to other racial types. Those people just wanted to talk to someone. They didn't even care that I couldn't understand English, so I couldn't help them. They just wanted to complain about their son or their son's wife.

An informant suggested that the language barrier, though it hampered communication, may have contributed to the smoothness of relations between the issei and their employers. The issei could not "hear" insulting or denigrating comments. One worker confirmed this by saying that she had never minded being a domestic but had she understood English, she might have gotten into quarrels with her employers. It does appear that the issei were less likely than the nisei or war brides to admit being bothered by the asymmetrical relationship with the employer. In addition to language, social and cultural differences may have helped to insulate the worker from feeling directly subordinated.

Ultimately, however, the personalism and asymmetry created contradictions in the employer-employee relationship. As Coser puts it: "The dialectic of conflict between inferior and superior within the household could never be fully resolved, and hence the fear of betrayal always lurked behind even the most amicable relationship between master and servant."[16] The fear is evident in issei women's complaints about employers who distrusted them. Mrs. Takagi once found money left under the corner of a rug. She carefully replaced the rug without touching the money or saying anything about it; she had been warned by her father-in-law that employers sometimes tested the domestic's honesty by leaving valuables about. Mrs. Taniguchi indignantly reported an incident in which she was suspected of dishonesty:

> There was a place I was working temporarily. They asked me whether I had seen a ring. I didn't know what kind of ring they meant, so I just told them no. I hadn't seen any ring while I was vacuuming. They sounded a little skeptical, saying it's strange I hadn't seen it. I felt insulted then, as though they were accusing me of something.

The conflict took its most concrete form in a struggle between employer and employee over control of the work process. Mrs. Kishi echoed the sentiments of many of the women when she expressed her dislike for an employer who was *yakamashi* ("noisy," "critical"): "Really, where they don't say too many things the work is better. If they ask, 'Have you done this? Have you done that? Do you understand?'—there is that sort of place. Most people don't say such things because they know [better]." Some employers were not content with having the work done, but also wanted it done in a particular way—their way. Sachiko Adair declares:

> When you clean people's houses, they have different ways. One does it this way and another person another way. I don't mind having a job for housework, two or three houses a week, but sometimes it gets to me. They say do this, do this, how to do. I know already everything, but still people try to tell you different ways. I think other jobs are easier. If you know how to do it once, you don't have a problem. Anything—just like a hostess job is always the same thing. But in a house, some people want you to

vacuum, this and this and this, but then you have to stop.
You have problems.

Some employers feared that the worker would loaf or cut corners if she was not watched or monitored. Several women mentioned
quitting jobs because the employer constantly checked up on them.
Mrs. Fujitani complained about one woman:

> The lady was too particular and she's always watching
> you, following you, whatever you're doing. And Japanese
> people, you know, aren't the kind that you have to have
> them keep their eye on you. They're honest, they work. So
> I don't like anybody that has to follow me and see what
> I'm doing.

Mrs. Taniguchi stopped working for one woman who spied on her.
Most of her employers left the house while she worked; and if they
returned, they announced themselves loudly. In this case, though,
"the missus would come in very quietly without warning, so it made
me feel as if she was spying on me to make sure I wasn't doing
anything wrong. I disliked that a great deal."

Another arena of conflict was the amount and pace of the work.
Employers tried to squeeze as much work out of the worker as possible. Workers complained that if they finished their work ten or fifteen
minutes early, some employers demanded that they do something
extra. Mrs. Kawai said, "Yes, I had some ladies say, 'Ten minutes is
ten minutes, so find something to do.'" Another ploy that some
employers used was the household equivalent of the "speed-up." If
the worker accomplished the agreed-upon task within the designated
period, the employer added more tasks, forcing the worker to do
everything faster. Employers were thus able to exploit the worker's
conscientiousness. Miss Ishida explained how she got into a situation
where she was rushing madly around:

> It kind of escalated. He was a bachelor, and when I first
> started to work he did the washing. I did the ironing and
> putting away, because he didn't like to do it. But the
> longer I stayed, he kept leaving it. I didn't—can't—leave
> it, so I automatically did it. Then he got married and I had
> a little more work to do, but I cut down on the housework
> because they didn't use all the house, so I skipped one

week in some of the rooms that they never used. But that place I quit. No, I didn't really quit [laughs].

The domestic workers had only limited resources for resisting employers' attempts to control their work and the conditions of employment. Yet they struggled to wrest some degree of control over their work and their lives. The choice of day work can be seen as one means to gain greater autonomy.[17] Domestics working for several families were less dependent on one employer. Work hours could be adjusted to fit in with the workers' other interests and responsibilities. As Mrs. Murakami said about her change from full-time work with one employer to day work, "You're freer to yourself."

Within the structure of day work, the worker maneuvered to increase her control over the work process. One way was to minimize contact with employers. Mrs. Amano deliberately chose employers who went out during the day:

> I liked it best when nobody was there. The places I worked, they went out. The children were in school, and I was all by myself, so I could do what I wanted. If the woman was at home she generally went out shopping. I liked it when they didn't complain or ask you to do this or that. The places I worked, I was on my own. It was just like being in my own home and I could do what I wanted.

Her sentiments were echoed by other women who say they strongly prefer employers who leave the house. Mrs. Kishi, an issei, said: "I don't like it when people stay home. I like nobody home. It's more easy to work—everything is smooth." Other women said they stayed with employers who left them alone and kept out of their way. Mrs. Fujii, a nisei, said that one employer was so nice that she could not ask for a raise. When asked what was nice about her, she laughed, "You don't have to work very hard. She leaves everything to me. I do whatever I want to do. She doesn't care." Mrs. Hiraoka said her favorites are

> ladies that don't like housework. That house is easy to work for. Because then I can do the whole thing my way. I like to decorate, and so I like to [rearrange their furniture] my way. Some people are particular, and then I don't touch it. But certain people I like to [have my] way and move it around.

Mrs. Amano was among those who retained autonomy by adopting a utilitarian orientation toward their employers. She picked up and dropped jobs on the basis of convenience, rather than becoming attached to particular employers: "Sometimes I gave the job to someone else and looked for something else. I changed from this job to that job. If I had to walk too far to the bus or the people were too messy, I kept the job until I found a better one and then I changed." Other workers also talked about dropping customers that they did not like over the years, so that eventually they worked only for those with whom they got along. Mrs. Morita mentioned that the casualness of the work was one of its advantages. She and her friends used to trade jobs among themselves to find the most agreeable ones.

Some women maintained control over the work by defining and enforcing their own standards; they insisted on working on the basis of tasks, rather than time. The job was done when the tasks were accomplished to their own satisfaction. If they worked extra time, they did not want to be paid extra; if they accomplished the task in less time, they reserved the right to leave. Mrs. Osborne took this approach right from the start:

> I tell them the first couple or three times they have to give me time to get used to the house. After that I want you to tell me what I haven't done. Something that you expected. If you're not at home write a memo. . . . When I'm cleaning I like to move all the furniture into the middle of the room. And if they're dirty or not, I just like doing it that way. It's not my conscience; it's my satisfaction. I don't know whether they think it's good or not, but I think of my satisfaction—the way I like it. Actually I don't care about anybody else's feelings but mine; I'm really selfish. . . . They leave a check, and when I'm finished I pick it up. Sometimes I stay for fifteen minutes over; I'm not going to go after them to pay. I don't mind if it's necessary to work even two hours over. They don't have to pay, but they don't have to deduct, like a half-hour [if I finish early].

The final recourse, when all efforts to bring around a recalcitrant or unreasonable employer fail, was to quit. The announcement of resignation often brought apologies or pleas from the employer to stay. The worker rarely relented, for she had usually built up considerable resentment by the time she took the step. The domestic workers interviewed tended not to voice their complaints along the way. They felt that it was demeaning to complain about mistreatment and that employers ought to know how to act properly without being told. Therefore the decision to quit was usually irrevocable. It was an especially difficult step for the issei and older nisei because resigning was an admission of defeat and violated the principle of *gaman* ("endurance"). Thus, when they quit, they usually did so in a manner designed to save face for both their employers and themselves. If asked why they were leaving, they made up an excuse that avoided direct criticism of the employer. They said that they were retiring, or sick, or had family obligations that required them to cut back. Their own pride was also important; when talking about quitting, they stressed that they tried their best and put up with a great deal before leaving. This is evident in Mrs. Yoshida's description of how she resigned from a job: "There was one place that no matter how much you do, that person would let you do more. So I thought I would quit. That day I did a lot of work—more than usual—and finished up everything she gave me." By meeting the challenge, no matter how unreasonable, Mrs. Yoshida was able to leave with her self-respect intact.

CHAPTER 7
The Meaning of Demeaning Work

When asked who they are, people often name their occupation or the organization that employs them: "I drive a cab," or "I'm with IBM." In industrial society, where we work and the kind of work we do define who we are and where we fit in the world.[1] Of all the jobs in industrial society, private household service provides perhaps the slightest basis for pride and a positive self-identity. Although household work lacks some forms of degradation found in industry—detailed division of labor, machine pacing, and standardized procedures[2]—it nonetheless shares negative characteristics with de-skilled industrial jobs: it involves almost exclusively manual labor, provides few challenges, and offers few opportunities to learn new skills, advance, or gain recognition. And it poses greater problems for self-esteem than even the least skilled industrial jobs. It is typically viewed as "the lowest rung of legitimate employment" and ranked below the most menial of industrial jobs.[3]

Research on housewives confirms that they, like workers in industrial jobs, perform their work without giving it much thought. When asked for their reaction to various household tasks, a sample of over three hundred American housewives described their feelings about all tasks except childcare as neutral, using such terms as "routine," "necessary," "nondescript," and "mindless" (e.g., "when I'm cleaning, my mind turns off completely").[4] A sample of English housewives evaluated housework rather as alienated factory workers rate their jobs. They complained about monotony (doing the same thing over and over); fragmentation (doing a series of unconnected tasks); mindlessness (thinking of things other than the task at hand); excessive pace (rushing from one task to the next); and social isolation (being alone in the house too much).[5]

Paid domestic work may be even more alienating than unpaid housework for one's own family. The tasks that are hired out tend to be the most physical and least creative ones—scrubbing floors rather than baking cakes. Unlike the housewife, the domestic does not enjoy or use the final product of her labors: the clean kitchen, shiny furniture, and so on. Moreover, by selling her labor, the domestic employee is stripped of the rationalization available to the housewife that the work is being performed purely for "love."

Yet these areas of similarity between household work and lower-level manual occupations do not fully account for its exceptionally low status. Why is domestic service typically ranked below even the most routine machine-tending jobs? Skill, or rather the lack of it, might be the answer; however, as Caplow suggests, there is ambiguity about the extent of skills required. Different occupational ranking schemes give different standings to domestic work. One system places private household work below all other occupations, while another classifies domestics as slightly skilled and specialized servants, such as cooks and butlers, as semi-skilled.[6] Leslie points out the contradictions in public attitudes toward the skills of servants. Since at least the late nineteenth century, employers have lamented the lack of good, experienced help and deteriorating standards. Yet employers had little respect for domestic skills and were rarely willing to pay the price for good help: "Domestic skills were familiar and therefore easy to ignore. Most working class women had some experience in housework and childcare, simply because of their female upbringing."[7]

This statement still holds today. Caplow suggests that what places domestic work at the bottom of the occupational hierarchy is not skill level, but rather the widely held assumption that personal service is inherently degrading. A corollary is the view that it is "less honorable to be employed by an individual than to be employed in the same capacity by an organization." After puzzling over the inconsistency of skill ratings of domestics, Caplow concludes that "no great harm is done by classification of domestic service as a low status function if only because of the limitation of personal freedom which is usually involved."[8] Caplow says nothing more on the subject and leaves unstated why personal service and employment by an individual are inherently degrading. However, his remark about the limits on the personal freedom of domestic workers furnishes an important clue. I suggest that the feature that makes domestic service demeaning is the worker's *personal subordination*. This interpretation makes sense of the finding that even machine tending is accorded higher status than domestic service. Pacing by a machine is a form of impersonal control, in contrast to the personal direction imposed by a superior. Similarly, working as a cleaner for a firm is less demeaning than performing the same work for an individual because in the former case a formal hierarchy of authority and impersonal rules replaces the face-to-face superior-subordinate relationship found in domestic service. As noted in the previous chapter, the most disliked aspect of the employer-employee relationship was personal subordination: being treated as a servant, being looked down upon, being given no greater importance than the furniture.

Another feature of domestic work is also critical to its low status. Domestic work shares with other low-level service jobs the involvement in what Hughes has labeled "dirty work."[9] Most occupations involve some "dirty work"—tasks workers find distasteful on physical grounds (e.g., cleaning up) or moral ones (e.g., disciplining subordinates). In high-status jobs these elements are usually incidental and can be partially or wholly delegated to underlings. In many low-status jobs, tasks regarded as repugnant by most members of society are the central activity—for example, streetcleaning, garbage collection, janitorial work, and housecleaning. Tasks done on a small scale with low-level technology, such as housework, appear the most petty and therefore especially demeaning.[10]

The "dirty" jobs named above require the occupant to deal literally with dirt, but above and beyond this literal level are the moral implications of "dirt." It is significant that the domestic workers in the study said that they had an aversion to dirty houses and quit clients who were too messy. Dirt and mess were associated in their minds with character flaws; a messy person was likely to be described as lazy, alcoholic, or otherwise morally defective. This is ironic, since it is partly because they clean up after other people that domestic workers are accorded low status.

In short, domestic work confronts the worker with two problems. The first is to find some form of satisfaction in work that most people consider unchallenging at best and repugnant at worst. The second is to maintain self-esteem and an independent identity in a situation where one is personally subordinated and accorded little respect. The remainder of this chapter will explore how these issues affected issei, nisei, and war bride domestics, and how they coped with them. We look first at the sources and nature of satisfaction, and then at the sources and nature of self-esteem and identity.

Sources of Satisfaction

Studies of worker satisfaction have found that workers trim their expectations to fit the constraints of the job and therefore pronounce themselves relatively satisfied even in objectively unsatisfying jobs.[11] Those in less skilled, varied, and responsible positions tend to focus on extrinsic satisfactions, such as pay,[12] and center their interests on their lives outside work hours.[13] Do Japanese American domestic workers respond in the same way? Do the three cohorts find similar or different satisfactions on the job?

In the interviews, the women were asked what they liked and disliked about domestic work, why and how they entered the field, and what were its advantages or disadvantages. Their responses to these open-ended queries, as well as spontaneous remarks during other parts of the interview, were examined to identify major themes around the issue of work satisfaction. One of the most important themes—social relations with employers—has already been discussed in detail in Chapter 6 and will not be raised again here, except incidentally.[14] Instead, three other themes will be discussed: the content of the work (mental involvement in and feelings about the tasks), the structure and organization of the job (pressures, responsibilities, and autonomy), and extrinsic characteristics (pay and hours).

Content Several issei, nisei, and war brides disclosed an awareness of the mental-manual distinction when they described the work as not requiring much mental involvement. "You use your body, not your mind" (Mrs. Hiraoka); "You don't use your head, so even the dumb can do it" (Mrs. Frankel); "You don't have to use your head" (Mrs. Fujitani). Others referred indirectly to a lack of mental involvement when they described the work as not taxing their capacities: "If I were smart, I might think this kind of job is silly, but I don't know anything, so it's easy" (Mrs. Togasaki); "Once you get used to it, there's nothing hard" (Mrs. Ito). Nine women in all talked about the work as "easy" or "just play," or used other terms describing it as unchallenging.

Yet the work was not seen as completely lacking in opportunities for stimulation. In fact, many women spontaneously mentioned various sources of interest. First, jobs were often characterized as challenging in that they forced the worker to meet new standards and to learn better ways of doing things:

> Some people are very difficult, but if I could [learn to] get along with them, I could learn something from them— quite a bit sometimes. When I worked for the lady in San Francisco, I had a very hard time, but I learned things there. So if you think about your experiences later on, you'd think, "That was nice." (Mrs. Noguchi)

The issei and war brides were apt to feel that domestic work exposed them to the lifestyles of the dominant culture, which helped to broaden their tastes and expand their horizons. Mrs. Takagi, an issei, said about one employer, "She taught me a lot of things. It's nice. Every place you go, it's different, so you learn a lot of things." For Mrs. Sentino the contact with other tastes led to vicarious enjoyment of a higher style of life:

> *What do you like best about domestic work?*
> Every place I go, I could feel like it's my own home. And a beautiful home each place I go. I think of her household when I'm shopping. How they put the house, how they're living. I share an interest with each family. They have a different idea on living and about the house. First time I go to this house I don't know what to do. I know Japanese style. I don't know anything about how to cook or housework.

Interaction with employers was also a means of keeping abreast of fashion. Mrs. Langer liked working for cultured and educated people because they discussed music and other interests. Mrs. Kono, a kibei, said that more educated employers kept her on her toes. She fondly described one of her customers, an 88-year-old English-born woman, as "very hard-headed":

> I think she's very smart—all there. I learned a lot from her. Every day I had to read something in order to have a conversation with her. [We'd talk about] children, and newspapers, how I felt about some killing, things like that.

Perhaps the greatest mental challenge was to read the employer accurately—to be sensitive to the employer's preferences and moods in order to anticipate her needs, as quotations in the previous chapter suggested. In addition, several women mentioned that although they felt sufficiently skilled in housework from doing it at home, they did not always know how to do the work the way the customer wanted it done. Each client had somewhat different expectations, and the worker had to figure them out and adopt new techniques and standards.

Aside from these incidental forms of stimulation, when all is said and done, the actual content of the work, housecleaning, is still the major source of interest or lack of interest in the job. Overall, twelve women indicated that they disliked the work. Six considered it too heavy; it was a strain and required too much effort: "I don't like to clean house, too heavy, you know" (Mrs. Takagi); "I don't like it; it's hard work" (Mrs. Kaneko). Three said that they would prefer to do something at which they were skilled, such as typing or sewing, indicating that they were not able to use their full capabilities on the job: "I'd rather do what I'm good at" (Mrs. Watanabe). The others did not specify why they disliked the work; they simply did not enjoy cleaning: "It's obvious—I'm no housekeeper" (Mrs. Morita).

A slightly smaller group, ten women, volunteered that they enjoyed cleaning or at least the results they achieved: "It's kind of fun to get things straightened out" (Mrs. Ito); "I like housework. After housecleaning the house looks beautiful, nice and shiny" (Mrs. Inaba); "Well, I feel good about cleaning. That's the main thing. I like to clean. I don't know if they're joking or what when they say domestic is artistic too. One of my teachers said it" (Mrs. Simeone). Thus, for these women the actual content of the work provided some degree of interest.

The remaining women could be classified as either neutral or mixed in their feelings. The neutral category encompassed two major stances. In one the worker said she neither liked nor disliked housework: "I can't say I like it or dislike it. After ironing, housecleaning is extra. I like to iron because I don't have to move around; and with housework you have to move around" (Mrs. Amano). In the second the worker rejected the relevance of liking or disliking the work: "It's not as though I like it, but—how shall I say it? It's good because I don't have to work eight hours" (Mrs. Suzuki); "There's nothing special to like or dislike. I just can't help it. I can't do any other sort of job, so I have to do it" (Mrs. Kishi). Among these women, housecleaning is taken for granted and arouses neither strongly positive nor strongly negative sentiments, an attitude shared by many housewives.

Other women enjoyed certain tasks and found others distasteful. The preferred tasks tended to be those that were more creative (e.g., arranging flowers, baking cookies), skilled (sewing, nursing), or service-oriented (e.g., care of the elderly), and those that were more circumscribed (cleaning bathrooms) or less strenuous (ironing). The most disliked aspects were the heavier physical tasks, such as scrubbing floors and washing windows. For women with differentiated feelings, a good job was one that involved a higher ratio of liked tasks to disliked ones. Thus, one strategy for maximizing interest was to pick jobs according to the mix of activities involved; another was to add enjoyable tasks to the regular load. Mrs. Hiraoka, quoted in the previous chapter, preferred working for women who disliked housework or lacked confidence about housecleaning, for then she was left to do everything her own way. She also arranged ornaments and moved furniture, activities that she liked despite a general aversion to housecleaning. Mrs. Langer chose to work for the elderly so that she could make use of her nurse's training: "I don't like housework, but I like to take care of people." She watched over her elderly employers when they bathed and felt rewarded when they told her that she was no ordinary domestic.

Structure and Organization   Given the content of the work, one might expect workers to feel little pressure to perform and little sense of responsibility. This is not the case. Time constraints and work standards create pressures. In order to clean a whole house or apartment in four hours, the domestic had to work at a constant pace; she could not rest or leave things to be done the next day, as she might do at home. Mrs. Fujii preferred her other part-time job, sewing aprons for a store, because it was piece work and she did not have to hurry. When employers piled on too much work, it was not just the time pressure but also the inability to do a good enough job that was frustrating. Mrs. Ito complained: "You've got to take your time, or you won't finish it as clean as she wants you to. That way she's losing out in the end." It is not just the employers' standards but the workers' own criteria as well, that were violated. Miss Ishida grumbled about having to cut corners when her employers gave her more work than she could handle. Mrs. Kishi expressed the dissatisfaction women felt at having to work too quickly to satisfy their own sense of workmanship. If the employer gave her too many jobs,

> I just do a quick job. I cannot spend too much time, you know, no time. I don't like that. I like to clean everything good. It takes time to clean good. I like that. Some people give me too much work, lots of work in one day. I can't do too much like that. I don't want to say something, so I just do it quick—everything quick.

Younger kibei and war brides were more aggressive in dealing with employer-created time pressure. Some forestalled the problem by seizing the initiative right from the beginning. The first day on the job, they announced that they were trying out the job to see what needed to be done and how long it took, in the manner of an expert consultant. Mrs. Hiraoka said that she never felt pressure because she always insisted on six hours:

> Certain people ask for a short time, but I usually ask for plenty of time. If they tell me they only want me for four hours, I tell them I have a certain way I have to work. I can't do it in four hours. Even a small house I work more hours. You need plenty of time to do it neat so you don't rush.

Even without external time pressures, however, internalized standards drove some women to work harder than they felt they ought to. Mrs. Inaba said that she was such a fussy worker that she always did everything by hand and had "worn out" her body over the years. An element of compulsiveness was evident in some women; they did not like to stop and rest until everything was done. Mrs. Rybin was typical of these women:

It's very hard work, especially because—I don't know other people, but—when I start to work, I can't do sloppy work. I shouldn't say sloppy, but I can't kill time in an idle way. When I start, I want to do it. I don't even take a coffee break or nothing. They call a coffee break, but I don't want it. When I start, I want to continue straight. So it's a hard job, a very hard job.

Aside from time and performance pressures, the greatest source of tension was responsibility for the employers' possessions. In the course of cleaning, they had to handle cherished or valuable goods. As Miyoshi Farrow observed, "In someone else's house you have got to take care. I don't want to break it or make chips." The risk of damage was always present, and the women worried about it. When asked to describe a bad day at work, Mrs. Fujii answered: "Well, sometimes a mistake. Oh, in domestic, I was ironing, and I had the heat on too high on this particular material and ruined it. Something like that, oh, I feel so terrible." Mrs. Sasaki replied to the same question:

Well, if I break something or drop something, it does affect me.
Have you ever broken anything valuable?
So far—I have to cross my fingers, no. There's a lot of valuable things in the house, and you have to handle it and you worry a lot.

Women recalled accidents vividly and in great detail. Mrs. Noguchi once broke a tray and felt so guilty that she bought a replacement to substitute secretly for the damaged one. She was still uncomfortable enough about the deception that she subsequently quit the employer. Some women were so intimidated by the possibility of damage that they refused employment in homes where there were too many expensive things around or else refused to handle fragile items. Mrs. Ito had a few bad accidents, including breaking a large punchbowl when a crystal from a chandelier fell, and became nervous about breakage:

Nowadays I don't like to handle valuables. Some places they have a bar and the glasses are around fifteen or twenty dollars apiece. I said, "I'll clean around, but I won't touch the glasses." She said, "If you don't feel comfortable, then don't do it."

Compensating for the pressure and responsibility was the broad discretion most women were given by the employer. Autonomy and freedom to do the work as they pleased was perhaps the major source of satisfaction in domestic work. Over half of the women mentioned autonomy—being their own bosses—as the main advantage of domestic work. In most cases this was possible because the employer was out of the house or stayed out of sight; often workers selectively retained employers who were willing to leave them alone.

Do they tell you what they want done?
No, usually at first, but nowadays they don't know what goes on. You know, just leave it up to me. It seems I'm my own boss. (Mrs. Ito)

Did you receive detailed instructions from the owner of the house?
No, no, not at all. They didn't say anything, just left the money and went out of the house. So I would just go ahead in my own way. (Mrs. Uchikura)

How do you feel about working in a house by yourself—do you get lonesome?
No, I like it. . . . I don't think I ever liked people watching me all the time or where I have to communicate with other people, I don't like. Housework, I'm my own boss. I feel so big. I feel free. (Mrs. Sentino)

Mrs. Sentino was also typical in not viewing social isolation, a frequent complaint of housewives, as a problem. The other domestics in the study agreed. When asked whether she ever felt isolated, Mrs. Sasaki said, "No, I feel better when I'm alone. It's easier to work." Even when employers did not complain or interfere, their presence could be disturbing. They might want to chat, and this slowed the work down. Working while the employer was visibly idle also made the worker uncomfortable. Mrs. Kishi mentioned both aspects:

How do you feel about working alone?

Oh, it's easiest when they're not at home. If they're at home, sometimes she comes and talks and I can't work. If you're talking then you're just resting.

When you do housework in someone else's home, you don't meet people. Do you like that or not?

I don't care, but I don't like it when people stay home. I like nobody home. It's more easy to work. Everything is smooth. When people are at home, I'm so warm and they're not doing anything. They just sit and say it's cold and put on the heater. It's so hot! (Laughs.)

Because they gain satisfaction from successfully accomplishing the work, these workers prefer autonomy even at the cost of being somewhat isolated.

Pay and Hours   For industrial workers, pay and hours have been found to be the main focus of satisfaction or dissatisfaction. How did Japanese American domestic workers feel?

They judged the fairness of their pay in relation to the going rate (i.e., what others were getting); the wealth of the client (what she could afford); and the amount of effort (how hard one was expected to work). On those grounds most of the women were "satisfied" with the level of pay. In relation to judgments of what they liked or disliked about domestic work, however, pay was not a large factor. Four women mentioned low pay as a disadvantage of domestic work compared with other types of work, and only two women reported that the pay was better than it was in other lines that they might have gone into. In both cases the women were receiving a flat $20.00 or $25.00 for a half-day. The only other monetary advantage, especially for the war brides and other casual workers, was not having to report the income and pay taxes on it.

If pay was mentioned relatively infrequently, hours were the most often named advantage of domestic work. Six women—issei, nisei, and war brides—said that they liked domestic work because the hours were short. They did not want to work eight hours a day. Another thirteen, all nisei and war brides, mentioned the flexibility of the hours and the ability to take time off. Flexibility has a dual significance. It is a source of freedom that allows a woman to exert control over her work life, and it is a requirement dictated by the demands of home, children, and husband. Both meanings can be found in most women's statements. The freedom from constraint is emphasized in the following:

What do you like or dislike about day work?
Well, the advantage is that you're more free to yourself. That's what I like about it. Because you're not tied down. Well, one day if you have something to do, you just call them up the day before and say that you're not coming. And sometimes they might be going away and they didn't want you. (Mrs. Murakami)

Like when I went to Japan for five weeks, I just didn't go to work at all. It doesn't tie me up—that's what I'm trying to say. It's not like you have to punch the clock. I'm talking about mine [employer]. . . . When my husband's on vacation, I just take off. (Mrs. Loring)

What are the major advantages of doing housework?
I can work any days I want to, actually, and my time—I usually prefer to work in the mornings, so I work from eight to twelve. That leaves me free to do what I have to do at home, you know, cooking and shopping and house-cleaning, whatever. (Miss Ishida)

The flexibility they enjoy "frees" them to meet their other obligations or to fit their work in with other people's schedules. The aspect of "necessity" is greater than consideration of autonomy in the following:

What's the main reason you went into domestic work?
When you have kids you can't work all day. I want to be home when the kids come home from school. I don't want to work full-time. In the morning I make sure they go to school and help them get ready. If you leave them behind, you don't know what they're doing. I took domestic work so I can go any time I want. (Mrs. Suzuki)

I didn't want to go to full-time job, because you have children. Housework, you could take time off when you

want and you could replace another day for it if you can't
go. Like instead of Tuesday, I could go Wednesday. (Mrs.
Simeone)

Overall, then, the flexible hours, like other aspects of work life
for these women, had a double meaning. The need for short, flexible
hours arose from the family obligations that limited their pos-
sibilities; yet the flexibility gave them some control over their lives by
allowing them to honor their own priorities.

Work and the Self

What are the connections between domestic work and Japanese
American women's sense of themselves? In order to deal with the
issue of how the self is experienced in relation to low-status work, this
section addresses three more specific questions: (1) To what extent do
issei, nisei, and war brides share the general societal view of domestic
service as low-status work? (2) To what extent is the status of the
occupation reflected in their self-evaluations? (3) To what extent is
the work role incorporated into their social identities—that is, their
social roles and positions in the family, community, and larger
society?

The Status of Domestic Work   The women's evaluations of the
status of domestic work are complex and contradictory. They vary
between cohorts and among women in a cohort. Judgments differ
according to the social context used as a reference point. The three
possible reference points were traditional Japanese society, the Japanese American community, and American society in general. Each
of the cohorts had a different relationship to each of these reference
points, so that issei, nisei, and war brides had distinct patterns of
responses.

The issei attitudes were perhaps the most complex. The traditional Japanese society in which they grew up was still stratified
according to the feudal caste system, and the Japanese remain highly
class-conscious even today. The issei were acutely aware of the low
station of household servants in Japan. Mrs. Togasaki, when asked
about the sort of people she liked working for, answered:

I don't know. It's different from Japan. I thought they were nice people. They didn't make me feel bad.
Is it different from Japan, then?
In Japan employees bow to their employers like this, and they even wear clothes different from their employers'. It's changed now. They don't even call them their "maidservants" anymore. If you don't treat them right, people won't work for you in Japan.

To the extent that the issei identified with traditional Japanese values, therefore, they saw domestic work as degraded. I suspect that many of the issei kept the nature of their employment secret from relatives in Japan. Unfortunately I did not explore this issue at the time of the interviews. However, informants indicate that, having left Japan to fulfill specific goals, unsuccessful issei were embarrassed and ashamed. Many did not return to Japan or lost track of friends and relatives because they did not want to face them as "failures." Mrs. Fujii's mother, an issei now living in Japan, urged her not to let her relatives know that she was working as a domestic:

> The issei don't want to be interviewed about domestic work. They're ashamed and don't want it known that they do housework. In Japan being a maid is considered the lowest thing. When I went to Japan in 1968, my mother told me not to tell anyone I was doing housework. "Tell them that you're just at home." In Japan they would assume you're very poor (*bimbo*) if you're working as a maid. To me all work is okay. All the same to me. But the issei are still old-fashioned. They think domestic work is dirty work.

If the issei felt this way in relation to Japanese society, however, they seem to have long ago come to terms with the "shame" as far as their lives in America were concerned. Several factors helped to insulate the issei from status degradation. As long as they felt like sojourners, menial work could be viewed as temporary—a means to an end, and not a real vocation. The issei were also influenced by the Meiji work ethic, which lent an aura of respectability to their endeavors. Mrs. Togasaki's remarks illustrate both of these elements. When asked whether it bothered her to work as a domestic, she replied:

We came to America to work, so we don't mind working, whatever the job. Once we took a job, we thought that's our job. It's a different story from Japan. If I could have understood English, I might have had bad words with the missus [laughs]. So I just thought I was doing my job and they also felt the same way.

Another mitigating factor was the presence of the ethnic community, most of whose members worked in similar low-level occupations. Even the most cultured and educated people were gardeners and domestics. Since everyone did the same kind of work, no particular stigma was attached to domestic service. Mrs. Iwataki noted the importance of the ethnic community both as a reference group and as a source of support when asked if she thought people thought poorly of those who did domestic work: "The places I went to, the people weren't the sort with bad feelings. Very kind. Myself, I never thought to be ashamed. We had to do any sort of work. Also, our friends were doing that sort of work and we used to talk."

Mrs. Togasaki's and Mrs. Iwataki's answers point to another factor alleviating feelings of status inferiority—the contrast the issei saw between the extreme subordination of maidservants in Japan and the relatively democratic treatment accorded them by their American employers. This contrast, as well as the language barrier that prevented the issei from hearing subtle insults, may have made the relationship seem more egalitarian to them than it would appear to an outside observer.

The nisei had no direct experience of Japanese society, so the traditional Japanese status system had only indirect influence on their evaluations—through their parents. Their main points of reference were, first, Japanese American society, especially the nisei community, and second, American society in general. As might be expected, urban women and those with more education or experience in non-domestic employment had higher aspirations and more awareness of American middle-class attitudes. They were thus more sensitive to the status implications of domestic work. Mrs. Nishi came from an acculturated family; her mother had studied western classical music, and her father had come to the United States to attend university. She was quite touchy about being a school girl: "I suppose this was my way of surviving, but I had such contempt for those people [her employers] because I thought, 'They're so gauche.' " Another urban nisei, Mrs. Watanabe, had secretarial training and experience, which colored her attitude toward domestic service. She saw it as inappropriate for someone with her skills: "I never liked the idea of working in a family."

For the most part, however, the nisei's attitudes toward domestic service were grounded in the experience of their ethnic peers. Those who started working before World War II were well aware that even college graduates had had to settle for menial jobs. Thus, Mrs. Morita was typical when she said:

No, the status—that didn't bother me, because every other person was working housework. Everybody, every other person, that was trying to save some money was working housework. I mean, people that wanted to be a little better [might work as clerks], but the pay was the same, and their expenses were higher.

As noted in Chapter 5, many nisei interpreted their situations in ways that neutralized the status implications of the job. They saw their jobs as "domestic skills" training, as a substitute for further education, and as a short-term activity until marriage.

The war brides and the kibei who returned after the war were the most disquieted by the status of domestic service, probably because their attitudes were the most grounded in Japanese values. The three kibei who returned to the United States after World War II all expressed sensitivity about the status of domestic work in relation to relatives and friends in Japan. Mrs. Hiraoka, for example, said that her mother, who lived in the United States, understood, but other relatives and friends did not: "When I go to Japan and say it to my friends, I'm not comfortable."

For some of the war brides, the entry into domestic work in the United States was viewed as a comedown. Six war brides claimed that they had employed servants themselves in Japan. Three came from middle-class families and had grown up in a household with servants. Two of these and three others had maids after they married. Mrs. Sentino, the daughter of a police chief, noted the irony of her situation. When asked what kind of people she liked working for best, she replied:

What kind? You know, I'm surprised. I had a maid before, when I was young. I didn't know how to treat her. I thought I was better than her. I had—but this place [United States] is equal. I like it. All equal. Never put down anything. Everyone respects me, so I enjoy it.

Because of feelings of status degradation, ten out of twelve war brides reported that they kept their employment as domestics secret from families and friends in Japan.[15] Mrs. Howell's was the bitterest response:

Would you tell your family in Japan that you were doing this kind of work?
No, I don't think my parents would like to find out. I'm mad at myself sometimes. I say, "Why come to the United States and have to work in somebody's house? You know, dirty bathroom. It's not right. You know? You don't have an education, you have to starve. I say Japanese people should stay in Japan. You belong in Japan.
Is that how you feel?
Yeah. I was born in Japan, I'm supposed to stay in Japan. We had a big dream in coming to the United States. Anyway, that's how I feel.

Mrs. Howell had internalized the degradation, as had two other war brides. In all three cases the husband had a negative attitude toward the job. Mrs. Rybin's southern-bred husband saw domestic service as "colored people's work," while Mrs. Bentley's college-educated husband, an accountant, saw his wife's job as inappropriate to his position.

Most of the women declared that they themselves were not ashamed of their occupation, but that family and friends in Japan would "not understand" because of their ignorance of American society. Mrs. Simeone typified the majority when she disavowed Japanese status values, saying that she preferred the egalitarian values of the United States:

How about the way people look at domestic work; is that a problem for you?
If I'm here I'm not ashamed. But I don't tell my sisters what I'm doing, when I'm doing housework. Because they're going to be shocked. That I came here to do it. But no, I don't feel—I tell anybody I'm doing house-

work because issei and some nisei are doing it. So I like American, no matter what you do you're not ashamed. People don't look down. But in Japan, it depends on what you're doing. They decide what kind of class. In Japan they classify people—samurai family or farmer, they're divided. But here I felt there's not anything like that. So I don't feel any shame.

To sum up, all three cohorts viewed domestic work as degraded in particular contexts. The issei, kibei, and war brides experienced status degradation when they used Japanese society as the frame of reference, whereas the nisei did so primarily when they judged domestic service from the perspective of middle-class American society. For all three groups the main ameliorating factor was the awareness that their ethnic peers were in the same boat. The perception that "everyone was doing it" was most powerful for the issei because of the uniformity of their occupational situations before the war. It was less effective for the nisei because of the greater heterogeneity of their peers' attainments in the post-war labor market. The war brides were most vulnerable to feelings of status degradation because their peer group was loosely constituted and they were exposed to negative assessments on two sides—from their families and friends in Japan and from their Caucasian husbands.

Self-Esteem   If domestic work is experienced at worst as degrading and at best as neutral, what are the implications for worker's sense of self? The evidence depends on the question asked.

Evidence for lowered self-esteem is found in answers to questions about why the women went into domestic work and what their aspirations are for their children. As might be expected, most women saw themselves as having few options. Some externalized the blame, citing discrimination or, more frequently, situational factors not under their control, such as family responsibilities, age, and health. Most women, however, assumed some blame, attributing their present job situation to their own shortcomings—the lack of what economists call human capital, needed to compete in the labor market. Inability to speak English was the most frequently cited factor among issei and war brides. In response to the question whether they had ever considered other types of work, a typical answer was "No, I didn't understand English, so I never thought about it." The nisei most often mentioned lack of education: "Well, I didn't go to high school, so I think domestic work is best for me." Other personal shortcomings mentioned were lack of job skills ("I don't know how to do anything else") and lack of work experience ("I wasn't in the habit—the routine—of working"). A few issei and nisei from rural backgrounds saw themselves as bumpkins: "I'm just a country person (*inaka mon*)."

Also indicating lowered self-esteem were women's responses to questions about their aspirations for their daughters. Although the issei and older nisei tended not to have specific occupational aspirations for their daughters, those who did mentioned only white-collar or technical jobs. Among women with daughters of college age or younger, only one, a war bride, said that she would not mind if her daughter went into domestic work. All the others hoped their daughters would choose some other line of work requiring specific educational qualifications. They wanted their daughters to have more choices than they themselves had had. The war brides used themselves as negative examples for their children, urging their daughters to follow a different path so that they would have better job prospects. Mrs. Adair, who had three teenage girls, lamented:

> I want a job, but I don't have any education myself. So I
> tell my daughters all the time, as long as you get a steady
> job, stay in school. I want you to get a good job, not like
> me. That's what I always tell my daughters: make sure
> you're not stuck.

These responses indicate that the women suffered wounds to their self-esteem from *being* domestic workers. If we switch the focus to *doing* domestic work, we find somewhat different responses. When women described the process of doing the work, they revealed considerable pride. Listening to the women's stories, one became aware that they were pleased by their own efficacy— their capacity to perform hard physical labor and to meet exacting standards.

Pride in sheer physical strength is particularly evident among women from a farm background, whether issei or nisei, and among the more robust war brides. Mrs. Yoshida, an issei, boasted that she never found housework arduous. Even at the time of the interview, she could work for hours in her garden without being aware of the passage of time because:

From the time I was a little girl, I was used to working hard. I was born a farmer and did farm work all along. Farm work is very hard. My body was trained, so nothing was hard for me. If you take work at a *hakujin* (Caucasian) place, you have to work hard. There was a place where the lady asked me to wash the ceilings. So I took a table and stood up on it. It was strenuous, but I washed the whole ceiling. So the lady said: "That was hard work, but next time it won't be so hard." She gave me vegetables, fruits, and extra money, and I went home.

Similarly, Mrs. Suzuki, a cheerful middle-aged kibei who grew up on a pineapple farm in Hawaii, strongly asserted that she was willing and able to do all of the heavy work disdained by others:

Some people, they tell you, "I don't do those things." I can do anything for them. They tell me, "Wash the kitchen." Okay, I wash the kitchen and everything. I should do everything. Okay, I wouldn't say no, you know? I say to everything, "Okay, I'll do it." I did laundry, ironing, change the baby, everything. Oh, yeah, and scrub. That's what they want you to do when they hire people. You know, kitchen floors, they don't want you to mop it, they want you to go on hand and knees and scrub it. They don't want you to be doing it and don't get it cleaned.

Closely related to pride in physical vitality is the self-respect gained from accomplishing difficult or arduous tasks, particularly when the standards are self-generated. Mrs. Inaba, a war bride, described herself as a very honest worker:

Me, I'm particular. If I see something dirty, I have to clean it. So I did wax remover too. In dirty places, I leave it on for five minutes and took the wax off and made it clean. I did it to that extent! Honest work. That's what everyone says. I'm particular, careful, so lots of people wanted me. And I didn't complain about being tired.

Pride in physical strength is common among male manual workers, but it is seldom seen as applicable to women in manual occupations. Similarly, satisfaction in accomplishing self-set goals is rarely attributed to women engaged in a job at the bottom of the occupational status ladder.[16]

Work and Social Identity

Like other low-status jobs, domestic work provides little basis for personal identity. Domestic workers would not mention their occupation in response to "Who are you?" Instead, work is viewed as a means to other, more valued identities. This was particularly evident in the case of five women—three war brides and two issei—who identified themselves in terms of other vocations. Mrs. Osborne, a war bride, worked half-time as an outreach worker for a community organization and called herself a "social worker," though she worked as a domestic on Saturdays and some weekday afternoons. Two other war brides had other vocations (minister and nurse respectively) that they could practice because of the money they earned or the contacts they made through domestic work. Two issei identified most closely with their role as church members. Mrs. Nishimura said that her children wanted her to do lighter work, but part-time domestic work was better because it allowed her the time to be president of the church women's club.

The role of domestic worker was also connected with the women's ethnic identity. As pointed out earlier, shared occupation led to common experiences and outlooks, which strengthened ethnic ties. The women saw themselves in their work roles as representatives of the ethnic community. For the issei and nisei especially, the community functioned as a reference group, similar to a large *ie* ("household"). Individual actions reflected on the community as a whole, so the reputation of the community depended on each individual's acting correctly. Being honest and hardworking was thus not merely an individual matter, but a group characteristic—the women proudly identified with the good reputation of the Japanese:

> It seems to be true of all Japanese—our work is really appreciated . . . because we don't do anything bad.

There aren't any Japanese who are disliked. (Mrs. Sugihara)

There's not that many people who you could trust and who'll do that type of work. So—that's why I think they like the Japanese Americans. (Mrs. Ito)

The Japanese all work hard. (Mrs. Farrow)

When employers distrusted them, the women felt that it was not just they themselves, but Japanese Americans as a whole, who were being insulted:

Japanese people, you know, aren't the kind that you have to keep their eyes on you. They're honest, they work. (Mrs. Fujitani)

But Japanese people in general don't do underhanded things. That's why we're trusted so much. (Mrs. Taniguchi)

This sense of "peoplehood," which is the essence of ethnicity, was linked with a sense of history. The efforts and sacrifice of early immigrants established high standards that later cohorts felt obligated to live up to. The tradition set by the issei was recognized by all who came after. Mrs. Rybin, a war bride, expressed the group sentiment:

I don't feel any kind of gap in the relationship with the issei because I always appreciate them. Because of how much hard time they had in this country it made a foundation for after we came here—the later-on peoples. So I feel sorry to them and I feel thank you to them. That's why I want to be nice to them.

Perhaps the most central identity that the work role made possible was that of mother/provider. As will be further discussed in the next chapters, working for the betterment of their children gave the women a sense of purpose when their own prospects for the future looked dim. In some cases the woman was the main breadwinner because the husband was ailing or absent; in others the women were equal supporters; and in still others the women's earnings provided the margin that allowed the children to continue their education. Whatever the case, working for their children infused their work with a sense of purpose beyond financial survival.

PART III
FAMILY

CHAPTER 8
Creating and Maintaining Family Life

As we shift from women's employment to their situation in the family we need to step back a moment to look at the larger picture once more. Just as we found it important to see how the larger labor market shaped women's work experiences, we need to consider the effects of the political economic system on women's relationship to family and household. That system was a hostile one to Japanese and other racial-ethnic families. It created special difficulties for Japanese American women on two fronts: they had to contend with gender inequality within the household, and also combat outside institutional assaults that threatened family life.

All women confront a basic duality in relation to the family. On the one hand, women as well as men need their families for emotional and economic support. In a society dominated by the impersonal values of a market economy, relations at the household level take on great emotional significance. The family is perhaps the only stable arena in which women and men can express intimacy and receive affection and love. In contrast to relations in the market, which are impersonal, competitive, contractual, and temporary, family represents "nurturing, enduring, and noncontingent relations governed by feelings of morality."[1] On the other hand, the family is an institution that has historically been, and continues to be, oppressive for women. As writers ever since Engels have pointed out, the traditional family based on monogamous marriage constricts women's freedom and personal growth, exacts a great deal of unpaid and unrewarded labor, and keeps them economically dependent on husbands.[2]

This duality of support and oppression is experienced in varying ways by women in different class positions and in different racial and ethnic groups. If most feminist writings can be taken to reflect the view of dominant culture women, the underside—the family as an oppressive institution—has become increasingly salient for white middle class women. Hartmann and Thorne have each described the family as politicized—as divided along gender, age, and generational lines, so that the interests of individual members are not synonymous.[3] In fact, they are frequently at odds. Men and women contribute unequal work and derive unequal benefits from their collective efforts. Women are exploited by the universal arrangement which assigns them primary responsibility for reproductive labor: they perform a disproportionate share of work in the household, while men receive disproportionate advantages in the form of services and access to income. In this view the household itself is the locus of conflict, as men and women struggle over the division of labor and resources.

When individuals and families confront economic deprivation, legal discrimination, and other threats to their survival, however, conflict over inequities within the family may be muted by the countervailing pressure on the family to unite against assaults from outside institutions. Thus writings on black women and families stress the other side of the coin—the family as a "culture of resistance."[4] This view emphasizes the solidarity among family members and their common interest in shoring up the family. Bound together by economic and social interdependence, women and men become partners in confronting adversity. Women's reproductive labor—that is, feeding, clothing, and psychologically supporting the male wage-earner and nurturing and socializing the next generation—is seen as work on behalf of the family as a whole, rather than as work benefiting men in particular. The locus of conflict, in this view, lies outside the household, as members engage in collective effort to create and maintain family life in the face of forces that undermine family integrity.

Much disagreement has been generated between those who emphasize division within the family and those who give priority to the struggle between the family and external forces. Proponents of the first position call for abolition or a radical restructuring of the conjugal family, while proponents of the latter counter by pointing out that working class and racial-ethnic women need strong and intact families to survive in a racist, capitalist society.[5]

I would suggest that for Japanese American women both positions are accurate; both aspects constitute concurrent realities. For issei, nisei, and war brides the family was simultaneously a resource in the struggle for survival and an instrument of gender subordination. Japanese American women confronted this contradiction: their reproductive labor maintained the family as a bastion of resistance to race and class oppression, while at the same time it was the vehicle for their oppression within the family. The dilemma for them was, could they defend and hold together the family while overhauling the structures that subordinated them?

In this chapter I focus on one side of the dialectic by sketching the history of struggle by Japanese Americans and other racial-ethnics to establish and maintain families. I make two related arguments. First, issei and nisei women's reproductive labor was essential to the creation and maintenance of the Japanese American family and of ethnic culture. Second, an intact family system characterized by strong kinship bonds and clear ethnic identity enabled the issei and nisei to withstand economic and psychological hardships and to develop a positive sense of self in a society that devalued people of color. The lack of a coherent ethnic family system made the war brides more vulnerable to these external forces, and they suffered greater personal disorganization as a result.

The two chapters that follow focus on the other side of the dialectic: I examine gender politics within the family, looking first at the issei and then at the nisei and war brides. These internal politics were conditioned by the larger struggle between the family and the dominant society, which is described below.

The Dual Labor System and the Racial-Ethnic Family

Asian Americans, latinos, and blacks were incorporated into the United States explicitly for the exploitation of their labor. These groups were slotted into a labor system designed to extract maximum profits from them as *individual* units of labor. Migrants from less developed regions are initially cheap and malleable because the areas from which they are drawn have lower standards of living and the workers themselves are often impoverished. The problem comes when they have spent some time in the advanced region, have become familiar with the prevailing standards, and are exposed to labor unions and organized efforts to improve wages and conditions. What is to prevent them from becoming as intransigent and expensive as native workers? The solution historically has been to impose various forms of constraint on migrant workers. First, the kinds of workers permitted to enter can be limited to the most productive and un-problematic: for example, single, uneducated men with no background of political activism. Second, immigrant groups can be put into a special legal category outside the basic system of civil rights and social welfare coverage. They are therefore highly vulnerable and cannot afford to take militant action. Third—and this is the area that will be elaborated here—the family system of immigrant groups may be manipulated to ensure greater profitability from their labor. The family is a target for dominant group control because it holds the key to both the cost of labor and its pliability.

The most stringent form of control is to exclude the family—that is, the conjugal or extended household—from the metropolitan center. This approach has been used in Western Europe with "guest-workers" and in South Africa with blacks employed in labor camps or in areas designated for whites. Only prime-age men or women are recruited and permitted entry; children, spouses, and other relatives are not allowed to accompany the worker. Detaching the individual worker from the household saves the state and the employer the cost of reproduction. Workers can be housed collectively in barracks or dormitories; amenities can be kept to a minimum, and an expensive infrastructure of social services avoided. Reproduction must still go on—the current labor force has to be maintained and future generations of workers have to be created—but the burden is shifted to the kin group left behind in the home region. They carry the responsibility for housing, feeding, and clothing dependents, providing care for the ill and infirm, and nurturing and educating children; in addition, they frequently augment the inadequate earnings of the migrant worker through subsistence production, including farming.

Besides saving the employer and the state reproductive costs, the absence of family ties in the "host" society makes the single migrant a more flexible source of labor, an important ingredient in profitability. Detached workers can be moved to meet short-term labor needs. They can be expelled when no longer needed.

However, even the single, detached laborer is not infinitely malleable. The capitalist is operating, as Braverman, Edwards, and others have noted, in a resistant medium.[6] Workers do not passively acquiesce in their own exploitation. The detached worker may have less to lose by refusing to comply with the rules of the game. She or he may be freer to quit a job or defy the boss's authority. In cases where a more reliable and docile work force is required, the employer may find it expedient to allow or encourage family ties, since having dependents to support may bind the worker to his or her job. An example of this strategy is the rise of family groups among migrant Mexican farm workers in Colorado in the 1920s. Prior to that date landowners in the South Platt region preferred single male migrants for seasonal field work because of their greater productivity. However, growers came to believe that family groups, despite their lower productivity per unit, were a more reliable work force. They could be counted upon to return year after year, and they were less likely to be involved in drunkenness, fighting, and gambling. Hence, growers supported the Mexican migrants' desire to be with family members by hiring parents and their children to work in the fields as a unit.[7] Another example comes from recent historical scholarship on the slave family. This literature suggests that in some places and periods, primarily in the upper South prior to the boom in cotton, some slave owners encouraged permanent conjugal households, not for humanitarian reasons, but in the belief that married slaves were less likely to rebel or run away.[8]

Where exclusion is unfeasible, then, family formation will be allowed, but under conditions imposed by the dominant society. Constraints are deemed necessary because strong kin ties pose a challenge to the dominant system. Loyalty to kin competes with allegiance to institutions of the dominant society, and the influence of the kin group over the individual worker may conflict with the authority of the employer. The family itself is the institution that most controls the workers' orientation toward the world; there, self-identity is formed, and children are prepared for their place in society. It is therefore the major medium for the reproduction of social relationships and the transmission of culture. An intact ethnic culture offers an alternative value system that enables members to resist the racist and capitalist ideologies that are used to justify their subordination.

Historically, black, hispanic, and Asian American families have been subject to both direct and indirect assaults on their integrity. Slavemaster control over all aspects of family life, including marriage and reproduction, was an essential element in the subordination of the slave population. Even after emancipation, family life among blacks was rendered difficult. The stability of urban black families was undermined by a labor system that forced them to work long hours under exhausting or dangerous conditions and subjected them to seasonal layoffs and devastating unemployment. Many black families were "broken up" by the premature death of black fathers.[9] In the Southwest Chicanos experienced extensive intrusions on their native institutions, including the family, following the Anglo takeover of the territories where they lived. Anglos imposed laws that weakened the traditional rights of the extended kin group—for example, whereas under Mexican law a deceased wife's relatives inherited her property, under Anglo law the husband came to inherit. The family's role in the enculturation of children was attacked. Public schools instilled values conflicting with those of traditional culture. Mexican American families sometimes responded "by withdrawing their children from the schools or protesting their methods of instruction."[10]

For both blacks and Chicanos, adversity in some ways strengthened kin ties. The family, including the larger kin group, was a continuing source of sustenance, and women kept many customs alive by cooking ethnic foods, organizing traditional celebrations, practicing folk healing methods, and transmitting folklore.[11]

The Struggle Against Family Exclusion: Asian Immigrants

In the case of Asian immigrants, families were deemed altogether expendable. The goal was the maximum exploitation of Asian male workers as temporary, individual units of labor who would fade away when they were no longer productive or needed. The policy was to prevent family formation altogether by excluding women and children, preventing laborers from bringing in spouses, and barring intermarriage with whites. As a result of these measures, Asian immigrant workers faced a bleak choice. They could return permanently to Asia, where they faced the same economic circumstances that impelled them to emigrate in the first place, or they could remain in the United States as bachelors or absentee husbands who saw their wives and children only during infrequent return visits. If they did not wish to or could not afford to return permanently to Asia, they would be bereft of any semblance of normal family life.

Measures designed to prevent family formation or reformation by Chinese immigrants distorted the development of the Chinese American community. Though some used loopholes or extralegal means to bring in spouses, most Chinese men were unable to establish conjugal families in the United States. The consequence was a radically unbalanced population. In 1890, when the Chinese population reached its peak of 107,475, there were 26.8 males for every female.[12] The men created a bachelor society within the Chinese ghetto. They formed kinlike organizations, made up of men with common last names or from the same districts within China, for mutual aid and protection.[13] Like other predominantly male societies, Chinatowns were beset by problems, including prostitution, gambling, tong violence, and drug use. As late as 1920, few households made up of husband, wife, and children were visible in the environs of Chinatown, despite seventy years of Chinese presence in the United States.

Policies preventing family formation were extended to the Japanese when they succeeded the Chinese. Women were prohibited from entering, or discouraged by special scrutiny: officials suspected Japanese women of being prostitutes or of harboring loathsome diseases.[14] Though a substantial proportion of Japanese men succeeded in bringing in spouses despite the difficulties, many issei men were unable to afford passage for a wife or did not act quickly enough before the 1924 Immigration Act took effect. The result was a substantial imbalance in the population. In 1930 among Japanese ten years of age and older, the ratio of males to females was 1.65.[15] A sizable number of issei men were marooned in the United States and remained bachelors all their lives. Some became itinerant seasonal agricultural workers; others worked in the city and resided in rooming houses and hotels; and still others were almost hidden as live-in servants in white households. It was only as the immigrant generation passed away in the 1960s that the ratio of males and females approached normality.

The interests of native workers, who feared competition from Asian laborers, and those of capitalists, who wanted to keep Asian laborers as an exploitable labor force, coincided in the drive to prevent Japanese family formation. This merging of interests may have added a measure of virulence to the assault on Japanese settlement. The practice of bringing over wives was widely attacked by anti-Japanese elements. The alleged fecundity of Japanese females was pointed to as evidence of their subhuman character. Because of their age at entry and their concentration in rural areas where children were considered an economic asset, issei women did have a high birth rate in the initial years after immigration, although the rate would have tapered off as the Japanese population approached a more normal age distribution.[16] Propagandists warned that these high rates of reproduction would overwhelm the white race. V. S. McClatchy, the publisher of the *Sacramento Bee* and a director of the Associated Press, projected that the Japanese population in the United States would grow to a hundred million by the year 2063. He testified before the U.S. Senate Japanese Immigration Hearings, apparently convincing many, that

> the Japanese are less assimilable and more dangerous as residents in this country than any other of the peoples ineligible under our laws. . . . They come here specifically and professedly for the purpose of colonizing and establishing here permanently the proud Yamato race. They never cease being Japanese. . . . In pursuit of their intent to colonize this country with that race, they seek to secure land and to found large families.[17]

The Struggle to Maintain Families: Japanese Americans

The establishment of conjugal households did not end the struggle for Japanese American families. Great effort was required to keep the family together and to preserve family bonds in the face of racism and a stratified labor system. In the issei generation particularly, participation in a labor system that consigned Japanese American workers to the most backward areas of the economy made economic survival precarious. Long, exhausting hours of work meant that men and women often had little energy to put into personal relations in the family. There was little time or money for leisure or recreation to relieve family tensions.

Issei women often gave birth at home, sometimes with no outside assistance, then rose within a few hours to work in the fields or tend to housework and childcare. They fought to safeguard their children's health, despite primitive sanitary facilities and inadequate medical care. They combatted racism daily by helping their children develop a sense of self-worth in a society that attacked their humanity and impugned their character.

In a racist society where members were exploited as individual units of labor, the family was a necessary counterforce. It was the one institution that Japanese Americans could turn to for comfort, affection, and an affirmation of their individuality and self-worth. It was also in the family that ethnic culture was preserved and transmitted on a day-to-day basis: Japanese was spoken at home, ethnic foods were cooked and eaten, Shintoism and Buddhism were practiced, and folk wisdom passed on. Women, through their reproductive activities on behalf of the family, were central to this daily creation and perpetuation of ethnicity.

The contemporary Japanese American family has inherited this legacy of struggle. Because of the continuing stratification of American society, the family has retained its importance as a defense against racism. Although the old absolute color lines have been breached and racial vilification is no longer openly broadcast, Japanese Americans are still subject to stereotyping. They are aware of the deep-seated racist sentiment lying just under the surface and ready to break through whenever tensions are elevated. The influx of Vietnamese and other Indo-Chinese refugees and the current economic competition between Japan and the United States have already produced antagonism directed indiscriminately against all Asian-looking people. Reports of racially motivated assaults, mob violence, and murders of Asian Americans have become common. The nisei have become aware that even positive stereotypes are attempts at control and are beginning to reject them. The "model minority" designation contains an indirect threat that stepping out of bounds— for example being "aggressive"—will lead to retaliation.[18]

The nisei have strived to maintain strong and inclusive kinship ties. The hardships endured by issei grandparents, and their own struggles, provide object lessons that parents use to develop ethnic pride in their sansei children. The awareness that they are the descendants and heirs of courageous pioneers not only spurs achievement, but strengthens their resistance to racist assaults.

The war brides are not direct inheritors of this historical tradition, and thus are not protected in the same way as the nisei. Their vulnerability testifies to the importance of the ethnic family as a culture of resistance. With its juxtaposition of dominant and subordinate cultures, the conjugal war bride family lacks a coherent ethnic identity. War brides strive to pass on aspects of Japanese culture to their children, but there is no larger kinship group or community to support that effort. War brides also find it harder to help their children form a clear self-identity. Interracial children are in a marginal position. They cannot identify simply as Japanese or Japanese Americans, and yet they do not belong in the dominant culture either. In the absence of a direct intergenerational tradition of sacrifice, the war brides do not have strong, positive images to pass on to their children. As we shall see in Chapter 10, they use their own lives as negative examples to spur their children to achieve. The emphasis on avoiding their mothers' mistakes, however, does not give the children a specific direction for their lives. And because the war bride family lacks the unified outlook of the issei and nisei family, it is more vulnerable to fragmentation as it confronts not only personal differences and opposition from parents and kin, but also hostility from the larger society.

CHAPTER 9
Gender Politics in the Family: Issei

In every society the family is the central institution defining women's place and social identity. Its importance was magnified for issei women because of the encompassing nature of the family system in Japanese society. Its very structure embodied Japanese cultural values and was the means by which traditional patterns of male dominance and privilege were perpetuated. Yet the family, though conservative, was not impervious to change; its internal dynamics were supported by other economic and political institutions in Japanese society. Thus, the internal structure and politics of the immigrant family underwent realignment in response to new external contingencies. The issei had to adopt family strategies that would enable them to contend with the stratified labor market, cultural assaults, and other constraints described in the previous chapter. In particular, the incorporation of men and women into the labor force as *individual* wage workers created a fundamentally different form of family economy. The nature of the transformations can be better appreciated if one first considers the family system in which the issei themselves were raised.

The Family System in Southern Japan

The household, or *ie,* was the fundamental social unit in the towns and villages of late nineteenth- and early twentieth-century southern Japan. The concept of *ie* is central to an understanding not only of

Japanese family life, but of Japanese society as a whole.[1] The term referred to a residential unit consisting of all those living together in a single household, whether related by blood or marriage or neither, including servants. Beyond this basic meaning, *ie* referred not just to the physical structure and contemporary membership, but also to an ongoing entity having continuity over time. Its existence extended into the past through ancestors and into the future through descendants.[2]

The *ie* operated as a corporate economic body for property ownership, production, and consumption. Land and businesses were held in common; members cooperated by contributing unpaid labor to the household enterprise, whether it involved rice growing or trade. Profits accrued to the household, not to individuals, and each member was fed, clothed, and provided for out of the joint production.

The household was also the basic social unit for organizing legal, political, and religious life. Village size was reckoned in terms of numbers of households. Clusters of geographically contiguous houses formed the next-highest social unit, the *buraku,* which cooperated in maintaining roads and bridges, planning festivals, and carrying out ceremonial functions. Several *buraku* made up the *mura,* or village, the basic rural administrative unit. Each household was expected to contribute labor or goods as a unit to *buraku* or *mura* activities.[3]

The *ie* was hierarchically structured according to three principles of stratification: gender, age, and insider-outsider status. Males took precedence over females, older people over younger, and those born in the household over those born outside it.[4] Authority, work responsibilities, and privileges were assigned according to these three axes of stratification.

The head of the household was usually the eldest male born in the household, who thereby had high status on all three grounds and was accorded ultimate authority. In the outside society, he was recognized as the legal representative of the household and the manager of the family enterprise. Inside the family, at least in theory, his rule was absolute. Other family members were required to be obedient and respectful. His status was acknowledged by an elaborate code of deference: "He always had a fixed seat at the head of the table, received the choicest part of the evening meal, was served first, and had the first use of the evening bath."[5] Other members tended to fear him, and consequently his relationships with them were likely to be formal and distant.

In contrast, the position of the mistress of the household was not well defined. Her power and prestige depended on specific circumstances. According to the social ideal, females were subordinate. Women were denied any role in the public domain and could not represent the family in legal or political dealings. However, the ideal of feminine subordination and the legal restrictions on women obscure the actual extent of informal female power. Women could, in fact, attain considerable leverage if they contributed substantially to family income, were skilled, worked hard, had forceful personalities, or were clever in manipulating others. A woman gained informal power as she moved through the life cycle. After her mother-in-law died, she became the mistress of the house and ruled over her daughters and daughters-in-law. Moreover, in contrast to the often distant relationship between father and sons, the mother-son tie was usually intense and emotionally close. The bond was forged during infancy and early childhood, when the son slept with the mother and spent a great deal of time at her side. It was sustained when the mother acted as a cushion to soften the father's often harsh treatment. When her eldest son succeeded to the headship, a woman might wield great influence over him. So, although Japanese women found it difficult to attain power through their husbands, they often succeeded through their sons.[6]

In the younger generation members were similarly ranked by gender and age. Because of the principle of primogeniture, the eldest son (*chonan*) was the most favored offspring and accorded deference second only to the male head. He succeeded to the headship of the *ie*, and with it he inherited the common land or business and the main house; he assumed responsibility for carrying on the family enterprise, caring for elderly parents, and worshiping ancestors.[7] Younger sons followed in status. They might inherit portions of land or household goods if there was sufficient property. However, they were expected to form separate, economically independent households upon marriage.[8] Daughters, because they left the household upon marriage and did not count in the continuity of the household, were accorded a low position. Since marriages were usually contracted between partners from different *mura*, a woman's involvement with members of her household of birth was necessarily limited after marriage. The order among siblings, reflected in the terms by which they addressed each other, was: elder brother, younger brothers, elder sister, and younger sisters.

Falling below even the youngest sister was the newly arrived bride, a young female outsider.[9] The trials of the new daughter-in-law were legion. She was assigned the most menial and onerous tasks. She was expected to rise before anyone else and stay up until everyone retired. She had to work under the supervision and critical eye of her mother-in-law, who judged her by how well she fitted in with the ways of the household. As a stranger in the community, she had few or no friends or kin to turn to for support or comfort. Her main reason for being was to work and bear children, especially a male heir. Any children she bore belonged to the household; if she left or was divorced, she had to leave them behind. Yet she herself could not initiate a divorce. If she ran away and returned to her parents, they were obligated to send her back.

The legal, political, and personal oppression of Japanese women was certainly extensive. Yet it is important not to overstate the extent of their subordination in the family. In farm families, the economic need for the wife's labor seems to have given women a great deal of de facto power. According to Embree, an American sociologist who spent eighteen months in the mid-1930s in a southern Japanese village like those from which the immigrants came: "In farm work man and wife are equal, so that in a farmer's household a woman has comparatively higher status than in a shopkeeper's house. If a man did not get along with his wife on the farm, his own income and food supply would be endangered."[10] In addition, farm women seem to have had more personal freedom than the ideal suggests. They participated regularly in village festivals and were involved through female work groups in cooperative ventures, such as manufacturing hair oil. Older women especially had considerable latitude to drink, joke, and tell ribald stories.[11]

Pre-War Japanese Americans: Farm and Entrepreneurial Families

Despite dramatic changes in the external circumstances of family life following immigration, certain factors encouraged continuity in issei family values and household structure.

Gender Politics in the Family: Issei

In the first place, because of their sojourner status, immigration did not sever the ties between the issei and their households of origin. Issei generally kept one foot in each society by retaining kinship obligations in both countries. From the actors' perspective, migration itself was not an individual act but a family strategy. The immigrant was "sent abroad" to work and remit money for the support of the kin group. The immigrant took on the role of economic provider while the kin group at home assumed much of the reproductive burden.[12] Even those who formed conjugal families abroad still retained obligations to kin in Japan and were expected to provide for parents and other relatives there. Mrs. Yoshida, for example, came to the United States originally to work for a few years and save enough so that her husband's parents could retire in comfort. Mrs. Taniguchi mentions scrimping in order to send money to her husband's father, who was having trouble hanging on to the family property because of the profligacy of his own father. Several women also sent money to their own parents and siblings. In return, the relatives at home could be called upon to perform services for the immigrants. As will be described later, children were sometimes left behind or sent back by parents who were working in America. An issei's parents, brothers, sisters, aunts, and uncles might be called upon to take them in and raise them for years at a time. Immigrants who became too old to work or who needed medical attention also returned and were cared for by relatives.

This suggests that the conjugal unit in the United States was often unable to be completely self-sufficient as a domestic and economic unit. The larger kin network provided extra flexibility and could be mobilized to absorb some of the burden produced by the multiplicity of problems the issei faced. Domestic cooperation thus spanned international boundaries. To be sure, the issei's attachment to kin in Japan faded over time as their kin network of children and grandchildren in the United States expanded. Nonetheless, the *ie* retained some hold at least until the death of the issei's parents. As long as it did so, the issei kept the values associated with their original households.

A second factor that fostered continuity of household structure among a large segment of the issei was their specialization in farming and ethnic enterprise. Their household economy resembled that of agrarian and small business families in Japan. Among this segment there was little break with tradition, since the *ie* system was easily transplanted to the new setting. As in Japan the household served as the basic unit of ownership, production, and consumption. The husband was the ultimate authority; he managed the farm or store and oversaw the unpaid labor of wife and children. According to one researcher, pre-war issei in the Seattle area, who were overwhelmingly concentrated in small enterprises, retained traditional Japanese family patterns:

> The division of labor was organized on age and sex criteria, and the hierarchy of household relationships structured work relationships. Family and business were one unified entity rather than two separately conceptualized domains. Second, like the irrigation rice farms of Japan, these enterprises were labor-intensive. Although the economic return per unit of labor was small, all household members could add to the family's labor output. The benefits accrued for the collective made the small return per worker acceptable. Finally, the economic resources of the community were controlled primarily by kinship units. Given the racist climate of the times, there was little opportunity for employment outside the community other than in menial, low-paying jobs. Consequently, the Issei and Nisei were dependent on the kinship-controlled economic resources of the community. Sons were dependent on fathers—not for land, but for capital or an established business with which they could make a living. Those whose fathers could offer them neither of these resources were dependent on wider kin and community ties.[13]

The one notable difference lay in the generational composition of the issei household. Since most of the issei's parents were left in Japan, their households consisted of only two generations, even where the husband was the eldest son. Issei women were for the most part spared the experience of being lowly daughters-in-law. When the parents did immigrate, the pattern of domination by the mother-in-law recurred. Three of the younger issei women in the study had parents-in-law living in the United States when they arrived. Two lived with their in-laws for several years and both suffered in the traditional daughter-in-law role. Mrs. Takagi said that her father-in-law was kind because he was her uncle, but describes her mother-in-law as "mean" and "cold." Mrs. Nishimura, who arrived as a bride at age 15, described her initial years as "hard" because of her youth. She had to take care of her husband's four younger brothers and felt that her health suffered because of the pressures of living with her husband's parents: "While I was living with them, I always had some kind of ailment. But after my son was born [and we moved out] my health improved." In all three cases by the time the women had several children, their in-laws had returned to Japan, leaving them free to run their own households.

Given the similarity in the economy and structure of farm and small business households in Japan and the United States, it is not surprising that women's roles did not differ either. There was no separation of "work" and "family life," since production, consumption, maintenance, and childcare activities were carried on more or less simultaneously and in the same setting. Women continued to work under the authority of their husbands. They earned no independent income, so they had little control over economic resources. Husbands continued to make major decisions, rarely consulting their wives.[14] Women were also prevented from meeting new people and forming relationships outside the family. The reader may recall Strong's remark, quoted in Chapter 4, that his interviewers were unable to obtain information from women because their husbands refused to allow them to be interviewed.

Pre-War Japanese Americans: Wage-Earning Families

What about the issei who were drawn into wage labor? The family economies of this large segment, which included the domestic workers in this study, differed considerably from those of farm and small-business families. Husband, wife, and older children were individually employed, mostly in marginal, low-paying jobs. Each worker's earnings were small, but the pooled income was sufficient to support a household and to generate some surplus for savings, remittances, and consumer goods. Tilly and Scott call this pattern (found among working-class urban families in the nineteenth and early twentieth centuries and among working-class ethnic families today) the "family wage economy."[15]

The strategy of the family wage economy was in some ways consistent with the values of the Japanese *ie* system. Because several wages were needed, economic interdependence among family members was preserved. Further, the employment of women was consistent with the assumption that women were full economic contributors. In other ways, however, the strategy marked a departure from the traditional structure. Wage work represented a form of economic organization in which the individual, rather than the family, was the unit of production, and in which work and family life were separate. The employment of wives outside the home violated the principle that husbands had exclusive rights to and control over their wives' labor.

These contradictions are reflected in the ambivalence of issei men toward their wives' employment. Some men opposed their wives' employment on the grounds that their services were needed at home. Other men demanded that their wives pull their full weight and take a job, regardless of the women's own inclinations. Thus, whereas Mrs. Amano defied her husband's wishes by going out to work secretly, Mrs. Togasaki indicated that she felt pressure to seek outside work:

> My husband didn't bring in enough money, so I went out to work. I didn't even think twice about it. If I didn't take a job, people would have started to call me "madam" [i.e., would presume that she considered herself too much of a lady to work]. It was like a race; we all had to work as hard as possible.

The contradictions extend to the effects of wage work on women's position in the family. To the extent that the traditional division of labor and male privilege persisted, wage work added to the women's burdens. But to the extent that wage work reduced women's economic dependence and male control over their labor, it helped women transcend traditional gender roles in the family. Evidence of both tendencies emerges from issei women's accounts, though the increased burdens are more obvious.

Male Privilege and Female Overload   The major responsibility for housework and childcare remained with women, even if they were employed. All but one of the issei women interviewed claimed that their husbands did little or no work in the home. Mrs. Nishimura was the most explicit in citing the sense of male privilege assumed by husbands:

No, my husband was like a child. He couldn't even make tea. He couldn't do anything by himself. He was really Japan-style. Sometimes I had too much to do, so although I would always iron his shirts, I might ask him to wait awhile on the underwear, but he'd say no. He'd wait there until I would iron them. People used to say he was spoiled. He was a completely Japanese man. Some people divorced their husbands for not helping around the house, but that never entered my mind. I thought it was natural for a Japanese.

Although Mr. Nishimura might be viewed as extreme even by other issei, all the women agreed that issei men expected to be waited upon. The frequency with which the issei women used the term "Japanese" to describe their husbands is striking. They saw their husbands' intransigence as peculiarly Japanese and attributed it to their early upbringing. One can detect in Mrs. Nishimura's statement a perverse pride in her husband's obstinacy and her ability to meet his most unreasonable demands. When asked whether they had ever wished that their husbands would help more around the house, the typical response was, "Yes—I sometimes felt that way. Some men help their wives, but mine never did."

The pattern of male privilege was so firmly entrenched that even when the wife was the sole earner, as was the case if the husband was ill or unemployed, she continued to do most of the housework. In a subculture that placed a premium on male superiority, unemployed men may have had a special need to avoid losing status by taking on "women's work."

The result of male privilege was that women experienced considerable overload. The men worked long hours, often at physically exhausting jobs, but the women's days were longer. Their work began before other members of the household arose with the preparation of the morning meal, and ended after others were relaxing with the clean-up following the evening meal. In between they had to fit in laundry and cleaning. Some women were endowed with natural vitality and got by on little sleep. They maintained an immaculate house and did extra work, such as making clothes for children. Mrs.

Nishimura described her schedule during the years she was working as a garment operative:

> Since I had so many children, I asked my mother-in-law to take care of the children. I would get up at five o'clock to do the laundry—in those days we'd do it by hand—and hang up the laundry, then go to Oakland. I would come home, and since my husband didn't have much work then, he'd get drunk and bring the children home. I would cook and eat, and then go to sleep. They all asked me how long I slept at night. But since I was in my twenties, it didn't affect me too much.

Others, like Mrs. Togasaki, who worked as a laborer in a flower nursery, were exhausted at the end of the day and let things slide at home: "My house was a mess. I went to work in the morning, and when I came back from work, I'd cook a little and then go to sleep, and that's about all."

Childcare and Kin Ties in Japan As Mrs. Nishimura's account indicates, women's outside employment created a problem that did not exist under the family production system—the need for separate childcare arrangements. Employers of domestics and laundry operatives sometimes allowed them to bring a young child to work. In other kinds of jobs and with more children, other arrangements had to be made. Friends, neighbors, older children, and husbands were recruited to babysit. Women with school-age children often set their work hours to the school schedule. As a last resort, kin ties in Japan were mobilized on behalf of the nuclear unit's economic strategy. Three of the fifteen issei women interviewed sent their children to Japan to be raised by relatives so that they could work. Mrs. Taniguchi, for example, had quit working after the birth of her second child. When her husband became seriously ill, however, her father-in-law, who was returning to Japan, took the two children with him so that she could go back to full-time work in a laundry. Like other issei, the Taniguchis planned to return to Japan eventually and felt that their children would benefit from a proper Japanese upbringing. Moreover, the children's presence in Japan would commit them further to returning. Mrs. Taniguchi's father-in-law "insisted that [her older daughter] return to Japan to receive a Japanese education. By doing so, he thought we would all go back to Japan. But it didn't work out that way." Mrs. Taniguchi and the other two women who sent children to Japan settled permanently in the United States and were eventually rejoined by their children.

Internal Reallocation of Responsibilities Most issei families did not resort to such drastic measures as sending children to Japan. Instead, in response to new economic circumstances and the need for women to work, families shifted responsibilities internally. The most common adjustment was for husbands to assume some childcare duties. Even Mr. Nishimura, the "completely Japanese man," transported and minded his children when he was out of work. Mrs. Sugihara claimed that her husband did quite a lot around the house, including dishes:

> He was considerably Americanized. He was young when he came over, and he was a school-boy [i.e., an apprentice domestic], so he was used to the American way of doing things. Even when we quarreled, he wouldn't hit me, saying it's bad in this country for a man to hit a woman, unlike Japan. In Japan, the man would be head of the family without question. "Japan is a man's country; America is a woman's country," he often used to say.

Some respondents and community informants reported cases of role reversal between husband and wife, though none occurred among the fifteen issei interviewed. Role reversals were most common when the husband was considerably older than the wife. Many issei men were married late in life to younger women and were in their fifties by the time their children reached school age. As laborers, their employment prospects were poor compared with their wives', since women could easily find jobs in domestic service. Mrs. Tanabe, a nisei raised in Alameda, recalled that her father was "retired" while she was still a young girl:

> The Hiroshima men in Alameda were the laziest men! Their wives did all the work. My dad raised me while my mother went out and did domestic work. He did the cooking and kept house and did the shopping and took

me when I went to school. So he didn't do much really.
But in Alameda they're known for being the lazy ones—
most Hiroshima men are—so no one's rich.

It may be that domesticity was considered appropriate for older men.
Another nisei, Mrs. Aoki, reported that her father, a widower, acted
as housekeeper and babysitter while she and her husband went out to
work.

Patterns of Leisure Women's non-work time was also affected
by immigration, settlement, and wage work. Like peasants everywhere, Japanese farm families worked long hours according to seasonal demands. However, accounts of village life indicate periodic
release through seasonal and religious festivals. Men and women also
got together for communal projects that combined work and socializing. Spurred on by a desire to get ahead and return to Japan, and
hampered by discrimination, immigrant Japanese worked even harder than they would have in Japan. Most of the women agreed that
their lives would probably have been easier, though perhaps less
materially comfortable, had they stayed in Japan. Women found less
in the way of regular leisure and release from the daily grind in
America. There were few communal projects and little seasonal re-
spite from work. Many struggling immigrant families never took any
time off and were isolated from the community. Arthur Yoshida, son
of one of the women interviewed, responded to a question about his
parents' activities in the community:

> Well, what I can recall, having ten children [my folks]
> were too tied up with the daily hassles of trying to make
> it, so they didn't have the time to contribute toward the
> activities of organizations. The only leisure was Sunday,
> as far as the church.

His mother confirmed this, noting that although the family lived a
half-block from the local movie theater for thirty years, she had never
attended a movie.

Scarce leisure time was rarely devoted to shared husband-wife
activities. The rural Japanese *ie* was characterized by what Bott has

called segregated conjugal role relationships.[16] Husbands and wives had separate rather than shared interests. Embree observed that in village life

> the predominance of a unified household in eating, working and sleeping is in sharp contrast to the way it acts in public. Man and wife are never seen to walk down the street talking together. The man will go alone or with a group of men, the wife alone or with some other women. . . . Both man and wife, however, usually come to strictly family affairs such as weddings and funerals, though even here men and women are seated on opposite sides of the room.[17]

The issei retained this pattern to a marked degree. Many community affairs were restricted to men only, and men and women sat in different sections of the church on Sunday. In general women's orbit was more restricted than men's. Their activities were limited to informal socializing in the course of shopping or doing chores, with occasional outings for weddings, funerals, or church affairs. District associations (organizations of those from the same district in Japan), credit associations, athletic events, and most other organized activities were strictly male domains. In addition, men typically gambled, drank, and socialized with male friends. Mrs. Nishimura complained that she had sometimes stayed up until two in the morning serving snacks and drinks to her husband's friends when they came over to play cards, and then had had to get up at five to go to work.

Tension and Conflict   Issei men frequently turned to drink for solace. Some drank alone at home; others drank in the company of convivial others, swapping stories and engaging in horseplay. Men's drinking seems to have been a source of considerable discord in many families. Heavy drinking was accompanied by the usual problems—financial difficulties and domestic violence. Two women's lives were tragically affected by the husbands' drinking. Mrs. Takagi's husband did not work regularly, and he had frequent accidents. Mrs. Shinoda's husband was killed in a judo mishap while intoxicated. Perhaps

a more typical story is Mrs. Iwataki's. Her husband's health deterio-
rated as a result of regular heavy drinking. She described him in these
terms:

> Not so much nice, but not so bad.
> *Was he old-fashioned?*
> Just like a Japan boy! So I did everything—cook, wash,
> keep house. My husband drank. He drank so much his
> stomach went bad. Once we married, he would have five
> or six drinks every day—sake. All his life he did that. But
> he did work hard.

Money spent on alcohol or going out with the men drained off
scarce income. Thus, the conflict over drinking often involved a deep-
er conflict over control of family resources. Women did not know
exactly how much their husbands earned, since many of them were
gardeners or self-employed. Some husbands felt that they had a right
to withhold a portion of their earnings for their own entertainment.
An extreme case, Mr. Takagi, refused to turn over any of his earnings,
which left Mrs. Takagi to support herself and their sons by working
as a domestic.

The extent of drinking among issei men can be gauged by the
fact that women whose husbands did not drink heavily thought it
worthy of comment. Mrs. Amano was initially reticent about discussing her husband, but she finally said: "He was not quarrelsome;
he didn't gossip about other people. He didn't get drunk, that is, not
knowing what day it was or falling down. If he drank, he fell asleep."
Another issei, Mrs. Sugihara, saw her husband as a paragon of virtue.
She felt fortunate that he was straitlaced:

> Yes, I've been lucky. I worked, of course, and encountered
> social problems [discrimination], but I didn't suffer at all
> with regard to my husband. He didn't smoke, drink, or
> gamble. Very serious Christian with no faults. Everyone
> else was drinking and gambling. Park Street was full of
> liquor stores, and so they'd all go there. But my husband
> led such a clean life, so I was lucky.

Thus, while issei marriages were extremely stable, one should
not romanticize them or exaggerate the degree of harmony within the
family. Nor should one assume an underlying unity of interest. Eco-

nomic interdependence and common cultural values bound members to each other. However, gender divisions generated serious conflicts: the discrepancy in power and privilege, the unequal division of household labor and childcare, and the separation of male and female social and emotional worlds made men's and women's interests fundamentally different. Overwork and poverty exacerbated conflict. Far from responding passively, many women actively contended with their husbands. Mrs. Taniguchi, who had to send two children to Japan and work in a laundry to support her sickly husband said:

> My life in the United States was very hard in the beginning because my husband was ill so much and we had such totally different personalities. We were both selfish, so we had many problems. But after I started going to church, I became more gentle. So we had fewer quarrels. I think that is a gift from God.

Mrs. Nishimura also reported that she and her husband quarreled a great deal:

> Well, he was rather short-tempered. . . . There were times when I thought he was stubborn, but we were far apart in age, so I would attribute our differences to that. Being apart in age does create quite a lot of differences . . . but I bore it all.

Though Mrs. Nishimura attributes the conflict to an age difference, one needs to read between the lines and think about what being older implies in this context—especially being an older male. A plausible interpretation is that her husband tried to exert his patriarchal authority and expected her, as a younger female, to acquiesce to his dominance. Both she and Mrs. Taniguchi expressed the traditional Japanese attitude that women must bear up under any hardship. Yet it is evident that they did not do so silently.

Did Women Gain?

Migration from the economic periphery to the advanced center is often thought to have a liberating effect for women, as traditional patterns of family life give way to individualism and as women gain economic independence through outside employment.[18] The experiences of Japanese immigrants in the pre-war period supports the argument that women's entry into the labor force, rather than exposure to "modern" ideas, is a crucial factor in the realignment of gender politics in the family. Farming and small-business families who were engaged in household-based production reproduced traditional relations in the household. In contrast, issei families whose economies shifted to multiple wage earning displayed greater discontinuity.

Changes accompanying the shift to a family wage economy were not, however, uniformly liberating for women. The changes had contradictory implications for women's reproductive work and for conjugal relations. The tradition that women contributed economically was easily adapted to the requirements of wage labor; women simply transferred their productive activities from the household to the labor market. The parallel tradition of male privilege was harder to alter. One suspects that buttressing the deeply internalized ideology of male superiority was the implicit threat of physical domination. Therefore, it was only under special circumstances in which that threat was inoperative that the weight of household labor shifted. One such circumstance—a fairly common one—was the husband's being considerably older than the wife. If a man was in his fifties or sixties while the wife was in her vigorous thirties or forties, he might take on most of the housekeeping chores while she assumed the main income-earning role.

In many ways, the immigrant situation increased women's overall workload. Women had to compensate for the inability of issei men to bring in adequate income in the stratified labor system, not only through employment outside the home, but also through increased labor in it. They had to produce clothing, basic foodstuffs, and other goods at home to stretch the budget. The sojourner strategy of working hard and sacrificing short-term comfort, combined with the externally constrained work rhythms of wage labor, made for a more relentless and constant pace of work. Women had less relief than they would have had in the village. There were fewer seasonal variations in the amount of work, fewer occasions for communal projects that combined work and socializing, and fewer festivities to provide periodic release. Additional problems were created by the shift to wage work, the most notable being the lack of adequate care and supervision of children. Under the family production system, children were surrounded by caretakers, both parents, and sometimes grandparents and other relatives. Issei women were left on their own to make arrangements for having their children minded while they were out working.

The gains that women made with migration and entry into the labor force were more subtle than the costs. There was, of course, the tangible benefit of added income, part of which could be retained for individual savings or spending. A less tangible but perhaps more significant gain was some degree of control over their economic circumstances. In Japan women were ultimately at the mercy of their husbands' ability or willingness to provide support. Mrs. Takagi's mother suffered extreme poverty as a result of her father's irresponsibility and heavy drinking. His debts eventually led to the loss of their family farm. Although her own husband drank and rarely contributed to the family income, Mrs. Takagi felt less victimized than her mother because in America she was able to work to support herself and her children. The ability to provide for their children fulfilled issei women's deeply ingrained belief in *oyakoku*, the reciprocal obligation that existed between parent and child. Sacrifice and hard work for the sake of children enhanced issei women's self-esteem and also their reputation in the community. According to Kitano, "The story of an aging parent living practically on bread and water in order that his children could gain a college education is not an unusual one in issei culture."[19] Though Kitano uses the male pronoun, his statement is probably more applicable to women, who were much more likely to stint themselves than their husbands were. Mrs. Nishimura was happy to work so hard:

> This is my best time, but my happiest time was then, when my children were small. I was poor and busy then, but that might have been the best time. It was good to think about my children—how they'd go through high school and college afterwards.

The very difficulty of their circumstances and their ability to "bear it all" were sources of pride. Looking back, the issei women expressed amazement at their own capacities.

The analysis of women's role and work in the wage-earning issei family underlines the dialectical nature of the immigrant family, described in the previous chapter. Family cooperation enabled the issei to cope with adversity, and cohesiveness was fostered by the need to confront external oppression in a united way. Nevertheless, the interests of individual members were not synonymous. Divisions and inequality along gender lines created conflict between men and women. The issei family was simultaneously a unity, bound by interdependence in the fight for survival, and a segmented institution in which men and women struggled over power, resources, and labor.

CHAPTER 10
Gender Politics in the Family: Nisei and War Brides

The Nisei

The development of the nisei family followed logically from the course taken by the issei family. The strategies adopted by the issei family to cope with conditions of life in the United States set precedents for the next generation. Thus, the notion of married women contributing to family income through outside employment was more or less taken for granted in the nisei family, and wage work for women was the accepted norm. Certain traditional elements retained by the issei were also continued by the nisei, or at least by the oldest segment of the nisei cohort, who married and started raising children before World War II. In the pre-war period, nisei marriages were still often arranged by parents, and their households were structured according to principles of hierarchical authority and sex segregation.

The political and social conditions that affected Japanese American family life were radically transformed by the internment and post-war economic developments. Most of the changes served to weaken traditional structures of control in the family and community. The internment eroded the political and economic basis of patriarchal authority. The issei father's alien status and inability to speak English disqualified him from acting as head of household in relation to the Caucasian administrators and bureaucrats who controlled the internees' lives. The nisei became the mediators and official representatives of the family. The economic interdependence of the family unit was also undermined. All members of the conjugal family, women and men, parents and children alike, were fed and housed by the government and no longer had to rely on the family unit for their material wants. Parents complained that family cohesion broke down in the camps as teenagers ate with their own friends rather than with their parents. The post-war resettlement brought further changes. Geographic dispersion weakened the power of the ethnic community to reinforce traditional family values. Before the war the potential approval or disapproval of the larger community had been a powerful tool used by parents to curb their children's misbehavior, to encourage conformity, and to spur achievement.[1] With the community scattered, it could not operate as a face-to-face reference group. Perhaps the most decisive change was in the economic circumstances of family life. As opportunities expanded, family life was less dominated by the daily grind of work and anxiety about making ends meet. With greater affluence came time and money for leisure. Even the families of gardeners and domestics could afford some luxuries.

Because of these changes the material base and the social climate for conjugal relations and raising children were markedly different for different age subgroups among the nisei. The oldest group, those born before 1910, for the most part had married and started raising children before the war. Their households were the most similar to those of their issei forebears. Indeed, there was some overlap in that many of the oldest nisei women married issei men, leading to a mixed issei-nisei family constellation. The youngest group, born after 1920, generally married and started their families during the internment or after the return from the camps. This group usually had "free" marriages, and their conjugal households were characterized by relative egalitarianism, shared decision making, and companionship between husband and wife. The family patterns of the large middle group, born between 1911 and 1919 and married around the time of the internment, are instructive because they display transitional features. For this reason, this account will focus primarily on the family complex of the middle group, with reference to the younger, more "acculturated" group or the older, more "traditional" group when their divergence is in some way enlightening.

Work and Family Life Despite growing up in a community where women routinely worked outside the home, the nisei subscribed, at least in theory, to the dominant culture's norms about "women's place." They agreed that women with small children should stay at home. They added that sometimes it is economically necessary for mothers to work. In their own cases, they said, circumstances required them to help out with family finances, and the precedent set by the issei made it natural for them to go out to work. I found no evidence of conflict over the decision or of husbands' opposition to their wives' employment. Most of the women (fifteen out of nineteen) had been employed prior to marriage, twelve as school girls or domestics. Although only three women continued domestic work without interruption, the rest resumed it after an interval most commonly spent bearing children and performing unpaid work for the family farm or business. For some, continuity of employment was impossible because the internment occurred shortly after their marriages. Four of the women were not employed before marriage, and they began working after returning from the camps, also out of necessity and without any fuss being made over it.

Fourteen of the women worked while their children were fairly young. Like the issei, they adopted a variety of strategies for childcare. Some women delayed working until their children started school, and then arranged their work schedules to correspond with school hours. Some women left school-age children to fend for themselves and put them in charge of younger children. Two women had neighbors available to babysit for them. Unlike the issei, the nisei could also call upon extended kin networks. Six women reported that relatives—a father, sister, or mother-in-law—helped with the care of pre-school children. Mrs. Kaneko, for example, traded off babysitting with her sister, who also had children, so that both could work part-time as domestics.

The Division of Household Labor The nisei accept in principle certain ideals of the dominant culture. They feel that a woman should be responsible for housework if she is not employed, but agree that the husband should share household labor if she is. Like most employed wives, the nisei have been unable to achieve this cooperation in practice. Mrs. Suzuki, a Hawaiian kibei married to a main-land-born nisei factory worker, exemplified the disjunction between belief and practice. She always did all the housework, no matter how many hours she worked. When asked whether husbands should help with housework, she said, "Nah, I don't think so. Not if he has a full-time job. I don't believe in that if the wife is home." Then she added:

> If the wife is working, it's different. When a wife is work-ing full-time like my daughter and her husband has a day off, he should help. My son-in-law doesn't help. You know D——— makes more money than he does. And you know she has to wash the clothes and clean the house and do all those things. It's hard on her.

For Mrs. Suzuki, as for other nisei, gender equality was an abstract ideal that had little bearing on her own situation. She seemed quite resigned to doing most of the housework in her own household and voiced no complaint about her own husband. It was only in relation to her daughter that she expressed anger at the unfair division of labor.

Only four of the nisei reported that their husbands helped with housecleaning on a regular basis. Most of the rest said that their husbands helped occasionally. Washing or wiping the dishes was the most common task; the second most common was vacuuming, which the husband did occasionally when the wife was pressed for time. Although the amount of labor men contributed was minimal, even occasional assistance was more than most husbands of issei were willing to provide in the pre-war years. Unexpectedly, the degree to which husbands of nisei participated in housework did not depend on age or generation: issei, nisei, and kibei men were equally likely to take on household chores. The issei husbands of the two nisei women who worked the longest hours (more than forty hours a week) both helped regularly with housecleaning. Two husbands, an issei and a nisei, began to help when the family moved from their farm to the city and the wife began wage work. In most cases, however, the husbands did not increase their contribution to household maintenance when their wives were employed. Instead, children, especially daughters, were pressed into service at an early age. Mrs. Ito, when asked how she managed both employment and home care, never mentioned her husband:

Well, I sort of worked it out. Every weekend we had to
have a houseclean. So the children all chipped in and did
their share of it, even with the cooking. As we went along,
I taught them how to cook and things like that when I'm
not around.

Unlike the issei, none of the nisei described their husbands as
"Japanese" in their attitudes. Nonetheless, the principle of male privilege with which the nisei grew up retained its hold. Older nisei and
kibei men expected to be waited upon, as their fathers were. Mrs.
Yamamoto, when asked about what kind of person her husband was,
said:

Only thing is, he doesn't do anything for housework. I
have to come in and serve him. He just sits down and
reads the newspaper. . . . When I was sick, he cooked,
but not too delicious! I tell him, "What if I die? You better
learn how to cook."

Several women felt that their husbands made substantial contributions to household maintenance through yard work and other
outdoor chores. They spontaneously described an inside-outside division of labor between wife and husband. Mrs. Ito, whose husband
was a gardener, made a point of saying that he did all the outside
work:

He's not too good about cleaning the house or things like
that. He's more of an outside person, so he took care of
completely—one hundred percent—the outside. I don't
bother about watering, so he does everything outside.
Sometimes he does wipe the dishes, now that there isn't
that much.

The inside-outside dichotomy parallels men's and women's occupational experiences. Whereas the women are employed literally to
work inside the house, most of the husbands are gardeners and
accustomed to working outdoors. Mrs. Watanabe makes the point
more explicit: "My husband has always been a gardener. His father
was a gardener, too. He likes the outdoors. He can't stand any indoor
work. He'd be sick. We have a dinner party and he doesn't feel good.
He has to be outside."

An inside-outside division of labor was never mentioned by any of the issei women, so this distinction probably reflects American, rather than Japanese, gender ideology.[2] Peasant women in Japan were not confined to indoor labor and in fact had responsibility for certain agricultural tasks. Fourteen of the fifteen issei women in the interview group had grown up on farms and worked in the fields. Many did the yard work even when their husbands were alive, and several later grew flowers or vegetables as a hobby. Thus, for them the inside-outside distinction by gender was not relevant. In contrast, although almost half of the nisei women had also grown up on farms, none engaged in gardening either as a major area of responsibility or as an avocation.

At the same time that the women paid lip service to egalitarian ideals and sighed or grumbled about their husbands' obstinacy, they also revealed that competence in domestic tasks was central to their identities as women. It was not at all clear that they would have relished their husbands playing a more active role, thereby encroaching on an area that was central to the women's self-esteem. They might even have seen husbands who actually did housework as not sufficiently masculine. I will quote Mrs. Watanabe's thoughts in detail, because they embody the complex and ambivalent attitudes held by many nisei women:

> As far as household things, I do it all. Some men are very domesticated. They'll vacuum for you, but mine doesn't. Well, my father brought us up that way, you know. He said a wife, a woman, is supposed to do a lot of things. [He said] you could tell a woman by whether the sink is clean; he used to tell me, "Always wash the dishes." His tone was put in the back of my mind all the time. So I try to keep my kitchen clean.

> If the wife works, the husband should help. She's helping with the financial part, so that I agree with. Yesterday, I went to church. I had to get up at seven o'clock to make stew for my husband. When I came back, he had washed the dishes, which I was surprised at.

This statement summarizes a number of themes that emerge from the interview material. Household work can be onerous; yet it is also the one domain over which the women exert a great deal of control. They are proud of their cooking and housekeeping abilities and feel that they have high standards that their husbands probably could not fulfill. They would like their husbands to help, but not necessarily interfere. They are pleasantly surprised when their husbands take on small chores without being asked. However, as long as women have to do most of the work, they want to stay in charge. The sense of proprietorship was particularly clear in Mrs. Noguchi's case. After her kibei husband retired from gardening, he began helping around the house, though he had never previously "touched a dish." Lately he had started accompanying her to her domestic service jobs and helping her with the work. They were able to finish in half a day work that used to take her a full day. Yet she was not altogether pleased by his efforts to keep busy, since he was intruding on her territory.

Conjugal Relations   The conjugal roles of the middle group of nisei followed the segregated pattern that has been described as characteristic of working-class families, rather than the companionate ideal of the middle class.[3] The western working-class pattern differs from the traditional Japanese pattern (which is also segregated) in that western women are not completely excluded from participation in the public realm. Among the nisei, women were active in social and community activities, though men and women usually clustered into separate groups at public gatherings. Recreation was also more family-centered than in issei culture, with the nuclear unit attending functions together rather than having separate events for men and women.

Among older nisei men and women, there was considerable separation of activities and interests. Like the issei, the nisei had relatively little leisure when their children were small. Later, when they did have leisure time, they tended to spend it with friends of the same sex. The men golfed or fished, while women shopped and attended Japanese craft classes. The women interviewed would like to do more with their husbands. However, the men were not inclined to include their wives in their male-oriented activities and were uninterested in the activities favored by their wives. For example, several women expressed a desire to travel but said that their husbands never wanted to go anywhere. Mrs. Hiraoka, exasperated, proclaimed, "If I had the money, I'd go myself."

The younger nisei couples more closely approximated the companionate model, though even here male interests took precedence. Mrs. Watanabe had a comfortable relationship with her husband. His interests, which included spectator sports, camping, and fishing, were stereotypically male. The Watanabes did things together because she shared his enthusiasm for athletics. He did not reciprocate by accompanying her to church functions. She explained:

> He loves sports, outdoor things. We go to the Warriors'
> and the As' and the Giants' games. I like them too. We
> always did things together. Only thing we don't do to-
> gether is when we have something at the church. He
> doesn't like to go to church too much. He doesn't like to
> sit still. He's not fussy; he's an easy-going person. Oh, we
> have disagreements, but not big disagreements, you
> know. We've had a lot of fun all these years. We were just
> mentioning it this morning. "We don't have much money,
> but we had a lot of fun."

The younger nisei couples also shared more emotionally, and when problems arose, they were likely to sit down and discuss them together. In contrast to the image of the strict and remote issei father, nisei husbands tended to be viewed by their wives as "easy-going." Mrs. Kono's husband was "almost a full-time boy scout leader":

> I think he's a very good scout leader. He's very patient. He
> never complains about little things. He'll complain about
> mothers complaining. The mothers complain—oh, al-
> ways complain—that on the overnight he didn't have any
> vegetables [laughs]. It doesn't bother him a bit! Some-
> how, he doesn't say a word, but everyone follows him.

Parent-Child Relations The traditional Japanese principle of mutual parent-child obligation (*oyakoku*) retained its hold on the nisei. They felt a deep sense of responsibility for their children's welfare and expected the children to reciprocate. They sacrificed and worked hard so that their children could get ahead and expected the children to work hard and conform to high standards of behavior.

The behavior of individual members was still seen as reflecting on the family, so children were admonished to study and stay out of trouble in order to uphold the family's reputation.

At the same time, the nisei generally claimed that they were less harsh as disciplinarians than their own parents and were closer emotionally to their children. Mrs. Noguchi explained:

Japanese parents are strict. [They say] girls shouldn't stay out and such things like that, which Japanese parents teach kids. My mother was much more strict than me. . . . I think it is better if you can be nice to your children. If you are too strict with them, they think you are too much. . . . I think the nisei are gentler to their own children because they have been disciplined strictly.

The nisei were more child-centered than the issei. That is, they emphasized the parents' obligation to understand and respond to their children's needs. Mrs. Morita fostered her eldest son's unorthodox ambition to be a dancer. At first she was shocked. ("I said, 'Are you crazy?' You know, a first son of a first son!") But when he got a paper route and saved to pay for lessons, she drove him to his classes without informing her husband. Nisei also organize many of the family's activities around the children's interests. While her husband devoted his energies to their sons' scouting, Mrs. Kono spent time with her daughters, having heart-to-heart talks and dispensing advice (e.g., "I told her to 'be yourself' "). When one son joined his high school baseball team, the Watanabes drove to the game every week, and Mrs. Watanabe arranged her work schedule so that she could drive her son to after-school practice.

Though they stress individuality more than the issei, orientation toward the group, including the family, remains strong. They are not as concerned about developing their children's individuality as parents in the dominant culture, perhaps because they realize that a person needs support from the kin group to succeed in a racist society. Although the nisei support and practice neolocal residence—that is, the newly married couple establishes a separate household—they do not believe that adult children need to distance themselves from parents in order to establish their own identities. They expect children to live with parents until they marry. Over half the children of the women interviewed attended college, but they lived at home and commuted to nearby state schools. Typically the parents provided housing and food, while the child worked part-time to pay for school expenses. Children frequently remained at home even after finishing college. Six women had daughters or sons over 21 living at home, and only one had an unmarried child living away from home. However, in contrast to the family wage economy of the issei family, employed teenage and adult children were not expected to turn over their earnings to their parents. Some of the nisei women commented on this difference from their own experience.

Except for two women, all aspired to college educations for their children. They saw education as the means for their children to do better than they had. As Mrs. Noguchi said, "Since I'm not well educated, I wanted my kids to get a good education." Paying for their children's education was a frequent reason for staying in domestic service. Mrs. Hiraoka disliked domestic service, but was postponing a career change until her daughter finished optometry school.

Although their educational aspirations for their children seemed typically middle class, the nisei domestics' ideas about college and career were vague. They believed that their children needed a college degree to get a good job, but did not know the requirements for particular careers. Asked if she had any hopes for her children when they were growing up, Mrs. Fujii said, "No, I thought they can do whatever they want." Mrs. Aoki confessed that she was so busy working that she never had time to discuss her children's plans with them. The nisei domestics' limited occupational experience limited their ability to give specific advice or guidance. A few expressed disappointment that one or more of their children had chosen not to go to college, despite their hopes.

The Extended Circle of Kin With the growth of three generations in the United States, nisei women have assumed an extensive and complex role in the larger kin network. This represents a major departure from the male-centered structure of the kin group as originally constituted in Japan. There the continuity of the lineage and of the household enterprise rested on the eldest male. Because they joined their husbands' households, women did not count in the family lineage and were cut off from kin connections. With the change to a family wage economy in the United States, the corporate unity of the household was broken. Sons were no longer dependent on the family business for their livelihood. The various aspects of inheritance that had all devolved on the eldest son no longer had to be combined in a single role. According to Yanagisako, nisei beliefs and practices tend to differentiate these aspects, and so, for example, nisei believe that all children, daughters as well as sons, should inherit equal shares of the parents' estate. If elderly parents have to live with one of their children, nisei believe that daughters are better suited than sons to take care of them.[4]

Furthermore, kin connections depend less on male lineage and on economic relations among men. Instead, Yanagisako found, connections among kin are maintained primarily by women. Among Seattle-area nisei, sets of female relatives—for example, a group of sisters and their mother—form a cooperative network. The women in the network exchange services, socialize, and organize gatherings to celebrate holidays and other occasions. Husbands are drawn into the wives' kin networks and see their own siblings and parents less frequently than they see the wives' relatives. Yanagisako calls this pattern of relations a "female centered kin network".[5]

The kin relations of nisei domestics in the study seemed to fit this pattern. When asked which members of the family they saw most often, they named married daughters most frequently. Although sons and their accomplishments were an important source of parental pride, women were emotionally closer to their daughters and in more frequent contact with them. Several women were the centers of a three-generation network consisting of their daughters, their sons-in-law, and their daughters' children. These women were intimately involved in their married daughters' lives. The daughters did not live in the same neighborhoods as their mothers, unlike the working-class women in East London described by Young and Willmott,[6] but they usually lived within a half-hour's drive. They were in daily or weekly contact in person or by phone. Daughters dropped by to eat or accompany their mothers on shopping trips. The exchanges were asymmetrical in that mothers did more for daughters than vice versa. Three of the domestics stopped working for long periods to babysit for an employed daughter or niece. They received nominal payment, less than they earned doing domestic work, but helping out a close female relative took priority. Other women participated less directly in the economies of their daughters' households, but they provided a variety of services, such as babysitting, meals, and sewing clothes for grandchildren.

Women adjusted their work hours in order to spend more time on kin obligations, and much of their income was expended on kin, rather than household expenses. Mrs. Yamamoto said about her earnings as a domestic:

> I don't make much, so I spend it. My husband's always mad at me. Before, I had my own bank account. Now we put it together in both our names. Most [of mine] I spend on birthday gifts, Christmas, grandchildren. The household expenses my husband pays.

Gender Relations Several features distinguished gender relations in the post-war nisei family from those in the issei family. Women's employment was taken for granted and did not generate conflict or ambivalence. Although the unequal division of household chores remained a source of tension, nisei women's husbands performed certain minimal tasks that most issei men shunned altogether. The division of labor was often predicated on an inside-outside dichotomy that delegated a considerable area of responsibility for household maintenance to men. Finally, nisei women were often the hubs in a female-centered kin network, which gave them an additional sphere of influence and autonomy that issei women did not have.

Gender and generational relations in the nisei family reflected a mixture of influences. Japanese values, as mediated by issei parents, were evident in the continued emphasis on mother-child obligations. The impact of middle-class American values was found primarily in verbal statements of norms—for example, about employment for women with children and men's role in housework. It would be surprising, given the pervasiveness of American, middle-class culture and the fact that these women work in white middle-class homes and interact with white middle-class women, if nisei women were completely uninfluenced by these ideals.

In terms of actual behavior, however, other factors came into play. Even though their ideological climate was dominated by middle-class values, the families of the women in the study were occupationally proletarian. Their day-to-day experiences were therefore rooted in the material and social conditions of working-class life. These conditions affected relations in the family in more direct ways than the ideological climate. Certain features of conjugal relations in nisei families—role segregation and reliance on female-centered kin networks—are consistent with those described as typical for families of manual workers in several different urban settings.

In the final analysis, many aspects of nisei family life cannot be attributed to any single source. They grow out of the juxtaposition of disparate influences. The emphasis on higher education and social mobility may grow out of the nisei's acceptance of middle-class American values, but it is also a logical outgrowth of Meiji-era Japanese values. The inside-outside division of labor between wives and husbands is consistent with both historical patterns in American culture and the day-to-day occupational experiences of nisei domestics and their husbands. In short, the gender system in the nisei family reflects a complex interplay between Japanese and American cultural influences and the material and social conditions of family life for nisei in the United States.

War Brides

In contrast to the extreme durability of issei and nisei marriages, war bride marriages were unstable and frequently disrupted by divorce. Among the twelve war brides in the interview group, only five were still married to and living with their first husbands. Two were divorced single parents; one was a widow; and four had remarried and were living with their second husbands. Even for those in long-term first or second marriages, marital conflicts and problems were much more conspicuous than among the issei and nisei. These issues were brought up and elaborated by most of the war brides in their interviews. At least at the conscious level, marital relationships were much more problematic for the war brides than for the other groups.

The dominant theme that ran through the war bride marriages was that of female powerlessness. As a result of the circumstances surrounding their marriages and immigration, these women had few resources (including social support) that would give them leverage in the conjugal relationship. Separation and often estrangement from kin, social isolation, inability to speak English, and restricted employment options placed these women at a considerable disadvantage vis-à-vis their husbands, as well as in relation to the larger society. As mentioned earlier, most of the war brides felt that they could not turn to kin for help or even sympathy when they ran into marital problems. They therefore tended to keep their unhappiness to themselves. Because they were bereft of parental and kin support, they had little validation for their perspective. Mrs. Inaba claimed that not having her parents' backing weakened her ability to stand up to her husband:

> He was the boss, always. He never consulted me. He decided [everything] himself. He would say, "That's all." That person had too much, what do you call it, stubbornness. He wanted to do it a certain way and he's got to do it that way. . . . That's why I did whatever my husband said. . . . In Japan I would have gone home to my parents. But since I'm an American, to leave the children would be a pity. But my parents said, "You're married, and no matter what problems you have, you can't come home." If my parents had said, "If you have problems, come home," I would have gone, but they said they wouldn't let me, so I just had to cry.
> *Were your parents opposed to your marrying an American (a nisei)?*
> Yes. My daddy and my whole family. He said, "American Japanese are American." So that's why I can't go back.

The support of kin in Japan might or might not have provided leverage, but lack of it left the women feeling alone and vulnerable.

Most of the war brides also lacked skills and resources that would have enabled them to live independently outside of marriage. Mrs. Howell's story illustrates how the combination of language difficulties, estrangement from kin, and social isolation (she said she had no friends) led her to jump into a second marriage and then kept her ensnared in it even though it has been unsatisfying and unhappy. Her first husband failed to make his child-support payments, after their divorce. With two daughters to support, she became desperate and thought of returning to Japan and throwing herself on her parents' mercy. A war bride friend urged her to move to San Francisco and try to make it on her own for six months. She had been struggling for a year to support herself and her daughters when she met her present husband. She remarried in haste and just as quickly regretted it. She intended to stick it out, however:

> If I got a good education, I could earn enough and I don't think I would have gotten married again. I think it's bad for my daughters. My second husband is not good for my children. . . . That's why Japanese people marry. As long as he's got a good job, got a good home, better stay even if the husband is terrible. . . . I stay in my life [because] one time mistake is enough. I don't want a second time. Because I don't want to make myself miserable any more.

Work and Family Life   In the absence of strong ties outside the conjugal household, women were almost completely dependent on their husbands both materially and emotionally. Outside employment was therefore their main connection with the outside world and the major arena for independent activity. Even the small earnings that part-time domestic work provided were significant because they had so few other resources. Their hunger for autonomy may explain why war brides were more likely than the issei and nisei to keep all their earnings separate from their husbands'. Four of the twelve war brides did not reveal their actual earnings to their husbands. None of the others put them into the family pool. They earmarked their earnings for special expenses or personal bills.

Employment also provided a set of ready-made relationships outside the conjugal family. For some women the relationship with specific employers met important personal needs. Mrs. Sentino said that her closest friends are her employers. These employers, who included a college dean, were part of the upper-middle-class world that she hoped her daughter would enter. Mrs. Howell, who worked primarily for elderly German Americans, preferred their company to that of women her own age. They took the place of the parents she wished she had. Midori Langer also enjoyed working for the elderly, whose old-fashioned values she found more congenial than those of her contemporaries. As mentioned previously, several war brides described one or more employers as "more like a friend" than a boss.

That employment was viewed by both husband and wife as increasing women's independence was revealed by the resistance offered by many husbands. The pattern was similar to that encountered by the issei women. Half of the war brides reported that their husbands were opposed to their being employed. And, like the issei women, they worked despite their husbands' objections. Miyoshi Farrow, who was married to a high school teacher, started working because she wanted to save enough to visit Japan.

> My husband didn't want me to do it at first; he wanted me to quit, but I kept doing it. He's not going to say anything any more because I'm not listening to him. One thing is, I'm not spending the money for crazy things. I'm saving for a big reason—to go to Japan to see my brothers and sisters, so he doesn't say any more, but he still doesn't want me to do it.

For the Howells, the disagreement over Shizuko's employment was part of an overall struggle for control in the family. Mrs. Howell and her three children from a former marriage formed an alliance that excluded Mr. Howell. He felt the isolation and attempted to get her to rely on him more, but she resisted:

> Oh, he's old-fashioned. My ex-husband was the same, but this husband is more old-fashioned. "Woman has to stay home; woman has to take care of the house" [laughs]. But I don't like it that way. Because I need fresh air. I don't have a good education, so I cannot use my mind. I *can* use my energy. . . . I got a house and husband and children and outside work. Most things I can handle myself because I don't want to depend on my husband. That's why my husband is mad, because I don't depend on him so much, but the kids depend all the way on me.

Some husbands claimed that what they objected to was not employment per se but domestic work. They felt that it was degrading for their wives to be housecleaners and that it reflected negatively on their own status. Etsuko Rybin ran a restaurant in Japan with her husband before immigrating and then worked as a seamstress after the couple arrived in San Francisco. Mr. Rybin never disapproved of his wife's working until she began domestic work:

> My husband doesn't like it. Southern people especially are like that. He said, "That's colored people's job." He

was raised over there [the South] like that. Oh, he didn't
like it! And he says, "I have pride too. I don't want you
to work like that."

It appeared that Mr. Rybin sincerely did not object to his wife's
being employed, but only to the *kind* of work she did. In other cases
the husband's objection to domestic work might have been a dis-
guised attack on his wife's being employed at all, since as far as the
women could see, they had very little choice of occupations. Either
they worked at a job that had low status, or they did not work at all.
Kimiko Bentley's husband, an accountant, "hates that I'm doing
housework; but there are no other jobs." Mr. Bentley suggested that
she first go to school to improve her English and then get a better
job. However, to become completely comfortable in English at this
stage in life would be very difficult and would take such a long time
that it would bar employment in the near future. Even if she mastered English, age, inexperience, and lack of current job skills would
constitute major stumbling blocks.

The Division of Household Labor Conflict over employment had consequences for the allocation of household labor.
Kimiko Bentley worked despite her husband's opposition. She said
that she had little to do at home once her daughter had grown up,
and she got lonely and homesick for Japan if she did not keep busy.
She therefore continued to work but had to make concessions at
home as a result:

> *In terms of your household here, does your husband
> help?*
> You mean clean the house? He doesn't; he never does.
> *Do you think husbands should help?*
> Well, sometimes I wish he would help when I'm very
> tired. Then he says, "Quit your job, it's a crummy job."

As Mrs. Bentley's remarks indicate, the circumstances under
which employment is undertaken may affect the leverage a woman
has in negotiating household responsibilities. Ferree has suggested
that the ostensible reasons for a woman's working affects whether
she gains power in the family through outside employment.[7] If a

wife's employment is viewed as financially necessary and if she undertakes it reluctantly, she can claim extra privileges for her contributions to the family economy. For example, she might be able to negotiate for her husband to take the children out on weekends so that she has some time to recuperate. However, if employment is viewed as something the wife does for personal fulfillment, she may actually lose leverage. Working itself is seen as a privilege. She may then have to perform not only her usual household duties, but also extra tasks to demonstrate that her job is not causing her to neglect her family. Thus, Mrs. Bentley and others who work in opposition to their husbands' wishes cannot call upon them for help with housework. Whether husbands would do more if they were not averse to their wives' employment or if their wives did not work is debatable, but their stance gives them a convenient excuse for refusing to help. Women are thus caught on the horns of a dilemma. All the women interviewed agreed that an employed wife was entitled to help with household tasks. Yet as long as her husband is opposed to her being employed and she insists on her right to work, she has no claim on his assistance.

Not surprisingly then, women once again wound up doing most of the cleaning and childcare at home. There were two notable exceptions. Mr. Sentino, a professional cook, did all the meal preparation, as well as much of the cleaning. He was described by Mrs. Sentino as completely homebound except for going out to work. His only interests were cooking and religion, and he therefore insisted on being in charge of cooking. The other exception was Mr. Rybin, who for almost fifteen years did most of the housework as well as caring for his disabled wife. The remaining women claimed that they did all the housework. Husbands sometimes helped with shopping or managed the finances. Several women referred to the inside-outside dichotomy noted in nisei families, and two described their husbands as "loners" or "unsocial" men who enjoyed puttering around the house, painting, and fixing things.

Like the nisei, the war brides agreed that men should help when their wives worked outside, but acknowledged that their own husbands did not. In a statement reminiscent of Mrs. Suzuki's, Miyoshi Farrow said, when asked whether men or women had harder lives:

Before, women stayed home, took care of children, so compared to the husband life was easier. Now women work and take care of the house and children. If they want children they have to carry the baby, birth it, and take care of it. So women have it harder. The other day my daughter was sick and in bed. She said, "I'm going to get up to fix dinner." I told her, "You better train your husband to cook and clean and wash the dishes."

Mrs. Farrow herself admitted that she did virtually all of the housework at home. Again we find women resigned to their own situations. It is easier to get angry on a daughter's behalf than to reform gender relations in one's own household.

Conjugal Relations   Among those interviewed, there seemed to be almost as many types of marital relationships as there were couples. Relations varied along at least three dimensions: degree of conflict, socio-emotional sharing, and equality. An example of one type of relationship is the Lorings', which displays male domination, little conflict, and moderate sharing of feelings. Aiko Loring described her marriage to her second husband, a sales executive, as harmonious. He did not care whether or not she worked, but told her she should do whatever made her happy.

I guess I feel more secure. I can depend on him a hundred percent. My ex-husband and him, it's like night and day, the different attitudes, and I hate to say this, but my present husband has more education, his thinking is more high, you know. . . . I learn a lot [more] from my present husband than I did from my ex-husband. . . . He's real thoughtful. He thinks a lot of my future.

Mrs. Langers' relationship with her husband is also without conflict and is more intellectually equal:

He's always taken such good care of me, and even the doctor is amazed that he is so patient with me. No matter what, he takes me to the doctor every day or encour-

ages me to try another doctor. On his days off, no matter
how tired he is, he takes me here and there. When he
comes home from work he used to force me to walk a
little outside even if I didn't feel like it. I'm lucky to have
such a husband.

The Langers communicated on a more intimate level than the Lorings, partly because Mr. Langer was knowledgeable about and in
tune with Japanese culture; he also spoke Japanese, the only non-
Japanese spouse to do so.

At the extreme of emotional distance were the Sentinos, who
had fundamentally different views of the world and diametrically
opposite values. Mr. Sentino was at home a great deal and imposed
his rather idiosyncratic standards on the household. Mrs. Sentino
evaded his scrutiny through a constant stream of outside activities:
taking classes at the local community college, playing tennis, and
working thirty hours a week. She ignored him as much as possible,
centering her energies on their teenage daughter:

Like right now my marriage is not happy, but my daughter doesn't understand why I want to stay with this guy. I
want to stay in my house. I divorced once. I don't want
to go through that again. My daughter says I should
leave——[she] says he's crazy. . . . Basically he's a nice
man, but doesn't have the best education. He's hard to
live with. He drinks a lot. This morning he got up at
5:00 a.m. and drank. He slept until 7:00 and got up to
drink again. Every weekend he gets drunk. On weekdays
he doesn't touch—he goes to work, but on weekends he
drinks all weekend. . . . He likes whisky. He has no hob-
bies, just drink and cook. He's religious, a Catholic, and
every morning he prays.
Does he get violent when drunk?
Yes, so I don't say anything. It's just a couple of hours. If
I open my mouth, it's a fight, so I wait until he goes to
sleep, so everything's all right.

The Howells were an equally alienated couple. However,
whereas Mr. Sentino's presence was intrusive, Mr. Howell was mar-

ginal in his household. Mrs. Howell was determined to maintain her autonomy and protect herself by remaining emotionally aloof. When asked if she got along with her present husband, she answered:

> In some ways, yes, because I don't trust anyone any more. I stay in my life because one time mistake is enough. I don't want a second time. . . . If I give too much love, I get more hurt, so no more. If he's nice, I'm nice back. But he tells me ten things. I believe about six, but four things I just let go. Then if he gives me a hard time, I'm not hurt so much. . . . Because my first husband I trust all the way. . . . [Later] He's got a good heart. But he's a hard head. He's a moody time. Sometimes kids say, "Hi, daddy," and he doesn't even say "hi."

These are the extreme cases. If one had to locate the group tendency, one would find that on the whole conjugal relations were fairly harmonious, but with a fair degree of separation in men's and women's emotional and social lives. Men ostensibly dominated— that is, wives "served" their husbands—but women managed to achieve some autonomy through employment and outside activities. Overall the women seemed to be more sociable and gregarious than their husbands. Husbands tolerated but were uninvolved in the women's social circles.

The war brides' Japanese upbringing conditioned them to expect a certain degree of distance between men and women. As Miyoshi Farrow expressed it, "Men's things should be for men, and women's things for women." Women routinely kept secret from their husbands certain matters that they discussed only with their female friends. Compared with Japanese couples, however, husbands and wives may have confided more in each other. Husbands did not take unilateral actions and were willing to sit down and discuss issues such as disciplining children. They did not order their wives around. And if war bride couples ran into difficulties, they might seek advice from a minister or marriage counselor. Thus, despite inequities, relations with American spouses appeared relatively close and egalitarian. Miyoshi Farrow described herself as "completely Japanese" in her outlook and cherished Japanese ways of relating to others. Yet she admitted that she would find it difficult to tolerate a Japanese marriage at this point:

> We're [women] in a bad position [there]. Two years ago I went to Japan and I went to see my brother's family there. They're typical Japanese. He's so much a boss. I couldn't stand what he says to his wife: "Masako, get this, bring that." I said, "Why don't you get it yourself?" He gave me quite a look.

Parent-Child Relations Aside from the conjugal tie, war brides' only close kinship bonds were with their children. Thus, relations with children were very important. At the time of the interviews, five women still had children living at home. Of the seven with children living away, five saw them at least once a week, and two saw them every two weeks or so. The war brides thus maintained contact with adult children but were not as deeply involved in their married children's lives as the nisei.

The war brides who had the most difficult times and felt disappointed at the way their own lives have turned out seemed to be the most emotionally invested in their children. Mrs. Osborne, a single parent, said: "My children come first. I'm working to upgrade my children. We stick together. We go to movies together, we go to restaurants together, and we sometimes just go, you know, around."

Mrs. Sentino submerged her own ruined aspirations and devoted all of her considerable energies to designing a happy life for her daughter Anne. She was intent on giving Anne every middle-class advantage she could afford. She not only enrolled her for piano lessons at age five, but took lessons herself for two years before that so that she could coach her. A large portion of her earnings from domestic work went to pay for private school tuition. She could not buy the kind of elegant house that most of Anne's schoolmates lived in, but she tried to make sure that Anne did not lack for anything else. She was able to provide her with an extensive wardrobe, adequate spending money, and, once she turned sixteen, a car.

The war brides internalized responsibility for the problems they encountered—marital breakups, low-status jobs, difficulty in dealing with authorities—so their self-esteem suffered. The inability to speak "correct" English not only limited their aspirations but also made them feel inadequate. Most of the war brides described themselves as "uneducated" even though they were high school graduates. Being unable to communicate fluently in English also affected their relations with their children. Unlike the issei, who spoke Japanese at home, the war brides were forced to deal with their children in English, a language in which they found it difficult to express complex thoughts. This made in-depth communication difficult. Furthermore, the children rapidly became more fluent than their mothers. The usual parent-child relationship, where parents were more competent and therefore authoritative, was reversed. The war brides felt powerless, and became, in a sense, negative role models. Many of the women, as noted above, explicitly used themselves as "bad examples" to motivate their children to do better. Sachiko Adair, a single parent, has kept her family afloat since her divorce only with great difficulty:

> If I'm educated maybe I have a good job. I wouldn't have to be scared people are going to fire me. Then I'd be settled at a desk until I retire. I always thought education is important. So that's what I tell them [her children] to do. "You don't want to be like your mother, just scared. You get a job, but you're scared you might get fired some time." I didn't want to raise them like I was raised. They should be more free.

Gender Relations   The war brides shared with issei women the basic experience of leaving their family environments, adjusting to a completely foreign culture and language, and confronting limited economic options. Issei women faced much more difficult economic circumstances and more virulent racism. Yet they also had certain advantages. They were married to men with whom they shared a common language and culture and even a similar class and regional background. As sojourners, the issei retained ties in Japan and maintained identities as Japanese. Their immersion in a cohesive community made up of others in similar circumstances reinforced a positive ethnic identity. In contrast, the war brides married men of completely different language and cultural backgrounds. Through their marriages they became estranged from their kin and alienated from Japanese society and their old identities. The absence of a homogeneous and cohesive peer group made the war brides almost completely dependent on their spouses for security and left them to make adjustments on their own.

These circumstances contributed to a sense of powerlessness. To overcome their isolation, the war brides had to build their own sources of support. Many exercised considerable resourcefulness in constructing friendship networks and carving out areas of autonomy. Like the issei, the war brides seeking employment encountered resistance from their husbands, who apparently viewed outside work as a threat to their authority in the family; but, again like the issei, the war brides persisted in their determination to work. Employment enabled them to earn an independent income, form relationships outside the family, and further their ambitions for their children. However, in part because they worked in opposition to their husbands' wishes, they had little leverage to shift the burden of household labor. In this respect, the war brides did not differ much from the issei and nisei, despite the cultural differences among their husbands.

APPENDIXES

Appendixes

APPENDIX 1
JAPANESE IMMIGRATION TO THE CONTINENTAL UNITED STATES, 1861–1923

| Decade | New Immigrants Admitted | Resident Population at End of Decade | | |
		All	Male	Female
1861–1870	218	55	—	—
1871–1880	149	148	—	—
1881–1890	1,637	2,039	—	—
1891–1900	27,440	24,326	23,341	985
1901–1910	54,839	72,157	63,070	9,087
1911–1920	51,956	111,010	72,707	38,303
1921–1923	3,996	138,834	81,775	57,059

Source: Yamato Ichihashi, *Japanese in the United States* (Stanford: Stanford University Press, 1932), tables on pp. 54 and 64, appendix C (tables 7 and 8).

APPENDIX 2
JAPANESE AMERICAN POPULATION BY GEOGRAPHIC REGION, 1890–1940

	1890	1900	1910	1920	1930	1940
Pacific States	1,532	18,269	57,703	93,490	120,251	112,353
California	1,147	10,151	41,356	71,952	97,456	93,717
Oregon	25	2,501	3,418	4,151	4,958	4,071
Washington	360	5,617	12,929	17,387	17,837	14,565
Mountain States	27	5,107	10,447	10,792	11,418	8,574
New England	45	89	272	347	352	340
Middle Atlantic	202	446	1,643	3,266	3,662	3,060
East North Central	101	126	482	927	1,022	816
West North Central	16	223	1,000	1,215	1,003	755
South Atlantic	55	29	156	360	393	442
East South Central	19	7	26	35	46	43
West South Central	42	30	428	578	687	564
TOTAL	2,039	24,326	72,157	111,010	138,834	126,947
% residing in Pacific States	75.13%	75.10%	79.97%	84.22%	86.61%	88.50%
% residing in California	56.25%	41.73%	57.31%	64.82%	70.20%	73.82%

(continued)

APPENDIX 2 (*continued*)

Sources: For 1890: U.S. Bureau of the Census, *Report on Population of the United States at the Eleventh Census: 1890*, pt. 1 (Washington, D.C.: U.S. Government Printing Office, 1895), table 19: "Population by Sex, General Nativity, and Color, of Places Having 2,500 Inhabitants or More, 1890." For 1900, 1910, and 1920: U.S. Bureau of the Census, *Fourteenth Census of the United States Taken in the Year 1920*, vol. 3, *Population, Composition and Characteristics of the Population by States; California* (Washington, D.C.: U.S. Government Printing Office, 1922), table 7: "Indians, Chinese and Japanese for Counties and Cities of 25,000 or More, 1920, 1910, and 1900." For 1930 and 1940: U.S. Bureau of the Census, *Sixteenth Census of the United States, 1940: Population*, vol. 2: *Characteristics of the Population*, pt. 1: *United States Summary and Alabama–District of Columbia, California* (Washington, D.C.: U.S. Government Printing Office, 1943), table 25: "Indians, Chinese, and Japanese, by Sex, for Counties, and for Cities of 10,000 to 100,000: 1940 and 1930," table F-36: "Race, by Nativity and Sex, for the City of San Francisco, 1940 and 1930," and table C-36: "Race, by Nativity and Sex, for the City of Oakland, 1940 and 1930." For 1950: U.S. Bureau of the Census, *U.S. Census of Population, 1950*, vol. 2: *Characteristics of the Population*, pt. 5, *California* (Washington, D.C.: U.S. Government Printing Office, 1952), table 47: "Indians, Japanese, and Chinese, by Sex, for Selected Counties and Cities, 1950." For 1960: U.S. Bureau of the Census, *Census of Population, 1960*, vol. 1, *Characteristics of the Population*, pt. 6, *California* (Washington, D.C.: U.S. Government Printing Office, 1963), table 21: "Characteristics of the Population for SMSAs, Urbanized Areas, and Urban Places with 10,000 or More, 1960." For 1970: U.S. Bureau of the Census, *1970 Census of Population*, vol. 1, *Characteristics of the Population*, pt. 6, *California* (Washington, D.C.: U.S. Government Printing Office, 1973), table 23: "Race by Sex for Areas and Places, 1970."

APPENDIX 3

JAPANESE POPULATION OF FOUR BAY AREA CITIES, 1890–1970

City	1890	1900	1910	1920	1930	1940	1950	1960	1970
San Francisco	590	1,781	4,518	5,358	6,250	5,280	5,579	9,464	11,705
Oakland	85	194	1,520	2,709	2,137	1,790	1,250	2,206	2,401
Berkeley	19	17	710	911	1,320	1,319	2,147	3,665	3,417
Alameda	37	110	499	644	822	700	457	457	683
San Francisco/Oakland SMSA[a]	—	—	—	—	—	—	—	22,444	33,587

Sources: For 1890: U.S. Bureau of the Census, *Report on Population of the United States at the Eleventh Census, 1890*, pt. 1 (Washington, D.C.: U.S. Government Printing Office, 1895), table 21: "Negro, Chinese, Japanese and Civilized Indian Population, Classified by Sex, by States and Territories: 1890." For 1900, 1910, and 1920: U.S. Bureau of the Census, *Census Taken in the Year 1920*, vol. 2, *Population: General Report and Analytic Tables* (Washington, D.C.: U.S. Government Printing Office, 1922), table 11: "Indians, Chinese, Japanese, and 'All Other' by Divisions and States, 1920, 1910, and 1900." For 1930: U.S. Bureau of the Census, *Fifteenth Census of the United States, 1930, Population*, vol. 2: *General Reports, Statistics by Subject*, chap. 2: Color or Race, Nativity and Parentage (Washington, D.C.: U.S. Government Printing Office, 1933), table 11: "Color or Race and Nativity, by Divisions and States, 1930." For 1940: U.S. Bureau of the Census, *Sixteenth Census of the Population, 1940: Population*, vol. 2, *Characteristics of the Population* (Washington, D.C.: U.S. Government Printing Office, 1943), table 22: "Population by Race, with Individual Minor Races, by Divisions and States, 1940."

ªFigures for Standard Metropolitan Statistical Areas available only for 1960 and 1970.

NOTES AND INDEX

NOTES

Chapter 1

1. Amey Watson, "Domestic Service," *Encyclopedia of the Social Sciences* (New York: Macmillan, 1937), 5:198–207.
2. U.S. Bureau of the Census, *Negro Population, 1790–1915* (Washington, D.C.: U.S. Government Printing Office, 1918), table 20.
3. David M. Katzman, *Seven Days a Week: Women and Domestic Service in Industrializing America* (New York: Oxford University Press, 1978).
4. Charles B. Keely, "Effects of the Manpower Provision of the U.S. Immigration Law," paper presented at the Population Association of America Annual Meeting, 1974.
5. George J. Stigler, "Domestic Servants in the United States, 1900–1940," Occasional Paper 24 (New York: National Bureau of Economic Research, 1946).
6. Segregated job markets for blacks and Chicanos are discussed in chap. 9, "The Job Ceiling," in St. Clair Drake and Horace R. Cayton, *Black Metropolis: A Study of Negro Life in a Northern City* (New York: Harcourt Brace, 1945); and Mario Barrera, *Race and Class in the Southwest* (Notre Dame, Ind.: University of Notre Dame Press, 1979). For a discussion of parallels in the employment patterns of black, Chicana, and Chinese American women, see Evelyn Nakano Glenn, "Racial Ethnic Women and Work: Towards an Analysis of Race and Gender Stratification," in Liesa Stamm and Carol D. Ryff (eds.), *Social Power and Dominance in Women* (Boulder, Colo.: Westview Press, 1984), pp. 117–50.
7. See Chapter 4 for tables based on U.S. census data.

8. These three groups can be characterized as cohorts in that each comprises an "aggregate of individuals who experienced the same events with the same time interval" and has a "distinct composition and character reflecting the circumstances of its unique origination and history." Norman B. Ryder, "The Cohort as a Concept in the Study of Social Change," *American Sociological Review* 30 (1965): 845.

9. An account of anti-Japanese activity up to World War II is found in Roger Daniels, *The Politics of Prejudice* (New York: Atheneum, 1973). For an insight into the virulence of anti-Japanese sentiments, see the documentary materials reprinted in Paul Jacobs and Saul Landau (eds.), *To Serve the Devil*, vol. 2: *Colonials and Sojourners* (New York: Random House, 1971). Testimony by various anti-Japanese groups and individuals is found in the proceedings of the State Board of Control of California, *California and the Oriental* (Sacramento: California State Printing Office, 1922).

10. Calvin F. Schmid and Charles E. Nobbe, "Socioeconomic Differentials Among Non-White Races," *American Sociological Review* 30 (1965): 909–22.

11. William Peterson's text *Japanese Americans* (New York: Random House, 1971) is the clearest examplar of the "model minority" ideology. The point can be made more generally that the achievements of Asian American groups—particularly Chinese, Japanese, and Koreans—are viewed as evidence that other groups could succeed if they tried harder or had different cultural values. An article titled "Success Story: One Minority Group" in *U.S. News and World Report* (December 26, 1966; reprinted in Amy Tachiki, Eddie Wong, and Franklin Odo with Buck Wong [eds.], *Roots: An Asian American Reader* [Los Angeles: Asian American Studies Center, University of California, Los Angeles, 1971], p. 6.) argues: "At a time when it is being proposed that hundreds of billions be spent to uplift Negroes and other minorities, the nation's 300,000 Chinese-Americans are moving ahead—with no help from anyone else." In a more scholarly vein, Ivan H. Light, *Ethnic Enterprise in America: Business and Welfare Among Chinese, Japanese and Blacks* (Berkeley and Los Angeles: University of California Press, 1972), attributes Chinese and Japanese success in business in large part to a strong sense of ethnic honor. He claims that blacks lacked such a sense of family and ethnic honor, which "would have provided a social standard against which poor blacks might collectively have measured individual conduct. This discipline would have permitted lower class blacks to mobilize themselves as a group in the interests of impersonal achievements capable of wringing respect from the most unsympathetic whites (p. 190).

12. Patricia A. Roos and Joyce F. Hennessy, "Assimilation or Exclusion? Attainment Processes of Japanese, Mexican Americans, and Anglos in California," paper presented at the meetings of the American Sociological Association, San Antonio, August 1984.

13. Yamato Ichihashi, *Japanese in the United States* (Stanford: Stanford University Press, 1932), has compiled the most extensive information on pre-1924 immigration.

14. Harry H. L. Kitano, *Japanese Americans: The Evolution of a Subculture*, 2d ed. (Englewood Cliffs, N.J.: Prentice-Hall, 1976), and Bok-Lim C. Kim, "Asian Wives of U.S. Servicemen: Women in the Shadows," *Amerasia Journal* 4 (1977): 91–115.

15. Discussions of immigrant labor in Europe are found in Ronald E. Krane (ed.), *International Labor Migration in Europe* (New York: Praeger, 1979), and Stephen Castles and Godula Kosack, *Immigrant Workers and Class Structure in Western Europe* (London: Oxford University Press, 1973).

16. Michael J. Piore, *Birds of Passage: Migrant Labor and Industrial Societies* (Cambridge: Cambridge University Press, 1979).

17. David S. North and Marion Houstoun, *The Characteristics and Roles of Illegal Aliens in the U.S. Labor Market: An Exploratory Study* (Washington, D.C.: Linton, 1976), p. 27.

18. Piore, *Birds of Passage.*

19. Latin American and Caribbean women and labor migration are discussed in Delores M. Mortimer and Roy S. Bryce-Laport (eds.), *Female Immigrants to the United States: Caribbean, Latin American and African Experiences,* Occasional Papers, no. 2, Research Institute on Immigration and Ethnic Studies (Washington, D.C.: Smithsonian Institution, 1981).

20. See "Introduction," in Lucie Cheng and Edna Bonacich, *Labor Immigration Under Advanced Capitalism: Asian Immigrant Workers in the United States Before World War II* (Berkeley: University of California Press, 1984), and Piore, *Birds of Passage.* The following description applies to labor migrants, who in the United States have tended to be people of color; the process was different for voluntary white European immigrants.

21. Piore, *Birds of Passage*, pp. 65–67, notes a major difference in orientation between immigrants who spent their formative years in the sending society and those who spent those years in the host society. S. Frank Miyamoto, in "An Immigrant Community in North America," in Hilary Conroy and T. Scott Miyakawa (eds.), *East Across the Pacific* (Santa Barbara, Calif.: ABC Clio Books, 1972), says that the rise of an American-born and educated generation was a major turning point for the

issei, who subsequently began to view their stay as long-term or permanent.

22. Making a slightly different point, Edna Bonacich talks about exclusion movements resulting from the conflict between "high-priced" (in this case native) labor and "low-priced" (in this case migrant) labor in her classic article, "A Theory of Ethnic Antagonism: The Split Labor Market, *American Sociological Review* 37 (1972): 547–59.

23. Robert Blauner, *Racial Oppression in America* (New York: Harper & Row, 1972, pp. 51–82), argues that this feature is one of several differentiating the experience of people of color ("colonized minorities") from that of European immigrants ("immigrant minorities").

24. Characteristics of a colonial labor system are discussed by Barrera, *Race and Class in the Southwest,* pp. 34–57.

25. Light, *Ethnic Enterprise in America,* discusses the Japanese and Chinese propensity for small business. Edna Bonacich, Ivan Light, and Charles Choy Wong, "Small Businesses Among Koreans in Los Angeles," in Emma Gee (ed.), *Counterpoint* (Los Angeles: Asian American Studies Center, University of California, Los Angeles, 1976), pp. 436–49, and Kenneth Wilson and Alejandro Portes, "Immigrant Enclaves: An Analysis of the Labor Market Experiences of Cubans in Miami," *American Journal of Sociology* 86 (1980): 295–319, discuss ethnic enterprise among Koreans and Cubans respectively.

26. Edna Bonacich, "United States Capitalism and Korean Small Business," paper presented at the Conference on New Directions in the Labor Process, Binghamton, New York, 1978.

27. Wilson and Portes, "Immigrant Enclaves."

28. Gary Becker uses a human capital approach to explain the disadvantaged position of minority workers in *The Economics of Discrimination* (Chicago: University of Chicago Press, 1957). For a review and critique of the human capital model as applied to women, see Donald Treiman and Heidi Hartmann (eds.), *Women, Work and Wages: Equal Pay for Equal Work* (Washington, D.C.: Academy Press, 1981).

29. Milton M. Gordon, *Assimilation in American Life: The Role of Race, Religion and National Origin* (New York: Oxford University Press, 1964).

30. Robert T. Averitt, *The Dual Economy* (New York: Norton, 1968).

31. See, e.g., Michael J. Piore, "Notes for a Theory of Labor Market Segmentation," in David M. Gordon (ed.), *Theories of Poverty and Underemployment: Orthodox, Radical and Dual Labor Market Perspectives* (Lexington, Mass.: D.C. Heath, 1972); Peter B. Doeringer and Michael J. Piore, *Internal Labor Markets and Manpower Analysis* (Lexington, Mass.: D.C. Heath, 1971).

32. The internal colonialism model was developed by black scholars and activists to describe black-white relations (Kenneth Clark, *Dark Ghetto* [New York: Harper & Row, 1965]; Stokely Carmichael and Charles V. Hamilton, *Black Power: The Politics of Liberation in America* [New York: Vintage Books, 1967]) and was later applied to Chicano-Anglo relations (e.g., Joan W. Moore, "Colonialism: The Case of Mexican Americans," *Social Problems* 17 [1970]: 464–72; Mario Barrera, Carlos Munoz, and Charles Ornelas, "The Barrio as an Internal Colony," in Harlan Hahn [ed.], *People and Politics in Urban Society, Urban Affairs* Annual Reviews [Beverly Hills and London: Sage Publications, 1972]: 465–98). The model has been most extensively developed by Robert Blauner in *Racial Oppression in America,* where he argues that it applies in varying degrees to blacks, Native Americans, hispanics, and Asian Americans.

33. See Harry K. Braverman, *Labor and Monopoly Capital: The Degradation of Work in the Twentieth Century* (New York and London: Monthly Review Press, 1974), pp. 257–70; Paul Goldman and Donald P. van Houten, "Managerial Strategies and the Worker: A Marxist Analysis of Bureaucracy," *Sociological Quarterly* 18 (1977); 108–77; and Alfred Dupont Chandler, *The Visible Hand: The Managerial Revolution in American Business* (Cambridge, Mass.: Belknap Press of Harvard University Press, 1977), p. 363. I use the term monopoly here to refer to the control of a market by either a few firms or a single firm.

34. Rick Edwards, *Contested Terrain: The Transformation of the Workplace in the Twentieth Century* (New York: Basic Books, 1979), argues that with the growth of monopoly capital there has been a shift from more personal forms of control toward organizational forms, such as internal labor markets.

35. See readings in Richard C. Edwards, Michael Reich, and David Gordon (eds.), *Labor Market Segmentation* (Lexington, Mass.: D. C. Heath, 1975).

36. Piore, *Birds of Passage,* p. 86.

37. Piore, for example, in discussing shifts in immigrants' orientations, says at one point: "*People* begin to anticipate their inability to maintain the ascetic existence they had originally planned, and they begin to bring their wives, and occasionally their children, from home" (*Birds of Passage,* p. 63; emphasis added). Piore is, of course, referring to men when he uses the term "people"; women appear as passive objects "brought" by husbands.

38. Lucy M. Cohen, "The Female Factor in Resettlement," *Society* 14 (September/October 1977): 27–30.

39. Books that discuss Asian immigration ignore or at most devote a few paragraphs or pages to female migrants; see, for example, Ichihashi, *Japanese in the United States,* and Stanford Lyman, *Chinese Americans* (New York: Random House, 1974).

40. Cohen, "The Female Factor in Resettlement."

41. U.S. Department of Justice, *Immigration and Naturalization Service Annual Report* (Washington, D.C.: U.S. Department of Justice, 1977).

42. Edna Bonacich, "The Development of U.S. Capitalism and Its Influence on Asian Immigration," unpublished paper, 1980.

43. Alexander Saxton, *The Indispensable Enemy: Labor and the Anti-Chinese Movement* (Berkeley and Los Angeles: University of California Press, 1971), p. 7.

44. Bonacich, "U.S. Capitalism and Korean Small Business."

45. William Bowen and T. Aldrich Finnegan, *The Economics of Labor Force Participation* (Princeton: Princeton University Press, 1969).

46. Bonacich, "The Development of U.S. Capitalism."

47. Saxton, *The Indispensable Enemy,* pp. 6–7. See also Paul Ong, "Chinese Labor in Early San Francisco: Racial Segmentation and Industrial Expansion," *Amerasia Journal* 8 (1981): 69–92. He shows that the Chinese were concentrated in industries that paid low wages, consisted of small firms, competed on the national market, or did not rely on skilled white craftsmen for some part of the production process.

48. Anti-Asian propagandists observed the concentration of Asians in female occupations and blamed the poor working conditions and low wages of women workers on competition from Asian labor. In 1888 John Tobin commented: "The coolie is the irrepressible foe of the female wage earner in every department of labor which requires merely the skilled use of hand and eye. He will cook, wash, iron, sew and do everything in the line of work which, in other climes and under more favored conditions, is considered the exclusive province of women." California Bureau of Labor Statistics, *Third Bienniel Report, 1887–1888* (Sacramento: 1888).

49. As Emma Gee aptly notes, most literature on the issei depicts them as "a nameless mass victimized by history. "Issei Women," in Emma Gee (ed.), *Counterpoint: Perspectives on Asian America* (Los Angeles: Asian American Studies Center, University of California, Los Angeles, 1976), p. 359.

50. Peter S. Li, "Fictive Kinship, Conjugal Tie and Kinship Chain Among Chinese Immigrants in the United States," *Journal of Comparative Family Studies* 8 (1977): 55–57, and Betty Sung, *Mountain of Gold* (New York: MacMillan, 1967), pp. 99–100.

51. Ichihashi, *Japanese in the United States,* pp. 291–96.

52. See Elizabeth H. Pleck, "A Mother's Wages: Income Earning Among Married Italian and Black Women, 1896–1911," in Nancy F. Cott and Elizabeth H. Pleck (eds.), *A Heritage of Her Own: Toward a New Social History of American Women* (New York: Touchstone, 1979), pp. 367–92; see p. 372 for a table comparing proportions of wage-earning wives and children in black, Italian, German, Polish, Russian Jewish, and Irish families.

Chapter 2

1. Sydney L. Gulick, *New Factors in American-Japanese Relations and a Constructive Proposal* (New York: National Committee on Japanese-American Relations, n.d.), p. 29, table b.
2. Yamato Ishihashi, *Japanese in the United States* (Stanford: Stanford University Press, 1932), p. 65.
3. Roger Daniels, "The Issei Generation," in Amy Takichi, Eddie Wong, and Franklin Odo, (eds.), *Roots: An Asian American Reader* (Los Angeles: Asian American Studies Center, University of California, Los Angeles. 1976), p. 142.
4. Alexander Saxton, *The Indispensable Enemy: Labor and the Anti-Chinese Movement* (Berkeley and Los Angeles: University of California Press, 1971), pp. 258–84.
5. Edna Bonacich, "The Development of U.S. Capitalism and Its Influence on Asian Immigration," unpublished paper, 1980.
6. For a discussion of Chinese return, see Stanford Lyman, "The Chinese Diaspora in America, 1850–1943," in his book of collected essays, *The Asian in North America* (Santa Barbara: ABC Clio Books, 1977), pp. 11–24. See Ichihashi, *Japanese in the United States*, for estimates of rate of Japanese return, pp. 65–66.
7. Melvin G. Konvitz, *The Alien and Asiatic in American Law* (Ithaca, N.Y.: Cornell University Press, 1946), pp. 79–96. Aside from legal attacks, the Chinese were victimized by periodic violence, including beatings, lynchings, and murder at the hands of hostile whites. See Lyman, *Chinese Americans*, pp. 58–62.
8. Saxton, *The Indispensable Enemy*, p. 7.
9. Stanford Lyman, "Strangers in the City: The Chinese in the Urban Frontier," in *The Asian in North America*, pp. 39–62.
10. Mary Coolidge, *Chinese Immigration* (New York: Henry Hold, 1909). The texts of the various laws are reprinted in Cheng Tsu Wu (ed.), *"Chink," A Documentary History of Anti-Chinese Prejudice in America* (New York: World Publishing, 1972), pp. 70–93.
11. Bonacich, "The Development of U.S. Capitalism."
12. Ichihashi, *Japanese in the United States*, pp. 3–5.

13. Daniels, "The Issei Generation," p. 140, and cf. Robert P. Dore, *Shinohata: A Portrait of a Japanese Village* (New York: Pantheon Books, 1978), pp. 39–42.
14. Ichihashi, *Japanese in the United States,* chap. 2.
15. Ibid., p. 90.
16. H. A. Millis, *The Japanese Problem in the United States* (New York: Macmillan, 1915), p. 31.
17. Ichihashi, *Japanese in the United States,* pp. 74–76.
18. Millis, *The Japanese Problem in the United States,* p. 5.
19. Ichihashi, *Japanese in the United States,* p. 10.
20. Ibid., p. 80.
21. Yukiko Irwin and Hilary Conroy, "R. W. Irwin and Systematic Immigration to Hawaii," in Hilary Conroy and T. Scott Miyakawa (eds.), *East Across the Pacific* (Santa Barbara: ABC Clio Books, 1972), pp. 40–55.
22. Shotaro Frank Miyamoto, "Social Solidarity Among the Japanese in Seattle," *University of Washington Publications in the Social Sciences* 11 (1939): 60.
23. Chie Nakane, *Kinship and Economic Organization in Rural Japan,* London School of Economics Monograph on Social Anthropology, 32 (London: Athlone Press, 1967), p. 32.
24. John F. Embree, *Suye Mura: A Japanese Village* (Chicago: University of Chicago Press, 1939), p. 79.
25. Miyamoto, "Social Solidarity Among the Japanese in Seattle," p. 60.
26. The first three periods are based on Miyamoto's ("Social Solidarity Among the Japanese in Seattle") analysis of stages in the development of the Seattle Japanese American community.
27. Edward K. Strong, Jr., *The Second-Generation Japanese Problem* (Stanford: Stanford University Press, 1934), p. 86.
28. Ichihashi, *Japanese in the United States,* pp. 106–77.
29. Ibid., p. 106, and Millis, *The Japanese Problem in the United States,* p. 28.
30. Ichihashi, *Japanese in the United States,* pp. 116–36.
31. Harry H. L. Kitano, "Housing of Japanese-Americans in the San Francisco Bay Area," in Nathan Glazer and Davis McEntire (eds.), *Studies in Housing and Minority Groups* (Berkeley and Los Angeles: University of California Press, 1960), pp. 178–97.
32. Cf. Murray Melbin, "Night as Frontier," *American Sociological Review* 43 (1978): 3–22.
33. Miyamoto, "Social Solidarity Among the Japanese in Seattle," p. 65.
34. Ivan H. Light, *Ethnic Enterprise in America: Business and Welfare Among Chinese, Japanese and Blacks* (Berkeley and Los Angeles: University of California Press, 1972), pp. 28–30.

35. Christie W. Kiefer, *Changing Cultures, Changing Lives* (San Francisco: Jossey-Bass, 1974), p. 11.

36. The matter is reported in U.S. Senate, *Japanese in the City of San Francisco*, message from the President of the United States Transmitting the Final Report of Secretary Metcalf on the Situation Affecting the Japanese in the City of San Francisco, Cal. Fifty-ninth Congress, Second Session, Document no. 147, December 18, 1906.

37. Ichihashi, *Japanese in the United States*, p. 65.

38. Ibid., p. 72.

39. Gulick, *New Factors*, p. 29, table b.

40. The *Yearbook of the Nichi Bei Times* is a directory of Japanese American residents, associations, and businesses in the Bay Area. Most Christian churches in the Japanese community were founded in the 1890s with the aid of white Protestant churches. The Buddhist churches, which were ethnically initiated, were founded and developed between 1900 and 1915. Oakland's church was the earliest (1901) followed by Berkeley's (1908) and Alameda's (1912). Japanese-language schools were usually attached to the churches. See *Buddhist Churches of America* (1975) and *Eighty-Fifth Anniversary of Protestant Work* (1974), volumes privately printed in Japan by the Buddhist and Christian churches respectively.

41. Information from several community informants.

42. Kitano, "Housing of Japanese Americans," p. 183.

43. Ichihashi, *Japanese in the United States*, pp. 296, 300–18.

44. Miyamoto, "Social Solidarity Among the Japanese in Seattle," p. 66.

45. Strong, *The Second Generation Japanese Problem*, p. 157.

46. Strong makes this point (ibid., pp. 208–51), as do community informants. John Modell found similar patterns of restricted opportunities in his study of nisei employment in Los Angeles in the 1930s: *The Economics and Politics of Ethnic Accommodation: The Japanese of Los Angeles, 1900–1942* (Urbana: University of Illinois Press, 1977), pp. 127–54.

47. Kitano, "Housing of Japanese Americans," p. 184.

48. Ibid., p. 184.

49. Harry H. L. Kitano, *Japanese Americans: The Evolution of a Subculture*, 2d ed. (Englewood Cliffs, N.J.: Prentice-Hall, 1976), p. 91.

50. Bok-Lim C. Kim, "Asian Wives of U.S. Servicemen: Women in the Shadows," *Amerasia Journal* 4 (1977): 98–100.

51. Akemi Kikumura and Harry H. L. Kitano, "Interracial Marriage: A Picture of the Japanese Americans," *Journal of Social Issues* 29 (1973): 67–81. See also John N. Tinker, "Intermarriage and Ethnic Boundaries: The Japanese American Case," *Journal of Social Issues* 29 (1973): 49–66.

52. This pattern is not much different from that found in most American organizations. See Diane R. Margolis, "The Invisible Hands: Sex Roles and the Division of Labor in Two Local Political Parties," *Social Problems* 26 (1979): 314–22.

Chapter 3

1. John F. Embree, *Suye Mura: A Japanese Village* (Chicago: The University of Chicago Press, 1939), pp. 8 and 190.

2. Edward K. Strong, Jr., *The Second-Generation Japanese Problem* (Stanford: Stanford University Press, 1934).

3. Edward K. Strong, Jr., *Japanese in California* (Stanford: Stanford University Press, 1933).

4. Although the women spoke of the decision as having been made by their parents, the father appears to have had the ultimate authority. The full range of attitudes among the women cannot be captured by a one dimensional scale; however, roughly arranging the women's attitudes from "most reluctant" to "most eager," the following range of feelings can be identified:
   1. Felt tricked, went reluctantly
   2. Were persuaded, inveigled by the parents with promises for the future
   3. Were "carefree," thought it would be a new experience
   4. Felt that the chosen mate or immigration to the United States was better than another alternative
   5. Aspired to come to the United States; parents concurred
   6. Aspired to come to the United States; had to overcome parents' reluctance

5. During this period, some Japanese women had to marry men who were emigrating because of the shortage of men remaining in Japan. This was a time of Japanese expansionism. Young men were colonizing Manchuria and Korea as well as seeking their fortunes in Hawaii and the mainland United States. Among the various destinations, the United States was viewed as offering the most favorable conditions for women. Mrs. Sugihara reports:
   > I was among the lucky ones, coming to America as I did. I almost wound up in Manchuria, you know. In Japan, the woman doesn't go out hunting for a husband. We used a go-between. The marriage arrangement offer from Mr. Sugihara came a week before the one from the person going to Manchuria. So my father rejected the latter offer.

6. Yuji Ichioka, "Japanese Immigrant Women in the United States, 1900–1924," *Pacific Historical Review* 49 (1980): 346.

7. Ibid., p. 347.

8. Financially better off immigrants could get outfitted in Yokohama before leaving. Mrs. Kono, a 91-year-old issei who was one of the non-domestic informants, went to a tailor there for dresses, hats, purses, and shoes, which were made by Chinese, and a parasol. She described the outfits as distinctive and always blue in color. The vast majority of women, however, arrived wearing kimonos and obtained western clothing after debarking.

9. Theresa Watanabe, "A Report from the Japanese American Community Study" (Department of Anthropology, University of Washington, 1977), p. 24.

10. Ichioka, "Japanese Immigrant Women in the United States," p. 350.

11. Harry H. L. Kitano, *Japanese Americans: The Evolution of a Subculture*, 2d ed. (Englewood Cliffs, N.J.: Prentice-Hall, 1976), p. 42.

12. Yamato Ichihashi, *Japanese in the United States* (Stanford: Stanford University Press, 1932). p. 71.

13. Dorothy S. Thomas and Richard Nishimoto, *The Spoilage* (Berkeley and Los Angeles: University of California Press, 1946), pp. 4 and 31.

14. Roger Daniels, *The Politics of Prejudice* (New York: Atheneum, 1973), p. 14.

15. Monica Sone, *Nisei Daughter* (Seattle and London: University of Washington Press, 1953), p. 22.

16. Christie W. Kiefer, *Changing Cultures, Changing Lives* (San Francisco: Jossey-Bass, 1974), p. 209.

17. Stanford Lyman, "Generation and Character: The Case of Japanese Americans," in Hilary Conroy and T. Scott Miyakawa (eds.), *East Across the Pacific* (Santa Barbara: ABC Clio Books, 1972), p. 285.

18. Alexander Leighton, *The Governing of Men* (Princeton, N.J.: Princeton University Press, 1954), p. 81.

19. Kitano, *Japanese Americans*, p. 189.

20. Ibid., p. 27.

21. Bok-Lim C. Kim, "Asian Wives of U.S. Servicemen: Women in the Shadows," *Amerasia Journal* 4(1977): 97–98.

Chapter 4

1. William Bowen and T. Aldrich Finnegan, *The Economics of Labor Force Participation* (Princeton: Princeton University Press, 1969), 159–64.

2. H. A. Mills, *The Japanese Problem in the United States* (New York: Macmillan, 1915), p. 20.

3. Percent of Japanese women ten years of age and over engaged in gainful employment calculated from U.S. Bureau of the Census, *Fourteenth Census of the United States Taken in the Year 1920, vol. 4, Population,* "Occupations" (Washington, D.C.: U.S. Government Printing Office,

1923), table 5: "Total Persons 10 Years of Age and Over Engaged in Each Specfied Occupation, Classified by Sex, Color or Nativity, and Parentage, for the United States, 1920." Percent of white women fourteen years of age and over gainfully employed from U.S. Bureau of the Census, *Historical Statistics of the United States, Colonial Times to 1957* (Washington, D.C.: U.S. Government Printing Office, 1960), series D 26–35: "Civilian Labor Force by Color and Sex, and Marital Status of Women, 1890 to 1957."

4. U.S. Bureau of the Census, *Historical Statistics of the United States, Colonial Times to 1970,* Bicentennial Edition, pt. 2 (Washington, D.C.: U.S. Government Printing Office, 1975), series D 49-62: "Marital Status of Women in the Civilian Labor Force, 1890 to 1970."

5. Edward K. Strong, Jr., *Japanese in California* (Stanford: Stanford University Press, 1933), pp. 108–9.

6. Only in the 1910 census were enumerators instructed to pay special attention to the gainful activities of women and children and to count unpaid family workers in agriculture. These special instructions led to a rise in the number of women reported as gainfully employed. See Joseph A. Hill, *Women in Gainful Occupations, 1870 to 1920,* U.S. Bureau of the Census, Census Monographs, 9 (Washington, D.C.: U.S. Government Printing Office, 1929), for a discussion of the issue.

7. This figure is lower than would be expected on the basis of geographic distributions. From 1900 to 1940, about one-half of the Japanese lived in rural areas, according to census figures compiled by Leonard Bloom and Ruth Reimer (*Removal and Return: The Socio-Economic Effects of the War on Japanese Americans* [Berkeley and Los Angeles: University of California Press, 1949], p. 8). The low figure for female agricultural workers in the census may be due to the underreporting of unpaid family workers, as mentioned in n. 6 above.

8. Definitive figures on Japanese employment in 1910 are unavailable. Occupational tables from that census display only aggregate data for Chinese and Japanese combined. However, since the Chinese female labor force grew very little between 1900 and 1920, the 1910 distributions for the Japanese can be estimated in the following way. We assume that the figures for the Chinese were the same in 1910 as in 1900. We then subtract the 1900 Chinese figure from each 1910 combined figure. The remainder in each category should be an approximation of the 1910 Japanese total. Using this method, I estimate that gainfully employed Japanese women numbered 1,800, of whom about 540, or 30 percent, were employed as "servants."

9. If data for issei and nisei are combined, the percentage in domestic work actually goes up slightly in 1940. This is because the nisei were more heavily concentrated in domestic work than the issei.

10. This information was provided by an issei community informant.

11. The concept of informal market work has been developed in the literature on women and economic development to designate income-producing activities that are overlooked in formal labor market analyses. See Lourdes Arizpe, "Women in the Informal Labor Sector: The Case of Mexico City," *Signs* 3 (1977): 25–31.

12. See n. 10.

13. Shotaro Frank Miyamoto, "Social Solidarity Among the Japanese in Seattle," *University of Washington Publications in the Social Sciences* 11 (1939): 76.

14. Edna Bonacich and John Modell, *The Economic Basis of Ethnic Solidarity: Small Business in the Japanese American Community* (Berkeley and Los Angeles: University of California Press, 1980), table 6:1, p. 99.

15. Ibid.

16. Ibid., p. 107.

17. Bonacich and Modell, *The Economic Basis of Ethnic Solidarity*, p. 96, and Bloom and Reimer, *Removal and Return*, pp. 106–9.

18. For 1930, U.S. Bureau of the Census, *Fifteenth Census of the United States: 1930, Population*, vol. 2, *General Report, Statistics by Subjects*, chap. 2: "Color or Race, Nativity and Parentage" (Washington, D.C.: U.S. Government Printing Office, 1933), table 3: "Urban, Rural-farm, and Rural-nonfarm Population of the United States, by Color, Nativity, and Parentage, 1930." For 1970, U.S. Bureau of the Census, *Census of the Population: 1970, Subject Reports*, Final Report PC(2)-1G, *Japanese, Chinese, and Filipinos in the United States* (Washington, D.C.: U.S. Government Printing Office, 1973), table 1: "Japanese Population by Sex and Urban and Rural Residence, 1970." The 1970 percentage is based on U.S. mainland only.

19. Bonacich and Modell, *The Economic Basis of Ethnic Solidarity*, p. 99.

20. Employment rates for all women by age group for 1960 and 1970 calculated from U.S. Department of Labor, *Handbook of Labor Statistics, 1974* (Washington, D.C.: U.S. Government Printing Office, 1974), table 3: "Civilian Labor Force by Sex, Color, and Age, 1947–73," and table 4: "Civilian Labor Force Participation Rates for Persons 16 Years and Over, by Sex, Color and Age, 1947–73." Employment rates for Japanese women by age group for 1960 and 1970 calculated from U.S. Bureau of the Census, *U.S. Census of the Population, 1960: Subject Reports: Non-white Population by Race,* Final Report PC(2)-1C (Washington, D.C.: U.S. Government Printing Office, 1963), table 39: "Economic Characteristics of the Japanese Population 14 Years and Over, by Age, for the United States, by Regions, Urban and Rural, and for Selected States, 1960," and U.S. Bureau of the Census, *Census of the Population, 1970: Subject Reports:* Final Report PC(2)-1G, table 2:

"Age of the Japanese Population by Sex and Urban and Rural Residence, 1970," and table 4: "Economic Characteristics of the Japanese Population by Urban and Rural Residence, 1970."

21. U.S. Bureau of the Census, *Census of the Population, 1970: Subject Reports:* Final Report PC(2) -1G, tables 2 and 4.

22. The dual labor market model has been explicated in a number of sources, including David M. Gordon (ed.), *Theories of Poverty and Underemployment: Orthodox, Radical and Dual Labor Market Perspectives* (Lexington, Mass.: D.C. Heath, 1972), and Peter B. Doeringer and Michael C. Piore, *Internal Labor Markets and Manpower Analysis* (Lexington, Mass.: D. C. Heath, 1971).

23. Anselm Strauss, "Strain and Harmony in American-Japanese War Bride Marriages," *Marriage and Family Living* 16 (1954): 103.

24. Gerald J. Schnepp and Agnes M. Yui, "Cultural and Marital Adjustment of Japanese War Brides," *American Journal of Sociology* 61 (1955): 48.

25. Harry H. L. Kitano, *Japanese Americans: The Evolution of a Subculture,* 2d ed. (Englewood Cliffs, N.J.: Prentice-Hall, 1976), p. 161.

26. See tables 5 and 7 for percentages of issei and nisei workers in domestic service. For percentage of white women employed in the occupation, see U.S. Bureau of the Census, *U.S. Census of the Population, 1960:* vol. 1, *Characteristics of the Population,* pt. 1, *United States Summary* (Washington, D.C.: U.S. Government Printing Office, 1964), table 205: "Occupation of the Experienced Labor Force and of the Employed, and Unemployment Rate, by Color and Sex, for the United States, 1960."

27. Patricia A. Roos and Joyce F. Hennessy, "Assimilation or Exclusion? Attainment Processes of Japanese, Mexican Americans, and Anglos in California," paper presented at the meetings of the American Sociological Association, San Antonio, August 1984.

Chapter 5

1. Amey Watson, "Domestic Service," *Encyclopedia of the Social Sciences* (New York: Macmillan, 1937), 5: 198; George J. Stigler, "Domestic Servants in the United States, 1900–1940," Occasional Paper 24 (New York: National Bureau of Economic Research, 1946); Janet M. Hooks, "Women's Occupations Through Seven Decades," U.S. Department of Labor Women's Bureau Bulletin no. 218 (Washington, D.C.: U.S. Government Printing Office, 1947). A comprehensive history of domestic service covering earlier labor forms, such as indenture, is beyond the scope of this review. For a description and analysis of domestic service in the colonial and post-revolutionary periods, see Lucy Maynard Salmon,

Domestic Service (New York: Macmillan, 1897; reprint ed., New York: Arno Press, 1972).

2. For example, David M. Katzman, *Seven Days a Week: Women and Domestic Service in Industrializing America* (New York: Oxford University Press, 1978); Theresa McBride, *The Domestic Revolution: The Modernisation of Household Service in England and France 1820–1920* (New York: Holmes and Meier, 1976); David Chaplin, "Domestic Service and Industrialization," *Comparative Studies in Sociology* 1 (1978): 97–127.

3. Genevieve Leslie, "Domestic Service in Canada, 1889–1920," in *Women at Work* (Toronto: Canadian Women's Educational Press, 1974), pp. 71–126.

4. Cf. Harry K. Braverman, *Labor and Monopoly Capital: The Degradation of Work in the Twentieth Century* (New York and London: Monthly Review Press, 1974), pp. 362–66.

5. Jane Addams, "A Belated Industry," *American Journal of Sociology* 1 (1896): 536–50; Lewis Coser, "Servants: The Obsolescence of a Social Role," *Social Forces* 52 (1973): 31–40.

6. Chaplin, "Domestic Service and Industrialization," p. 98.

7. McBride, *The Domestic Revolution;* Leonard Broom and S. H. Smith, "Bridging Occupations," *British Journal of Sociology* 14 (1963): 321–34; Margo L. Smith, "Domestic Service as a Channel of Upward Mobility for the Lower-Class Woman: The Lima Case," in Ann Pescatello (ed.), *Female and Male in Latin America: Essays* (Pittsburgh: University of Pittsburgh Press, 1973), pp. 192–207; Chaplin, "Domestic Service and Industrialization"; Arizpe, "Women in the Informal Labor Sector; The Case of Mexico City," *Signs* 3 (1977): 25–31.

8. For proportions from 1870 to 1930, see Katzman, *Seven Days a Week,* table 2-2, p. 53. For 1970, see U.S. Bureau of the Census, *Historical Statistics of the United States, Colonial Times to 1970,* Bicentennial ed., pt. 1, chap. D, Labor (Washington, D.C.: U.S. Government Printing Office, 1975) series D 182–232 (table): "Major Occupation Group of the Experienced Civilian Labor Force, by Sex, 1900 to 1970."

9. E.g., Addams, "A Belated Industry"; Salmon, *Domestic Service.*

10. Salmon, *Domestic Service,* pp. 78–80; Katzman, *Seven Days a Week,* pp. 66–69.

11. E.g., Lawrence A. Glasco, "Ethnicity and Social Structure: Irish, German, and Native Born of Buffalo, New York, 1850–1860" (Ph.D. diss., State University of New York at Buffalo, 1973); Susan Kleinberg, "Technology's Stepdaughter: The Impact of Industrialization Upon Working Women" (Ph.D. diss., University of Pittsburgh, 1975).

12. Glasco, "Ethnicity," quoted by Katzman, *Seven Days a Week,* p. 80.

13. Ibid., p. 67.
14. Albert Camarillo, *Chicanos in a Changing Society* (Cambridge: Harvard University Press, 1979), p. 91.
15. Mario T. Garcia, *Desert Immigrants: The Mexicans of El Paso, 1880–1920* (New Haven: Yale University Press, 1981), p. 326.
16. Mario T. Garcia, "The Chicana in American History: The Mexican Women of El Paso, 1880–1920—A Case Study," *Pacific Historical Review* 44 (1980): 326–27.
17. C. Arnold Anderson and Mary Jean Bowman, "The Vanishing Servant and the Contemporary Status System of the American South," *American Journal of Sociology* 59 (1953): 215–30.
18. David M. Katzman, *Before the Ghetto: Black Detroit in the Nineteenth Century* (Urbana: University of Ilinois Press, 1973), pp. 107–8; Katzman, *Seven Days a Week*, pp. 71–80; W. E. B. DuBois, *The Philadelphia Negro: A Social Study Together with a Special Report on Domestic Service by Isabel Eaton* (1899; reprint ed., New York: Schocken Books, 1967), p. 435–36.
19. Gerda Lerner, *Black Women in White America: A Documentary History* (New York: Vintage Books, 1973), pp. 238–40; Katzman, *Before the Ghetto*, pp. 104–8; Katzman, *Seven Days a Week*, pp. 73–74.
20. Katzman, *Seven Days a Week*, p. 76–80.
21. Diane Nilsen Westcott, "Blacks in the 1970s: Did They Scale the Job Ladder?" *Monthly Labor Review* (June 1982): 29–38, table 2.
22. Charles B. Keely, "Effects of the Manpower Provision of the U.S. Immigration Law," paper presented at the Population Association of America Annual Meeting, 1974.
23. E.g., McBride, *The Domestic Revolution*, pp. 82–95; Broom and Smith, "Bridging Occupations"; Smith, "Domestic Service as a Channel of Upward Mobility."
24. Salmon, *Domestic Service*, pp. 140–50.
25. Katzman, *Seven Days a Week*, pp. 14–21, 144.
26. Stigler, "Domestic Servants in the United States," pp. 6–7.
27. Katzman, *Seven Days a Week*, p. 90.
28. Camarillo, *Chicanos in a Changing Society*, p. 219.
29. Katzman, *Seven Days a Week*, p. 56.
30. Ibid., p. 55.
31. Ibid.
32. Di Vernon, "The Chinese as House Servants," *Good Housekeeping* 12 (January 1891): 20–22; Jean Faison, "The Virtues of the Chinese Servant," *Good Housekeeping* 42 (March 1906): 279–80.
33. Katzman, *Seven Days a Week*, p. 222, partly quoting Vernon, "The Chinese as House Servants."

34. Eliot Grinnell Mears, *Resident Orientals on the American Pacific Coast* (Chicago: University of Chicago Press, 1927), p. 314.

35. Alexander Saxton, *The Indispensable Enemy: Labor and the Anti-Chinese Movement* (Berkeley and Los Angeles: University of California Press, 1971), p. 7.

36. Roger Daniels, "The Issei Generation," in Amy Takichi, Eddie Wong, and Franklin Odo (eds.), *Roots: An Asian American Reader* (Los Angeles: Asian American Studies Center, University of California, Los Angeles, 1976), p. 139. However, because of their age and gender distribution and able-bodied status, they were undoubtedly a larger proportion of the labor force.

37. Yamato Ichihashi, *Japanese in the United States* (Stanford: Stanford University Press, 1932), p. 109.

38. Daniels, "The Issei Generation," p. 145.

39. H. A. Millis, *The Japanese Problem in the United States* (New York: Macmillan, 1915), p. 31.

40. *Alameda Argus,* May 1, 1900.

41. Ichihashi, *Japanese in the United States,* p. 110. See also the curious anonymous "autobiography"—"The Confessions of a Japanese Servant"—reprinted from an early labor periodical, in Leon Stein and Philip Taft (eds.), *American Labor: From Conspiracy to Collective Bargaining* (New York: Arno and the New York Times, 1971).

42. Mears, *Resident Orientals,* p. 313.

43. Edward K. Strong, Jr., *Japanese in California* (Stanford: Stanford University Press, 1933), pp. 115–17, 120–29.

44. *Alameda Argus,* January 25, 1909.

45. Mark S. Granovetter, "The Strength of Weak Ties," *American Journal of Sociology* 78 (1973): 1360–80, notes that a member of a cohesive network with strong ties gets much less extensive information—for example, about potential jobs—than an individual in a loose-knit but broadly cast network.

46. Daniels, "The Issei Generation," p. 147.

47. Mrs. Ikeda was not included in the main analysis because of an equipment malfunction that ruined the tape recording of her interview.

48. Mrs. Kawai is technically a kibei, though she is within the same age group as the issei and culturally similar to them. She was born in the United States, but was raised from age 4 in Japan. She returned to the United States in her mid-twenties, following marriage to an issei.

49. Robert J. Myers, *Social Security* (Homewood, Ill.: Irwin, 1975), p. 84.

50. The main exceptions to this pattern, aside from those who entered domestic work after World War II, were a kibei who entered day work immediately upon returning to the United States, a Hawaiian nisei

who was a laundress in a sorority house, and a rural nisei who obtained a full-time live-in housekeeping position as a teenager with no experience and eventually became a professional servant.

51. T. Scott Miyakawa, personal communication. Domestic work in Japan was ordinarily accorded low status. In this instance, however, it was viewed not as a job, but as a form of education and training. The prestige and position of the family in which one served lent respectability to the position.

52. Tamara Harevan found that age of marriage went up among daughters in French Canadian immigrant families employed in the textile mills. Presumably parents were anxious to delay the marriage of their wage-earning daughters because they contributed to household income. See Tamara Harevan, "Family Time and Industrial Time: Family and Work in a Planned Corporation Town, 1900–1914," *Journal of Urban History* 1 (1975): 365–89.

53. Relatives who found placements for the kibei included a mother, aunt, mother-in-law, and father-in-law.

54. U.S. Department of Labor, "Private Household Workers, Fact Sheet," (Washington, D.C.: Women's Bureau, 1970), p. 3.

55. U.S. Department of Labor, *Handbook on Women Workers, 1983* (Washington, D.C.: U.S. Government Printing Office, 1984), table II-7, p. 66.

56. Chaplin, "Domestic Service and Industrialization," pp. 123–24.

57. Kopp Michelotti, "Multiple Job Holding," *Monthly Labor Review* 97 (May 1973): 64–9.

58. Katzman, "Domestic Service: Women's Work," p. 380.

Chapter 6

1. Helen Campbell, *Prisoners of Poverty: Women Wage-Workers—Their Trades and Their Lives* (Boston: Little, Brown, 1900); Lucy Maynard Salmon, *Domestic Service,* (New York: Macmillan, 1897; reprinted., New York: Arno Press, 1972); Amey Watson, "Domestic Service," *Encyclopedia of the Social Sciences* (New York: Macmillan, 1937), pp. 198–207.

2. Perhaps the point is made clearer by Harry K. Braverman's remark in *Labor and Monopoly Capital: The Degradation of Work in the Twentieth Century* (New York and London: Monthly Review Press, 1974), p. 364–65, that although the work of a cleaner employed by a firm that sells cleaning services generates profit and thereby increases the employer's capital, the same work performed by a servant in the home actually reduces the employer's wealth.

3. Margaret Benston, "The Political Economy of Women's Liberation," in Edith Hoshino Altbach (ed.), *From Feminism to Liberation* (Cambridge, Mass., and London: Schenkman, 1971), pp. 199–210.

4. Edith Abbott, *Women in Industry: A Study in American Economic History* (New York and London: D. Appleton, 1910); p. 16; David Chaplin, "Domestic Service and Industrialization," *Comparative Studies in Sociology* 1 (1978): 99.

5. John F. Embree, *Suye Mura: A Japanese Village* (Chicago: University of Chicago Press, 1939), p. 80.

6. Chaplin, "Domestic Service and Industrialization," p. 99.

7. David H. Katzman, *Seven Days a Week: Women and Domestic Service in Industrializing America* (New York: Oxford University Press, 1978), p. 85.

8. Ruth Schwartz Cowan, "The Industrial Revolution in the Home: Household Technology and Social Change in the Twentieth Century," *Technological Culture* 17 (1976): 1–23.

9. Susan McCoin Kataoka, "Issei Women: A Study in Subordinate Status" (Ph.D. diss., University of California, Los Angeles, 1977).

10. Women's Bureau, U.S. Department of Labor, *1975 Handbook on Women Workers* (Washington, D.C.: U.S. Department of Labor, 1975), pp. 319–20; David M. Katzman, "Domestic Service: Women's Work," in Ann H. Stomberg and Shirley Harkess (eds.), *Women Working* (Palo Alto, Calif.: Mayfield, 1978), p. 383.

11. Katzman, *Seven Days a Week*, pp. 303–14; George J. Stigler, "Domestic Servants in the United States, 1900–1940," Occasional Paper 24 (New York: National Bureau of Economic Research, 1946), pp. 12–20.

12. Domestic workers were first covered by federal minimum wage laws in 1974 and by California wage laws somewhat earlier (Women's Bureau, *1975 Handbook on Women Workers*), pp. 319–20.

13. Jane Addams, "A Belated Industry," *American Journal of Sociology* 1 (1896): 536.

14. Lewis Coser, "Servants: The Obsolescence of a Social Role," *Social Forces* 52 (1973): 32.

15. On occasion the ties between employers and workers may even transcend generations, so that families are linked in a quasi-feudal relationship. Family members may carry on obligations contracted in the prior generation. Mrs. Ito, for example, started going to help an elderly couple for whom her mother-in-law had worked:

    His [her husband's] mother used to go and his folks used to do the garden. They used to be on L Street, but now they're on the P——. I haven't been working there that long. But she called me and every once in a while she loses somebody and she comes and asks me if I have time. So I finally go there and I don't think she's ever let me go . . . I usually go about nine o'clock and we have lunch together and have lots of things in common and discuss such things. They help me in a lot of things. They know him [her husband] before he came back from Japan too. [Her husband is a kibei.]

16. Coser, "Servants," p. 36.

17. Katzman (*Seven Days a Week*, pp. 176–79) points out that employers preferred live-in help and deplored the trend toward live-out help because the former system gave them greater control over the domestic's life.

Chapter 7

1. Studies of long-unemployed men show that the absence of work undermines workers' identities and the lack of the structure imposed by a job makes them dispirited and purposeless. See E. Wight Bakke, *The Unemployed Worker* (New Haven: Yale University Press, 1940); Eli Ginzberg, *Grass on the Slag Heaps* (New York: Harper, 1942); and Charles Winick, "Atonie: The Psychology of the Unemployed and the Marginal Worker," in George Fish (ed.), *The Frontiers of Management Psychology* (New York: Harper & Row, 1964).

2. Using Meissner's terminology, one might say that domestic work is subject to few *technical* constraints. It is precisely this lack of technological innovation that has rendered domestic work so anachronistic. See Martin Meissner, "The Long Arm of the Job: A Study of Work and Leisure," *Industrial Relations* 10 (1971): 239–60.

3. Theodore Caplow, *The Sociology of Work* (New York: McGraw-Hill, 1954), p. 48.

4. Catherine Berheide, Sara Fenstermaker Berk, and Richard A. Berk, "Household Work in the Suburbs: The Job and Its Participants," *Pacific Sociological Review* 19 (1976): 491–518.

5. Ann Oakley, *The Sociology of Housework* (New York: Pantheon Books, 1974), pp. 41–60.

6. Caplow, *The Sociology of Work*, pp. 32–33.

7. Genevieve Leslie, "Domestic Service in Canada, 1889–1920" in *Women at Work* (Toronto: Canadian Women's Educational Press), p. 82. The determination of skill levels is fraught with difficulty. The U.S. Department of Labor publishes the *Dictionary of Occupational Titles*, which rates jobs in terms of complexity on three dimensions: concepts, people, and things. A three-digit number is assigned to each occupation to represent its rating on each of the dimensions, a seemingly objective measure. However, a research group in Wisconsin found systematic

biases in the ratings so that traditionally female occupations, such as childcare, were scored artificially low, even on the "people" dimension. See Mary Witt and Patricia K. Naherny, *Women's Work: Up from .878, Report on the DOT Research Project,* final report for the Manpower Administration, U.S. Department of Labor (Madison, Wisc.: University of Wisconsin—Extension, 1975), pp. 28–30. Harry Braverman (*Labor and Monopoly Capital: The Degradation of Work in the Twentieth Century* [New York and London: Monthly Review Press, 1974], pp. 424–47) argues that most classification schemes are artificial and not based on actual evaluation of tasks. Jobs involving use of machinery, even if only machine tending, are assumed to be more skilled than those requiring "traditional" knowledge, such as fishing or lumbering. A reading of these sources suggests that skill ratings also reflect relative ease of access to training. Occupations for which access to training is closely controlled, making it difficult to secure, are rated as more skilled. This argument fits domestic work. Training in domestic skills is available to all females by virtue of socialization in the home; domestic work is thus seen as unskilled. In contrast, training in male-dominated crafts can be obtained only through closed apprenticeship programs, and these jobs are viewed as skilled.

8. Caplow, *The Sociology of Work,* p. 48.

9. Everett C. Hughes, *Men and Their Work* (Glencoe, Ill.: Free Press, 1958), pp. 49–52.

10. Large-scale cleaning using heavy equipment may take on a heroic cast. Thus, workers who operate large streetcleaning vehicles on city streets are accorded higher status than workers who push a broom and cart to accomplish the same task.

11. Barry Gruenberg, "The Happy Worker: An Analysis of Educational and Occupational Differences in Determinants of Job Satisfaction," *American Journal of Sociology* 86 (1980): 247–71.

12. Nancy Morse and Robert Weiss, "The Functions and Meaning of Work and the Job," *American Sociological Review* 20 (1955): 191–98; John Goldthorpe, David Lockwood, Frank Bechhoffer, and Jennifer Platt, *The Affluent Worker in the Class Structure* (London: Cambridge University Press, 1969).

13. Robert Dubin, "Industrial Workers' Worlds," *Social Problems* 3 (1956): 131–42.

14. In general, women's reactions to employers could be classified on the basis of two dimensions, the functional and the expressive. Functional responses were those relating to the employers' role in providing services or promoting desired goals. In this category were numerous responses indicating that good employers were those who (1) left workers alone to

do the job as they saw fit and (2) gave the workers positive feedback about the results of their work. Expressive responses were those indicating affectionate bonding—that is, attraction to the employer as a person, as distinct from utilitarian considerations. In this category were responses showing satisfaction with employers who (1) had similar viewpoints, philosophy, or values, and (2) showed mutuality in the relationship (i.e., reciprocal caring). See Edwin Locke, "The Nature and Causes of Job Satisfaction," in Marvin D. Dunnette (ed.), *Handbook of Industrial and Organizational Psychology* (Chicago: Rand McNally College Publishing, 1976), pp. 1297–349, for a discussion of these two dimensions in the employer-employee relationship.

15. In the other two cases the information was not obtained. After the third war bride I interviewed volunteered the information, I systematically asked the rest if they had told their relatives. All reported that they hid their employment from at least some of their relatives in Japan.

16. See Richard H. Hall, *Occupations and the Social Structure,* 2d ed. (Englewood Cliffs, N.J.: Prentice-Hall, 1975), pp. 232–33, for a discussion of the status of domestic servants.

Chapter 8

1. Frederick Engels, *The Origin of the Family, Private Property and the State* (New York: International Publishers, 1972). For later critiques and elaborations, see Karen Sacks, "Engels Revisited: Women, the Organization of Production, and Private Property," in Michelle Zimbalist Rosaldo and Louise Lamphere (eds.), *Woman, Culture, and Society* (Stanford, Calif.: Stanford University Press, 1974), pp. 207–22; Michele Barrett, *Women's Oppression Today: Problems in Marxist Feminist Analysis* (London: Verso, 1980), pp. 187–226; and Lise Vogel, *Marxism and the Oppression of Women: Toward a Unitary Theory* (New Brunswick, N.J.: Rutgers University Press, 1983), pp. 29–37 and 73–92 especially.

2. Barrie Thorne, "Feminist Rethinking of the Family: An Overview," in Barrie Thorne with Marilyn Yalom (eds.), *Rethinking the Family: Some Feminist Questions* (New York: Longman, 1982), p. 18.

3. Ibid., pp. 1–24; Heidi Hartmann, "The Family as a Locus of Gender, Class and Political Struggle: The Example of Housework," *Signs* 6 (1981): 366–95.

4. The concept of the indigenous family as a culture of resistance to colonial or neo-colonial domination was developed by Mina Davis Caulfield in her classic article "Imperialism, the Family and Cultures of Resistance," *Socialist Revolution* 20 (1974): 67–85. Other important formulations of the family as a source of resistance to oppression and

exploitation include Angela Davis, "Reflections on the Black Woman's Role in the Community of Slaves," *The Black Scholar* 3 (1971): 3–15 and Jane Humphries, "Class Struggle and the Persistence of the Working Class Family," *Cambridge Journal of Economics* 1 (1977): 241–58. Charles V. Willie (*A New Look at Black Families,* 2d ed. [Bayside, N.Y.: General Hall, 1981], p. 48 and pp. 183–85), asserts that even among affluent black families, the need to contend with racism promotes a more equal partnership between husband and wife and fosters a sense of a common family mission.

5. Rayna Rapp, "Family and Class in Contemporary America: Notes Toward an Understanding of Ideology," in Thorne and Yalom, *Rethinking the Family,* pp. 168–87.

6. Harry Braverman, *Labor and Monopoly Capital: The Degradation of Work in the Twentieth Century* (New York: Monthly Review Press, 1975), p. 139, talks about the "natural resistance" of the worker; Richard Edwards, *Contested Terrain: The Transformation of the Workplace in the Twentieth Century* (New York: Basic Books, 1979), pp. 11–16, discusses worker resistance as a feature of all workplaces.

7. Paul S. Taylor, "Mexican Labor in the United States: Valley of the South Platte, Colorado," *University of California Publications in Economics* 6, no. 2 (June 1929): 134.

8. Herbert G. Gutman, "Persistent Myths About the Afro-American Family," *Journal of Interdisciplinary History* 6 (1975): 181–210.

9. For a perspective on women's labor in the family under slavery, see Jacqueline Jones, "My Mother Was Much of a Woman: Black Women, Work and the Family Under Slavery," *Feminist Studies* 8 (1982): 235–69. The most comprehensive analysis of the black family both during and after slavery is Herbert G. Gutman, *The Black Family in Slavery and Freedom: 1750–1925* (New York: Random House, 1976).

10. Richard Griswold Del Castillo (*La Familia: Chicano Families in the Urban Southwest, 1848 to the Present* [Notre Dame, Ind.: University of Notre Dame Press, 1984], p. 79), discusses efforts to outlaw the speaking of Spanish in public schools in the Southwest, as well as Chicano initiatives to establish separate schools to preserve the language.

11. Mario T. Garcia ("The Chicana: The Mexican Women of El Paso, 1880–1920—A Case Study," *Pacific Historical Review* 44 [1980]: 315–37) makes the case that women were the guardians of Mexican cultural traditions in the family, including the retention of traditional folklore, songs, ballads, birthday celebrations, weddings, and other observances, as well as Mexican-style cooking and folk medicine.

12. Evelyn Nakano Glenn, "Split Household, Small Producer and Dual Wage Earner: An Analysis of Chinese American Family Strategies," *Journal of Marriage and the Family* 45 (1983): 38.

13. Stanford Lyman, "Strangers in the City: The Chinese in the Urban Frontier," in *The Asian in North America* (Santa Barbara: ABC Clio Press, 1977), pp. 39–62.
14. Yuji Ichioka, "Japanese Immigrant Women in the United States, 1900–1924," *Pacific Historical Review* 49 (1980): 339–57.
15. U.S. Bureau of the Census, *Fifteenth Census of the United States, 1930: Population*, vol. 5: *General Report on Occupations* (Washington, D.C.: U.S. Government Printing Office, 1933), table 6.
16. Theresa Watanabe, "A Report from the Japanese American Community Study" (Department of Anthropology, University of Washington, 1977), pp. 21–26.
17. V. S. McClatchy, U.S. Senate Japanese Immigration Hearings, 68th Cong., 1st sess. (Washington, D.C.: U.S. Government Printing Office, 1924), pp. 5–6, quoted by Roger Daniels, *The Politics of Prejudice* (New York: Atheneum, 1973), p. 99.
18. The gnawing fear that lies under the surface ease of even the most successful Japanese Americans as a result of the trauma of internment is articulated by Gene Oishi in "The Anxiety of Being a Japanese American," *New York Times Magazine* (April 28, 1985): 54, 58–59.

Chapter 9

1. Chie Nakane, *Japanese Society* (Berkeley and Los Angeles: University of California Press, 1970), p. 7.
2. Chie Nakane, *Kinship and Economic Organization in Rural Japan*, London School of Economics Monographs on Social Anthropology No. 32 (London: The Athlone Press, 1967), p. 7.
3. John F. Embree, *Suye Mura: A Japanese Village* (Chicago: University of Chicago Press, 1939), pp. 121–32.
4. Richard K. Beardsley, John W. Hall, and Robert E. Ward, *Village Japan* (Chicago: University of Chicago Press, 1959), p. 232.
5. Theresa M. Watanabe, "A Report from the Japanese American Community Study" (Department of Anthropology, University of Washington, 1977), p. 11.
6. This pattern of working through the son may help explain the frequently observed conflict between mothers-in-law and daughters-in-law. According to Watanabe, "A Report," p. 13, the intensity of the conflict stemmed less from jealousy over the affection of the son/husband than from competition for power, which could only be achieved through him. Because of their restricted opportunities for power, women fought over one of the few avenues through which they could achieve it.
7. The ideal was for the eldest biological son of the previous head to succeed him. However, circumstances sometimes prevented the realiza-

tion of this ideal. The eldest son might become incapacitated, be incompetent, or choose some other venture (such as emigrating). In such a case a younger son might inherit the headship. If he had no living son, the head might adopt a male heir, often a nephew or other relative or a daughter's husband.

8. Groups of households related through sibling ties were called *shinrui* or *shinseku* (similar to what westerners call "relatives"). Although the genealogical relations between the "main" household and these branch households were recognized, the bonds between them were primarily emotional, rather than economic. Among middle and lower peasants, related but distant households rarely cooperated economically. Instead, cooperation took place among physically contiguous households irrespective of kinship.

9. This situation was reversed in cases where the head adopted one of his daughter's husbands as a successor. This was called a *yoshi-muka* marriage. In this case the husband was the stranger and the wife the insider. He had the same legal rights as a son, but his lack of allies and outsider status undermined his position. Naturally men disliked this arrangement, and a man contracted such a marriage only if his own prospects were poor and the economic advantages of the marriage were considerable.

10. Embree, *Suye Mura*, p. 37.

11. See Robert J. Smith and Ella Lury Wiswell, *The Women of Suye Mura* (Chicago: University of Chicago Press, 1982), pp. 73–84, for descriptive details.

12. Evelyn Nakano Glenn, "Split Household, Small Producer and Dual Wage Earner: An Analysis of Chinese American Family Strategies," *Journal of Marriage and the Family* 45 (1983): 35–46, describes the division of labor between Chinese sojourners and kin in the home village.

13. Sylvia Junko Yanagisako, "Two Processes of Change in Japanese-American Kinship," *Journal of Anthropological Research* 31 (1975): 202.

14. Ibid.

15. Louise A. Tilly and Joan W. Scott, *Women, Work and Family* (New York: Holt, Rinehart and Winston, 1978), pp. 15, 104–6.

16. Elizabeth Bott, *Family and Social Network: Roles, Norms and External Relations in Ordinary Urban Families* (London: Tavistock Publications, 1957), pp. 52–96.

17. Embree, *Suye Mura*, p. 95.

18. Mirjana Morokvasic, "Women in Migration: Beyond the Reductionist Outlook," in Annie Pizacklea (ed.), *One Way Ticket: Migration and Female Labour* (London: Routledge and Kegan Paul, 1983), pp. 20–24.

19. Harry H. L. Kitano, *Japanese Americans: The Evolution of a Subculture,* 2d ed. (Englewood Cliffs, N.J.: Prentice-Hall, 1976), p. 43.

Chapter 10

1. Harry H. L. Kitano, *Japanese Americans: The Evolution of a Subculture,* 2d ed. (Englewood Cliffs, N.J.: Prentice-Hall, 1976), p. 26, and Shotaro Frank Miyamoto, "Social Solidarity Among the Japanese in Seattle," *University of Washington Publications in the Social Sciences* 11 (1939): pp. 82–98.

2. Different historical patterns underlay the division of labor in Japan and the United States. Although aristocratic women were secluded in Japan, peasant women worked in the fields. In contrast, white farm women in America generally did not do heavy field work. That work was allocated to men, while women were responsible for household maintenance, food preservation, and so on.

3. The segregated pattern has been described among working-class communities in Boston (Herbert J. Gans, *The Urban Villagers* [New York: Free Press, 1962]); Chicago (Mirra Komarovsky, *Blue Collar Marriage* [New York: Vintage, 1967]); and London (Michael Young and Peter Willmott, *Family and Kinship in East London* [Baltimore: Penguin Books, 1962]).

4. Sylvia Junko Yanagisako, "Two Processes of Change in Japanese American Kinship," *Journal of Anthropological Research* 31 (1975): 196–224.

5. Sylvia Junko Yanagisako, "Women-Centered Kin Networks in Urban Bilateral Kinship," *American Ethnologist* 4 (1977): 207–26. The similarity to kinship patterns found among the white working class (cf. Young and Willmott, *Family and Kinship*) and poor urban blacks (Carol B. Stack, *All Our Kin* [New York: Harper & Row, 1974]) is striking.

6. Young and Willmott, *Family and Kinship,* pp. 31–43.

7. Myra Marx Ferree, personal communication.

Index

10, 216; men's drinking and problems in, 213–15; men's participation in housework in, 211–12; men's role in childcare in, 211; men's withholding wages in, 214; parent-child obligation in, 217; role of daughters in, 54–55, 128; role reversal in, 211–12; services to, by kin in Japan, 206; sex segregation in, 212–13; shifts in domestic responsibilities in, 211–12; size of, 49; ties of, to kin in Japan, 205; two-generation composition of, 206; violence in, 213; wives' overload in, 209–10; women's wage work and, 215–18

Family, Japanese American: effect of affluence on, 220; effect of labor system on, 198–99; formation of, discouraged, 197–98; during internment, 219–20; post-war dispersion and, 220; and resistance to racism, 199; struggles of, 198–200; transmission of culture in, 199; women's role in preserving, 199

Family, migrant/immigrant: advantages to employers of supporting, 195; advantages to state of excluding, 194–95; constraints imposed on, 195; effects of labor system on, 193–96; exclusion of, 194; reproductive costs of, 194; and resistance to dominant group control, 195–96; women's labor in, 3–4

Family, nisei, 219–31; age cohorts compared, 220; aspira-

tions for children in, 228; bicultural nature of, 230–31; childcare strategies of, 221; child-centeredness of, 227; children's participation in housework in, 222–23; companionate model in, 226; compared to family in Japan, 225, 228–29; differences in, by age, 220; division of housework in, 221–25; and extended kin network, 221, 228–30; female-centered kin network in, 228–29; gender relations in, 230–31; group orientation in, 227; influence of issei patterns on, 219; influence of middle-class values on, 230; inheritance in, 229; inside-outside division of labor in, 223–24; lack of leisure in, 225; male privilege in, 223; material conditions of, 231; men and household maintenance in, 223; men's participation in housework in, 222; mother-child obligations in, 230; mother-daughter ties in, 228–29; parent-child relations in, 226–28; pre-war and post-war, compared, 220; sex segregation in, 225–26; wives' views of husbands in, 226; women's control of domestic sphere in, 224–25

Family, war bride: aspirations for children in, 240, 241; communication in, 238; compared to family in Japan, 239; conjugal relations in, 237–41; division of labor in, 235–37; economic dependence of wives in, 232–